D1291593

I Could Be Happy

I Could Be Happy

AN AUTOBIOGRAPHY

SANDY WILSON

LONDON

Michael Joseph

First published in Great Britain by Michael Joseph Ltd
52 Bedford Square, London, W.C.1
1975

© 1975 by Sandy Wilson

All rights reserved. No part of this publication
may be reproduced, stored in a retrieval system
or transmitted, in any form or by any means
electronic, mechanical, photocopying, recording
or otherwise, without the prior permission
of the Copyright owner

ISBN 0 7181 1370 5

Set and printed in Great Britain
by Tonbridge Printers Limited, Tonbridge, Kent,
in Bell eleven on twelve point,
on paper supplied by P. F. Bingham Ltd,
and bound by Dorstel Press at Harlow

ML 410
.W 716 A 3
1975 b

Contents

Illustrations

The
Nineteen
Twenties

THE BOY FRIEND was set, rather arbitrarily, in 1926; I was born two years earlier, not so much arbitrarily as unexpectedly. I arrived more or less in the middle of a decade which I was later to idealise, and my first memory of it is a party. It took place at the Johnstones, whose daughter, Winty, was a friend of my sister, Helen. Winty had a brother called Carly, who was considered very dashing, because he went in for Oxford Bags and co-respondent shoes. He also wore a long student's scarf, and at one point in the party, to amuse the others, he rolled it round and round me and then tugged the loose end, causing me to revolve helplessly and finally collapse on the floor. Surprisingly, I did not cry. Everyone was laughing, the gramophone was playing, and I sat on the floor and laughed too.

For my family the realities of the Twenties were somewhat different from my rosy memory of them. My father and mother had met and married in 1907, in India, where my father worked for a shipping company called Grahams. My mother, Elsie Humphrey, had two older sisters, Lilian and Nell, both of whom also found husbands in India: Lilian married Stanley Reed, later to be editor of the *Times of India* and to receive a knighthood, and Nell married a banker, Frank Bennett. My father, George Wilson, was the youngest son of a Scots family from Bannockburn, who had made a small fortune in woollen mills. My grandfather had bought Bannockburn House and given his children the best of everything, which for George meant education at a private school and at Harrow, where he distinguished himself in games and was made captain of the school football team. But while my mother was a Londoner, gay, imaginative and wilful, my father was a countryman, sober, meditative and possessed of a strong Presbyterian sense of duty: a match of contrasts, perhaps, but, to begin with at any rate, a happy one.

Their first daughter was born in 1909, in Karachi, and was named Christian, after the eldest daughter in my father's family, as is the

Scots custom. Their second daughter was born in Sussex in 1913, while my parents were home on leave, and was called Helen, after the second daughter in my father's family, and Lilian, after my mother's sister. During the 1914–18 War the family stayed in India, later moving to Burma, where the third daughter was born, in 1916. She was named Elsie, after my mother, but, since her birthday was December 26th, she was also christened Noël, and this was the name by which she was always known. Having had three daughters, my mother decided to call a halt, and in 1920 the family sailed for England on their first post-war leave. My mother had privately determined that she would remain in England when my father's leave was up, but in fact none of them was to see India again. On the eve of his return my father received a telegram from Grahams instructing him that his passage had been cancelled and he was to report to the London office. The rest of the family remained in Stirling, where they had been spending their leave, staying with their Aunt Christian, who kept house for her batchelor brother, Dan.

My mother described the change of plan as 'a blessed relief', since it meant that the family would remain together, and it seems clear that, for one reason or another, she had had enough of India. But as circumstances gradually changed for the worse, she began to look back on those Indian days as a kind of Paradise Lost. In the last few years of her life she was bedridden after suffering two strokes; but, although immobile, she retained all her other faculties in abundance and, to pass the time, decided to write her memoirs. They are disjointed and incomplete, but every now and then a passage recreates totally a phase of her past:

'The day in India was much better spaced out than in England, and I remember feeling quite at a loss to know what to do with myself when we came home. It sometimes began with friends calling in for Chota Hazri, which was a "little meal" on waking, consisting of fruit and tea. Then there would be a bicycle- or horse-ride, because all exercise had to be taken before breakfast – "big breakfast", that is. The early morning could be very pleasant: the sweepers would be watering the roads and there was a fresh smell everywhere. There would also be badminton parties, and some very energetic matches were played. Then it would be home to a hot bath, by which time the house would have been cleaned and dusted. Breakfast was a family affair, and the menfolk would be busy preparing to leave for their various offices. All sorts of vehicles were used: dog-carts, phaetons, victorias and ticca gharries, and, as the Monsoon drew on, they had to be equipped with suitable livery, the drivers in heavy mackintoshes, and the carriages, if open, with a huge water-proof apron which buttoned one in tightly all round.

One just drove through the rain, and a big umbrella was always ready for alighting at the shops or houses where one called. "Calling" was a great ritual: everyone had a box with their name on it, which at four o'clock was put outside on the gate-post. One drove around and dropped one's card into the newcomer's box, never entering the house. This would be followed by an invitation to tea or dinner.

'Entertainment was the life and soul of India and went on all day. There were so many well-trained "boys", who all enjoyed the "Bunda-bust", as they called it, of a party of any kind. "Tiffin" (lunch) was a very friendly meal, and it was nothing to have several mothers land on one, together with their babies and "ayahs" (Indian nurses). The ayahs would take charge of the babies, while the mothers enjoyed a gossipy meal followed by the inevitable siesta. The hostess would give word to the butler that she was resting, all doors were closed and the whole house, except for the servants, would sleep until about three-thirty, when one would be woken by the sound of the gardeners drawing water. Then the ayahs dressed the babies for the afternoon walk and went off to their nearest meeting-place, arriving back in time to return home.

'In the cool of the evening there were various sports to watch. Polo demanded great skill, and it was said that one man could turn his horse on a spot the size of a penny. Horse-races and point-to-points drew the crowds and pig-sticking was a great attraction for the menfolk at week-ends, though I do not remember eating any pork, and the natives of course would not touch it. So I suppose the poor beasts were buried where they fell, or did pig-sticking mean that you just left your mark on the animal and let it go at that? I never bothered to find out.

'As the then-Governor's wife, Lady Harris, was a niece of my god-mother, we were very lucky in getting invitations to At-Homes, Dinners and Dances at Government House, and very impressive occasions they were. There was always a supply of good-looking ADCs, whose object and duty was to look after the guests, and the evening dress of a white jacket with a scarlet cummerbund added greatly to their appearance. Dinner-parties held privately were called "Burra Khanas" and were arranged most beautifully, with exquisite flowers. They might be followed by a small dance, but usually everyone who could do so was asked to play their piece on the piano or sing a song, while the rest sat round in perspiring admiration.

'By the time that was over, it was the hour for seeking refuge in a well mosquito-proofed bed, which had been prepared at sundown, before the mosquitoes woke up. And one was thankful for the punkah moving to and fro above the bed all night, to keep one cool. But woe to the punkah wallah who drowsed on duty! A shout would go up and after a moment the punkah would start again.

'And so to the morning, when one was awakened by the cry, "Cha hai, Memsahib!", a welcome cup of tea was thrust through the net, and another Indian day had begun.'

My parents had no inkling of what a different life awaited them at home or how ill-equipped they both were to deal with it. But my mother did have one foretaste of the future:

'Just as we were preparing to leave for England a "wise man" followed me up to my room with the request, "Memsahib, tell fortune?" As I was very busy, I shooed him off, but he insisted; so I reluctantly listened to what he had to say. I must confess that as we already had three little girls and a long voyage ahead of us we did not want to enlarge the family. However his message to me was that I would have a son. This had always been a dream child to me, and I at once said, "No, I'm sure that will never be." But he insisted: "Yes, Memsahib, there will be a boy." '

The England they returned to was much altered from the England they had left in their youth. Severe war-time rationing was still in force, there was a housing shortage, and a flu epidemic was raging. For the time being my Aunt Christian's house in Stirling provided a home. But things were far from well in Scotland too. My grandfather had died in 1906, and the family fortunes were at a low ebb.

'He had a most generous disposition,' wrote my mother, 'and the outstretched hand of many an old friend was filled with money, to the detriment of his family's welfare. When he died, his affairs were found to be in a parlous state: Bannockburn House had to be sold, and the mills were also failing. The elder sons, Ben and Dan, tried to establish a carpet industry, as the Tartan trade was diminishing; but the luck of the place had vanished, and eventually it was sold for a laundry – a sad descent for a firm that, it was said, had done so well that no-one knew how much money they had.'

My sister Noël remembers being told by an aunt that when my grandfather died, he had £30,000 in investments that were worth nothing at all: 'He had so much money that he didn't know what he was doing, and he didn't care.'

On my grandmother's death the division of her belongings took place at Aunt Christian's house, St Margaret's. 'We were banished upstairs,' my sister Helen recalls, 'because we weren't "family". There were three brothers, Ben, Dan and George, and three sisters, Christian, Helen and Eliza (known as "Dizzy"), and everything had to be divided equally between them, to the absurd extent of each one receiving one cup and one saucer from a tea-set.' Ben's wife, Ada, was guilty of a fearful gaffe. 'They must have been desperately hard-up. But instead of taking all the bits and pieces to the pawn-broker's in Glasgow, she popped them in Stirling, and the next thing we knew was that Aunt Christian and Uncle Dan came back from a walk in a terrible state, because some of the things from Bannockburn House were sitting in a pawn-broker's window in the Arcade. So they all clubbed together and bought them back.'

And while the fortunes of my father's family were waning, his own were threatened by a débâcle in Grahams' affairs. The firm had been over-trading recklessly and was heavily in debt to American companies; they hurriedly began to retrench, and in 1922 my father was posted to the office in Manchester, where he set about finding a home in order to reunite his family. He eventually took rooms in a house in Didsbury.

'We were landed in a spot called Washway Road,' wrote my mother, 'which seemed to me to typify the atmosphere, for surely it rains more in Manchester than anywhere else in the world.' It was a miserable time for the whole family. 'We shared a house with a fat woman and her daughter,' Helen remembers, 'where we had two rooms. Christian and I were in one and Mother and Daddy and Noël were in the other. We went to a ghastly school, where the rain poured in through the roof while we sat and read *Lorna Doone*. I've never been able to read it since.'

The violent deterioration in their circumstances was beginning to strain my parents' relationship, as Noël soon became aware: 'I slept in the same room as Mother and Father and they quarrelled all night. She was going to go off and leave him, and he used to be on his bended knees begging her not to. Sometimes I wished that she would leave, and then he and I could go and live in a cottage in the country.' One day she came home screaming in terror. 'I had seen a woman walking down Washway Road with webbed feet, like a duck. The whole thing was so horrible, I've never got over it.' But my mother rallied her resources and decided that she could take care of the family on her own, since, although the landlady and her daughter were supposed to look after things, she found herself doing most of the work. 'So it suddenly struck me that it would be much more comfortable to have a house to ourselves. By that time we had made friends with people whom we met at Sale Presbyterian Church, and they told us of a furnished house in Sale Moor. I can see it now: it was a bright little house, and I set about it manfully, cooking and cleaning for the family. I had an extraordinary idea that it would all come easily, and friends were most kind, giving me tips and assistance. But I shall never forget my first pastry: you could have thrown it across the road and it would have remained intact.'

My mother could look back on it light-heartedly, but Helen saw the pathos in the situation: 'Mother simply hadn't been brought up to this kind of thing. She had five pounds a week to feed us all, and she couldn't even boil an egg. She had no idea whether you cooked potatoes in boiling water or cold water. What she must have gone through!' In an attempt to help, my father tried to grow vegetables in the garden, but he planted them the wrong way up, and when his brothers in Stirling heard about it, they laughed at him. It was, as Noël says, 'a horrible situation, and they neither of them had any idea how to cope with it.'

They were the poor relations. But Aunty Lil's husband, Stanley Reed, had grown wealthy from his time in India, and she took pity on the impoverished Wilsons and in 1923 invited them for a holiday to Newport in Pembrokeshire, where they had rented an enormous house for the summer. The weather must have been particularly balmy, because, as Noël succinctly puts it, 'There was a moonlight picnic, and the result was you.'

My father was furious, as the last thing in the world he needed was another mouth to feed. He went down with mumps, caught from Helen, who was always the first to succumb to any infectious disease, and then there was another move, to an unfurnished house called Rosegarth, in Irlam Road, Sale, where the family settled in to await what could hardly have been looked on as a happy event. 'I knew Mother was going to have a baby,' says Helen, 'and every night I prayed, "Please, God, may it be a brother!"'

I have no idea whether my mother was comforted during her pregnancy by the 'wise man's' prophecy, but certainly in later years she claimed that my arrival had been foretold to her, not by an angel, but by a ghost. During the holiday in Newport she and my father had been given separate bedrooms (which perhaps explains their behaviour at the picnic). The house was built on the foundations of a medieval castle, and my mother, who throughout her life was fascinated by the occult, was told that her room was haunted by a 'little lady in grey'. She never saw the lady, but each morning she was woken early by the sound of horse's hooves approaching the castle. She heard the rider bang on the gates, which were then unlocked and opened with a clang. As he rode into the courtyard she heard hooves clip-clopping on the paving-stones. With a clatter of armour he would dismount, enter the hall and climb the stairs. Nearer and nearer came his heavy tread until finally it stopped outside my mother's door. Every morning, with no

feeling of fear, she would jump out of bed and open the door, hoping to
see her visitor. But there was never anybody there. Eventually she
told her story to some local residents. 'Ah,' they said, 'that is the *real*
ghost of the castle.'

My mother was forty-three and her confinement was not expected
to be easy. A nurse was engaged, which must have considerably upset
my father's accounts, and Aunty Lil came to stay at a nearby hotel, so
as to be on hand when needed. Eventually, early one morning in May,
the baby was born, and, to the relief of everyone, was a boy. The
nurse took one look at me and said, quite unaccountably, 'One day
he'll be a bishop.' The remark made a deep impression on my mother,
and to the end of her days she claimed to feel disappointed that I never
showed the slightest inclination to enter the Church. My sisters were
given the day off from school, sent home and scrubbed clean by Aunty
Lil, and were then, at the appointed moment, ushered into the presence
of their baby brother. Christian and Helen were delighted with the new
arrival, but Noël, up till then her father's favourite, had a fearful
premonition: 'I realised I had been *displaced!*' My father's attitude
changed completely: 'His very footsteps,' wrote my mother, in a
slightly euphoric passage, 'were lighter with the joy of having a son
at last.' It was in this mood, presumably, that he entered me for
Harrow, despite the unlikelihood of his ever being able to afford the
fees. Following the Scots custom, I was christened after my father's
father, Alexander, and my Scottish grandmother's maiden name,
Galbraith.

Our material situation did improve slightly at this time, as my father
was made manager of Grahams' Manchester office. A nurse-maid was
engaged: her name was Louisa, and I was devoted to her. But we could
hardly be described as prosperous, and the family's entertainments
were of the simplest kind, far removed from the mad parties and hectic
dances which are thought typical of the 1920s. This was due not only
to economics but also to my father's Presbyterian outlook, which
deprived my sisters of most of the gaieties one associates with adoles-
cence. Liquor was taboo, music and dancing were frowned upon, and
the Theatre and the Cinema were, in my mother's words (but not in
her opinion), 'the source of all evil'. This makes my father sound like
a reincarnation of Edward Moulton Barrett, but so far from being a
despot he was a kindly man of unwavering religious and moral con-
victions who simply tried to live by standards which were rapidly
growing out of date. Sunday was observed with Puritan rigour: the
whole family went twice to church, throughout the day only certain

books could be read (the children were given volumes of an annual called *Chatterbox*) and the only games we played had to be of an educational kind such as 'Word-making and Word-taking', a primitive form of Scrabble. In the evening the children were summoned to recite a psalm which they had been set to learn during the day, and there were family prayers before bed-time.

In these unpromising circumstances, my mother somehow managed to make our existence a little more cheerful than it might have been. 'She did do her utmost to make what she could out of life. We were always allowed to ask our friends round, and on Wednesdays we put a W in the front window, for the Wall's Ice Cream Man to call, and we had pêche melba. Another treat was corned beef, with an onion sauce which was called "brains". Mother managed to make gay things out of ordinary things: she always had bright ideas.'

One of her bright ideas was to buy a gramophone with some money that had been left to her. It remained with us until late in the Thirties, and I remember it well: a cabinet model with doors which concealed the loudspeaker, and a shelf beneath for storing records. 'At first we only had two: Clara Butt singing *Abide with Me* and *Valencia*. Then Christian went down to London for a few days to stay with cousins and they took her to see *No, No, Nanette*. She came back with the record. We played it and played it, and she taught us how to Charleston. But of course we had to stop when Daddy came home from work.'

While the girls Charlestoned, their infant brother sat and watched and listened. More records were bought: *Funny Face*, *Mercenary Mary*, *Show Boat* . . . Totally unaware of family troubles and financial difficulties, I simply absorbed the songs and dances of the day and grew up convinced that they were what the 1920s were all about.

But the economic situation was beginning to tell on my mother, and matters reached a climax after a summer holiday at Bainbridge in Yorkshire, when I was three years old. 'We would take long walks across the moors,' she wrote, 'and during one of these I had a nasty fall and broke my wrist. I tied it up hastily with my handkerchief and said nothing, knowing that my husband would think it a careless sort of thing to do. We found a small hotel for lunch, and when the manageress saw I was in pain she produced a leather strap, which probably saved my arm. When we got back to our cottage, our doctor came out from Manchester and set it properly for me; but that and the strain of house-keeping and looking after Sandy brought on a nervous breakdown, and I wrote to my sister Lilian and asked if I could go to her.' But there was more to it than that, as Helen remembers: 'I was putting you on your pottie, when we were summoned downstairs. I pulled your trousers up and took you down, and we were all lined up and Mother said, "I'm leaving you." Aunty Lil came up and fetched Mother and told her, "You're never going back to that man." '

My sister Christian had left school and was studying Art at the Slade in London, and Noël had, with the assistance of Uncle Stanley, been sent to a boarding-school at High Wycombe called Godstowe. My father objected, but my mother insisted that it was necessary for the sake of her health for Noël to be sent away from Manchester. 'She also thought I was developing a Lancashire accent. I wept every night and I used to say, "Send Helen instead of me." ' But Helen, who would have given anything for the chance to go away to boarding-school, was left at home in Sale to look after her father and me. She had no-one else to turn to but her schoolfriends, in particular Winty Johnstone: 'She lived in the road next to ours, in a large house with a tennis court. She had two sisters and a brother: the elder sister kept house, and the second sister, Peggy, was at Oxford. Carly, the brother, was very handsome and had a moustache. Their mother was a vapid creature, who just drifted around. They can't have been very well off, because they had only one electric light bulb which they used to move from room to room. But the great thing for me was to be able to get out of the house and have a little gaiety. Of course there was never any question of having boy-friends at our parties, and we didn't dance; we just played games, like "Up, Jenkins!" and so on. I once went to a thé dansant at the Midland Hotel with another school-friend, who had two brothers. But there were never any boys in our lives.'

Meanwhile my mother's flight south was not turning out quite as she had hoped: 'At first the peace of my sister's lovely house and garden seemed, after Manchester, like Heaven. But then Lilian made up her mind that I had something worse than a break-down and sent for my eldest sister, as she was convinced I had gone off my head. As soon as Nell saw me, she knew that I was all right, but Lilian was still sure that I needed watching carefully, and while she and my brother-in-law were away in London, her butler was instructed not to let me out of his sight.' When she realised what was going on, my mother decided to escape, 'although I regret that to do so I had to borrow – really steal – some money from my sister.' She made her way to London and went to see her Aunt Kate, who reminded her of some savings she had put into a Building Society. This enabled her to travel to Eastbourne and take a room in a boarding-house, where she spent the evenings playing bridge with the landlady. She now decided that my health was also at risk in Manchester, and wrote to my father asking him to send me to join her. Helen, who always seemed to get landed with the uncongenial tasks, was instructed to take me to Eastbourne. 'We were met by Aunt Dizzy in London and she took us across to Charing Cross and put us on the train. It wasn't a corridor train, and halfway to Eastbourne you said "I want to go wee-wee", but I managed to keep your mind off it by drawing pictures and singing *Tea For Two*.'

Still unaware as I was of any breach in the family, the Eastbourne visit was to me just a prolonged holiday during which I had my mother all to myself. To begin with we spent the afternoons in long walks along the sea-front, which often terminated in the life-boat house, where there was a working model of a shipwreck at sea which could be set in motion by a penny in the slot. We would return to our lodgings in time for tea, and on the way Mother used to recite a sort of incantation, which I still sometimes use myself, 'Little finger, tell me true: will there be a letter for me? Yes, No, Yes, No' and so on, touching a finger for each word until she reached the little finger on her right hand. By varying the phrasing of the question one could also vary the reply. At the time it was just a game, but I realised later that she must have been wondering constantly how things were at home.

But winter was coming on and the weather was getting colder. It became a problem to find something to do in the afternoons, and Mother discovered a perfect solution in the Cinema. It was warm, it was entertaining, and, most important of all, it was cheap, for in those days one could get a good seat for fourpence. But while for her it was a convenience, for me it was the start of a love affair which lasted for nearly thirty years; a one-sided love affair however, because the Cinema has never made any advances to me, and on the whole I prefer it so, as I would hate to have my illusions shattered. Nowadays I go to the cinema much more rarely, because there are so few films I want to see; but in 1927 the choice was enormous: there were many more picture-houses, and the programme was changed at least once a week. My favourite film was Lon Chaney's version of *The Hunchback Of Notre Dame* which we saw every afternoon of its run. I suppose my father would have been horrified to learn that his only son was being seduced by the Silver Screen, particularly as he now had another reason to disapprove of it: one of the partners in Grahams had visited Hollywood and made a disastrous investment in the film industry.

But at the moment he was only concerned in reuniting his family, and this happened at Christmas, in Eastbourne. There must have been some sort of reconciliation, because after the holidays Mother, Helen and I returned to Sale, where I went to my first school, run by a lady called Miss Lowe. I remember very little about it, apart from my reluctance to leave home every morning, and in any case my attendance was constantly interrupted by coughs, colds and eventually bronchitis. Mother took me to Blackpool to recover, but as soon as we returned I fell ill again. It was finally decided, on the suggestion of the family doctor, that I should be sent south to boarding-school. Godstowe, where Noël was a pupil, was a girls' school, but had a kindergarten attached for younger brothers and sisters of the boarders, and I was entered there for the autumn of 1928 at the age of four and a half.

Once again Helen was left behind in Sale: 'The young man from Mr Plant's, the outfitters, came and he stood you on the dining-room table, because you were so small. He brought you the smallest of everything, and they were still three times too big. Then you went off to Godstowe, and that was the worst moment of my life, because I was left with Mother and Daddy and she was absolutely broken-hearted. The only thing that cheered her up was to play Al Jolson singing *Sonny Boy* on the gramophone. She had queued up to see the film by herself – it was the first of the talkies – and she came home and bought the record. To this day I cannot bear it. I used to come home from school for lunch and buy two cream slices on the way, and we'd sit there and eat them, and she wouldn't speak to me. I would rack my brains for things to say to her, to try and rouse her, but she wasn't interested.'

It was also a bad time for my father. A new man had joined the Manchester office, and he found himself being ousted. In 1929 he was posted to Liverpool and things improved for a while. He found a small house in the suburb of Wavertree, where the surroundings were a good deal more agreeable than in Sale, my mother came to life again, and even Helen's lot was improved, because, having matriculated from Sale High School, she was sent down to London to secretarial college, where Christian, whose artistic aspirations had proved abortive, now joined her.

After the first shock of leaving my home and family, I soon settled down quite happily at boarding-school. Although I saw very little of her, since we were in different houses, it was a comfort to know that Noël was within reach, and my house-mistress, Miss Billyeald, made a special pet of me and arranged for me to sit beside her at meals, so that I could surreptitiously hold her hand under the table, if I was feeling unhappy. Godstowe was situated on a hill overlooking High Wycombe and the school buildings were surrounded by ample gardens and playing fields. As it was a girls' school (in fact a preparatory school for Wycombe Abbey, where it was intended that Noël should go), the staff were, with one exception, women, and all my teachers' names began with W. There was Miss Willkins, who was plump and inclined to go red in the face with rage, if anyone misbehaved; there was Miss Willford, who was thin, wore glasses and had her hair in 'earphones'; and there was Miss Willby who had an Eton crop and a bark like a sergeant major. The Head Mistress of the school was a Mrs Turner, and her husband was the only male member of the staff. He was a huge, irascible man, who suffered from gout, and when Noël led me into the Turners' study to introduce me on my arrival at Godstowe, he glared at the small, frightened boy, with grey flannel shorts hanging well below his knees, and bellowed, 'What on earth have you got there?'

As it was the winter term, there were various entertainments in the evening, including a Fancy Dress Party, which I attended disguised as Rudolph Valentino in *The Sheik*. Then we were visited by a conjuror, and for a week or so afterwards I was determined to be one too. But my fate was sealed one evening when we were all summoned to the gymnasium to see a performance by Ben Greet's touring company. They gave us *The Tempest*, and Ben Greet himself played Prospero. Ariel was an actress with bright red frizzy hair which stood out all round her head, and I had never before seen anyone so beautiful. The whole thing was much more magical to me than any conjuror, and I made up my mind that night that when I grew up I would be part of it.

There was no theatrical tradition whatever in my father's family, and only a trace of it in my mother's, although she sometimes claimed to be descended from an actress who had born an illegitimate child to George III. Her brother, Frank, went into the Theatre against his parents' wishes and had compounded his error by abandoning his first wife for an American, Virginia Fox. He dropped the family name of Humphrey and as Frank Vernon was successful in the London Theatre both as director, actor and producer; but of course I had no idea of this at the time, and he was rarely, if ever, referred to, particularly not by Aunty Lil and Uncle Stanley. But in my family, in spite of my father's disapproval of the Theatre, there was a strong love of 'let's pretend', playing charades and other acting games. We had a 'dressing-up box', an old trunk full of bits and pieces of costumes, and now that I had seen one play I was forever attempting to mount entertainments of my own and pleading with my sisters to take part. We used to play a particularly long and elaborate form of charades, in which one side chose a famous name – the longer the better, I always felt – and thought of another famous name for each of its letters. Thus if one had chosen 'Napoleon', one had to act 'Nero', 'Arthur', 'Portia' and so on, and then 'Napoleon' himself, as a grand finale. Each charade was like some endless pageant, and the fact that the other side would have probably guessed the name after the first three letters never deterred us from acting it right through to the bitter end.

While I was at Godstowe, I visited London for the first time. The school held its Speech Day in the summer term: there was a service in the morning in the local church, and the afternoon was given over to speeches in the gymnasium, a concert and, after tea, a display of 'Greek' dancing on the playing fields. Everyone was then allowed to go home for the week-end, and, since Liverpool was so far away, my mother and I went to London and stayed with Helen and Christian. They were living in a hostel on the Embankment: 'It was called the Maybelle-Mary Egerton and it was where the Vickers building stands now. We shared a room with a curtain down the middle: Christian had the window and paid twenty-seven and six a week, full board, and I paid twenty-five shillings.' On the Monday afternoon I was taken to the theatre for the first time, to see a Variety bill at the Coliseum, featuring a famous clown called Noni who did an act with a horse, and during the summer holidays I tried very hard to be a clown. But the lack of dialogue defeated me – to say nothing of the make-up – and I resumed my devotion to the straight theatre.

In the following year Noël moved down the hill to Wycombe Abbey and I was now on my own at Godstowe; but I had made a lot of friends there, mostly among the girls, one of whom I had decided to marry later on. Her name was Prue and she had a large mouth and a very snub nose, and we arranged to meet on Paddington Station in 1940, by which time we felt we would be old enough to settle down together. Her parents were rich – at least in comparison with mine – and used to arrive at Godstowe in a large car, in which they whisked us off to a tea-shop in High Wycombe. On the way back we behaved appallingly: I threw peppermint lumps at the passers-by, which seemed to me a gesture of insane extravagance, and Prue stuck her head out of the window and shouted 'Help! I'm being kidnapped!' Unfortunately, before we had time to make a definite date for our reunion, her parents' marriage broke up, she was suddenly removed from Godstowe, and I never saw her again.

While we contemplated marriage, we had not the least knowledge of, or curiosity about, sex, and my first encounter with this fascinating subject came as a total surprise. During one holidays Noël repeated to me a limerick which had enjoyed a great success at Wycombe Abbey the term before:

There was a young lady from Spain
Who took down her knicks in the train.
A nasty young porter
Saw more than he oughter
And asked her to do it again.

It struck me as very funny and I could hardly wait to pass it on to my
girl friends at Godstowe. Before long it was all round the school and
inevitably came to the ears of one of the mistresses, who reported the
disgraceful affair to Mrs Turner. Somehow the limerick was traced
back to me and I was summoned to her study. However, after I had
admitted my guilt, I was not punished, but simply told in the kindest
possible way that such things were 'not nice'. Mrs Turner then went
on to impart a piece of information whose inaccuracy was only matched
by its irrelevance. 'Do you know,' she said, 'that when little babies are
sent from heaven, they all arrive dressed in a set of beautiful baby
clothes? Isn't that wonderful?' I agreed that it was and that ended the
interview. It was not until several years later, when I discovered how
babies actually arrived, that I realised the unlikelihood of their appearing
in the world fully clothed, and from that day to this I have puzzled over
Mrs Turner's motives in telling me such a tall story. Or perhaps –
dreadful thought – since she had no children of her own, she actually
believed it herself?

I was unaware of the Depression until near the end of 1930 when
my mother, who had a tendency to over-dramatize, announced in
gloomy tones that this year there would be no Christmas presents.
There were of course, and there was also my first visit to a pantomime.
It was *Robinson Crusoe* and the principal boy was Dorothy Ward. She
sang *When You're Smiling* and *On the Sunny Side of the Street*, and from
the moment she came on I have to confess that I forgot the red-haired
lady who played Ariel. Dorothy, with her tossing blonde curls, her
invincible swagger and her glistening tights, was my hero and heroine
wrapped into one. The next day I built a raft out of the living-room
furniture and to the sound of the Overture from William Tell on the
cabinet gramophone I recreated Crusoe's shipwreck. I pleaded with my
parents to see the pantomime again and finally my father, unaware
of the ambitions he was fostering, agreed to take me to a Saturday
matinée. He also found a song-sheet at Woolworths with the words of
On the Sunny Side of the Street which I learned by heart and sang to
anyone who could be forced to listen. After my second visit I wrote my
first fan letter: 'Dear Miss Ward, you are so beautiful that I would
like you to be my sister.' In reply I received a signed photograph of my

idol wearing a strategically draped length of white satin and holding a madonna lily. It struck me on looking at it that perhaps she did not see herself in a sisterly capacity, and the comments of my real sisters confirmed my apprehensions. I never did hear my father's opinion of the photograph, but by the time I returned home for the Easter holidays it had vanished for ever.

I also continued to visit the cinema, though not as often as I would have wished. Films were now All-Talking, All-Singing and All-Dancing, and the first musical I saw was *The Gold-Diggers of Broadway*. *Tip-Toe through the Tulips* and *Painting the Clouds with Sunshine* were quickly added to my repertoire, and I began to wonder vaguely if, as well as being an actor, I might also be able to make up my own words and music, which would of course be performed by several hundred chorus girls in the style of *The Gold-Diggers* and *The Broadway Melodies*, the first of which had just appeared. Like most families of that time, we had an upright piano in the living-room, on which my mother and my sisters occasionally played, and sometimes on Saturday evenings the family and friends would gather round to sing songs from the Scottish Students' Song Book: *Little Brown Jug*, *Riding Down to Bangor* and a ballad whose chorus went, 'There's nae lack aboot the hoose, there's nae lack at a' '. I tried playing the piano myself, in the hope that something like *On the Sunny Side of the Street* might result, but, since I had no musical knowledge whatever, it never did, and nobody suggested that I should take piano lessons, since quite enough was already being spent on my education.

Not only my education but the future of the whole family must have exercised my father's mind during 1931. The Depression was having a disastrous effect on business everywhere, and more often than not the report on the day's trading in his diary would be a laconic 'Nothing doing'. At least during the holidays life at home was more cheerful. There were usually games or charades after tea, and on January 2nd he wrote: 'Children acted after dinner. Sandy very keen' – little did he know how keen! A week later we were invited to the Hamiltons' next door, where Noël was taking part in an entertainment organised by their daughter, Lilian. The only item I remember is a rendition of Maurice Chevalier's current song-hit, *You Brought a New Kind of Love to Me*, by Lilian Hamilton dressed à la Dietrich in *The Blue Angel*, in black stockings and a top hat. My father's diary simply states that we were present.

Christian and Helen now both had secretarial jobs in London and when, at the end of January, Noël and I returned to boarding-school, my mother also departed for a long stay with Aunty Lil in Torquay, leaving my father alone in Liverpool. Though he complains in his diary only of occasional loneliness, the routine of his life must have been depressingly monotonous. Every week-day, including Saturday morning, he spent in Grahams' office in Liverpool, performing his duties as manager, although business was almost at a standstill. His evenings were usually spent at home alone reading; on Saturday afternoons he would take a walk or watch a local football match, and on Sundays he went, as was his life-long custom, to morning and evening service at the Presbyterian Church. At Easter Mother and Aunty Lil returned to the Reeds' house in Buckinghamshire, not far from High Wycombe, and Noël and I were invited to stay at the beginning of the school holidays. My father joined us there for a few days, after which we all returned to Liverpool. In the summer he took my mother, Noël and me up to Stirling for two weeks, and we stayed, as before, in Aunt Christian's big old house on Park Avenue, which was lit by gas and where a semblance of the old life still existed: she kept a cook and a maid, and there were family meals, taken with the utmost decorum round a big mahogany dining-table. My Uncle Dan had died, but in his study at the top of the house were all his books, and I retreated there after tea to read John Buchan and explore volumes of the Victorian *Punch*. Every day we went for walks over the moors and hills my father loved ('A splendid day for climbing. Sandy did very well, trotted all the way down from Ben Cleugh') and which, if Fate had been kinder, he would never have left.

The next month, October, he was notified by letter from Head Office that the Liverpool branch of Grahams was to close and a week later he himself was given his notice, his engagement to cease at the end of the year, when he would receive six months' salary. 'Gave notice to the staff,' he wrote on October 30th, 'very sorry to have to do so.' The next week-end Helen and Christian came up from London and a family conference was held to make some sort of plan for the future. With two daughters working in London and Noël and myself at school not far away, the obvious course was to move there. Since the 1890s Hampstead had been a colony for emigrant business-men from Scotland, who built themselves huge baronial-style houses, some of which still line Fitzjohn's Avenue and the adjoining streets, and the St John's Wood Presbyterian Church had a large and wealthy congregation. A cousin of my father's on his mother's side, Willie Galbraith, who lived in Netherhall Gardens, suggested we take a flat in the neighbourhood and offered to try and find my father employment in London. I have a copy of the letter my father typed out giving details of his previous experience. The last paragraph reads: 'As regards my financial position, you know all about Grahams' affairs, so I need not say anything on that point. As you can see, I have had a good deal of business experience, but have never had much to do with books; I am taking steps to remedy this. I am very anxious to find work of some sort and am prepared to do anything in order to earn a few pounds a week, so as to enable me to keep a home together and to do a little towards educating my two younger children.' He was nearly fifty-eight.

A home was found in a maisonette flat, which consisted of the two top floors and attic of a house in Denning Road, only a few minutes' walk from Hampstead Heath. At the end of November my parents began to pack up the contents of the house in Wavertree, and on the fourteenth of December the movers came and my mother left for London. 'Everything cleared out of the house before four o'clock,' wrote my father. 'Very sad to see an empty home.' As he was still working for Grahams, he was obliged to go and stay with friends.

I first heard of the impending move from Noël, who came up to Godstowe to tell me. Like my father, she has always preferred the country to the town, and she did not care for the idea at all. 'We're going to live in London,' she fumed, 'and it'll be beastly. There won't be anywhere for you to play or go walks.' Falling in with her mood, as I was in the habit of doing, I also became depressed. I was hardly to know that London, so far from being beastly, would turn out to be my natural habitat.

The Nineteen Thirties

IT was not only Noël who resented the move to the Metropolis;
Helen also objected, but for different reasons: 'I hated you all
coming to London, because we were thoroughly enjoying ourselves,
living a free life – although of course Christian always kept me in
order. I came back from work one evening and told her I had been
invited out to dinner by this very ordinary little man at the office, Mr
Clark, who used to loan us his tickets for the Proms. And she said, "Of
course you can't go out to dinner with a man like that." So I obediently
went back to him and said, "I can't go." ' So the 'free life' did not
include men; but compared with what they had left behind in the
North, London had a great deal to offer. Christian was working as a
secretary at one of the first British advertising agencies, the London
Press Exchange: 'Mr Therm was one of our most successful campaigns,
and Three Nuns tobacco, grown by those splendid bronzed Rhodesian
farmers! Ever-Ready Batteries and Cadbury's Chocolate were other
products advertised by us and most of the business was done on the
golf course or at lunches, but nothing like the mammoth expense
account gorging there is now. We managed to enjoy ourselves
amazingly cheaply. You could get into the gallery at the theatre for as
little as one and nine, and the pit, which was at the back of the stalls,
was three shillings. One had a jolly good lunch of a roll and butter,
cheese and coffee for ninepence – and that was being extravagant.' But
working hours were long, from nine in the morning until seven at
night, with one Saturday a month off, which, as Helen points out, 'was
a privilege and not a right. And three evenings a week I had to be
prepared to stay at the office until nine o'clock at night, if required – and
very often did. Friday was the worst, because I was paid after lunch.
Christian was paid before lunch and could walk to work from Westminster, but I had to have tuppence for my bus to the city and fourpence
for my lunch. So we always had to turn out our pockets and find
sixpence. Fortunately they had very good brown bread at the hostel,

so that if the worst came to the worst I used to stock up with that and take it to the office and then buy an apple, and that was my lunch. Still, I don't think it did us any harm.'

I came home for the Christmas holidays to find my mother and Christian and Helen installed in the flat in Denning Road, and in no time at all I had forgotten Noël's gloomy prognostication and become a Londoner, which I have remained ever since. True, we had no garden, but Hampstead Heath was almost on the door-step and was more like the country than anything I had known in Sale or Wavertree. With its hills and streams, its lakes, ponds and woods, it was the best playground imaginable and before long I had made part of it my domain, and even today when I visit it I can recognise every tree, bush and path. At that time Old Hampstead, as the area in which we lived was called, still had the look and feeling of a village: South End Road, which winds along past the Heath, across the North London Railway and down to the local cinema, was our high street, where we shopped at the old-fashioned Bakery, the Family Butcher and the Sweet Shop, which was also the Post Office. But if you turned right out of Denning Road instead of left towards the Heath, a few minutes' walk brought you to Haverstock Hill and Belsize Park Tube Station from where for threepence the Underground carried you in a flash to Leicester Square in the heart of the West End. I soon found that if I took the correct exit out of Leicester Square Station, I would emerge just beside Wyndhams Theatre and could walk along the front of it examining the photographs of the latest play, and then turn left down a passage, where the stools were lined up for the gallery queue, and which took me, past some rather strange bookshops, to St Martin's Lane and the New Theatre, where there were more photographs to see. Down St Martin's Lane, beyond the London Press Exchange, where Christian worked, was the Duke of York's and, opposite it, the Coliseum. Round the corner and into Charing Cross Road again, and there was the Garrick. Across the road to Leicester Square, where the Alhambra and Daly's still stood, before they were demolished and rebuilt as cinemas, and beyond lay Piccadilly Circus and Shaftesbury Avenue, with another whole row of theatres to be explored. By the time I was ten I knew my way all round the West End and could reel off exactly what was on at each theatre and cinema and who was in it.

But in the meanwhile a rather more important aspect of my education was being taken care of. It seems curious now, but it was a fact that the more our circumstances deteriorated, the higher went my father's aspirations for Noël and myself. She had decided to become a doctor, and Wycombe Abbey had fortunately granted her a scholarship in 1931 for the rest of her time there. There was a place waiting for me at the Headmaster's House, Harrow, but it was rapidly becoming obvious that I could only take it up if I too won a scholarship, and a substantial one at that. It now turned out that a school friend of my father's sister, Helen, had married Edward Sanderson, the headmaster of Elstree Preparatory School in Hertfordshire, which had a close connection with Harrow and a reputation for grooming boys for scholarships. The fees were high, probably among the highest in the country, but Aunt Helen's husband, Uncle Douglas, generously offered to contribute towards them. There was only one condition: I must learn to box. Aunt Helen wrote to Mrs Sanderson, and after the necessary negotiations it was arranged that I should go to Elstree in the autumn of 1932.

I celebrated my departure from Godstowe by producing my first play, in the drawing-room of the house-mistress, Miss Ewing, who had succeeded my beloved Miss Billyeald. During Speech-day week-end that year I had been taken to a matinée at the Open Air Theatre to see Robert Atkins' production of *A Midsummer Night's Dream*, in which he himself played Bottom, with Phyllis Neilson Terry as Oberon and Leslie French as Puck. What had most impressed me was the Mechanicals' play at the court of Theseus, particularly the fact that Thisbe was performed by a man in female disguise who assumed a squeaky treble voice. I decided on returning to Godstowe that I would produce my version of *Pyramus and Thisbe*, but I would go one further than Shakespeare: I would play Thisbe and all the male parts would be played by girls. At first my friends were reluctant, but they were soon won round by a combination of bullying and cajolery, and the performance was arranged for the last evening of term. The script was severely curtailed; in fact the only speech retained in its entirety was Thisbe's lamentation on discovering the death of Pyramus. This became the comedy high-spot of the play and was received with a very gratifying ovation. I had taken the first step in my chosen career!

The term at Wycombe Abbey began a few days before Elstree's, and that morning Noël and I went for a last walk together on the Heath and she gave me a few words of advice on how to behave at my new school: 'Whatever you do, don't swank about anything. And if you make friends with someone who is senior to you, don't call him by his christian name until he gives you permission.' I never had a chance to test the validity of her second maxim, because at Elstree no-one ever called anyone, no matter how intimate the friendship, by anything except his surname. But the first was certainly sound, and I soon discovered that 'swanking' or 'showing off' was only less reprehensible

B

[33]

than sneaking in the schoolboys' penal code. My father had no particular instructions for me except to say my prayers every night; but on
the evening before term began my sister Christian suggested that, if
any other boy attempted to get the better of me, I should simply say,
'My father was Captain of Football at Harrow', and that would put him
in his place. Thus armed, I set off the next afternoon with my mother,
by Underground to Edgware and then by bus to Elstree. The school
lay at the top of a steep hill, on the outskirts of Elstree Village. It was
an eighteenth century country house, with various more recent additions
and outbuildings, and it fronted on to the main road, on the other side
of which were the playing fields and the chapel, reached, for safety's
sake, by an underground passage. The bus stop was just beside the
chapel, which was fortunate for me and my family, as we had no car.

My mother and I were greeted by Mrs Sanderson, a gracious and
handsome lady not unlike Ethel Barrymore, with a penchant for
Pekingese, who gave us tea in her drawing-room along with the other
new boys and their parents, after which it was suggested that we
should take a look round the rest of the building. The classrooms and
dormitories were pretty much the same as I had been used to at
Godstowe, but when my mother and I reached the wash-room and
lavatories I was brought up sharp against something totally strange – a
urinal. Having no idea of the function of this row of white china stalls,
where water hissed and gurgled, I turned into one of the cubicles
opposite, which housed the more familiar receptacles, only to find to
my horror that not one of them had a door. For the first time I began
to feel apprehensive about what life would be like in a high-class
preparatory school.

We all returned to Mrs Sanderson's drawing-room, where we were
joined by the headmaster – a distinguished white-haired gentleman
with a military bearing – who informed us it was time to say goodbye
to our parents. While this was going on, I became aware of a noise
like a distant cattle stampede which penetrated the green baize door
separating the 'School Side' from the 'Private Side'. It turned out to be
our fellow-pupils returning and, when we had waved goodbye to our
parents as they disappeared down the drive, we were taken through by
Mr Sanderson to meet them. He shepherded us into the main classroom
or Big School Room, as it was called, and left us there, a bewildered
and rather frightened little group surrounded by a horde of shouting,
rampaging strangers. One by one we broke away and went off to try
and make contact with the natives. Suddenly I was confronted by a boy
a year or so older than myself who glared at me and said, 'Hello, new
squit! What's your name?' Remembering Christian's advice, I replied,

'Alexander Galbraith Wilson, and my father was Captain of Football at Harrow.' For a moment my interrogator was taken aback; then he shrugged and said, 'Well, I don't blame him,' and vanished into the mob. I was so baffled by this response to my magic formula that I never ventured to use it again.

It would seem, to judge from innumerable novels and memoirs, that the majority of English writers have unhappy memories of their preparatory schools, and I am afraid I am no exception. The five years I spent at Elstree were on the whole the most disagreeable of my life and looking back on them now I am amazed to think that I endured them with hardly a murmur of complaint, as indeed did most of the other boys who were there with me. I suppose it had been dinned into me so often how lucky I was to be going there that I never dared to tell my parents how awful it was. For a start, the food was appalling, worse even than any I had during my three years in the Army, and it was not only bad, it was inadequate. Our last meal of a long day was at six o'clock, when we were given bread and jam and tea, and nothing else, unless one's parents could afford to pay extra for either three or six eggs a week; my parents of course could not, so that as well as going hungry one was publicly exposed as coming from a poor family. Halfway through my time there so many epidemics broke out that a specialist was called in; he said at once that we were being underfed, and from then on we were given a hot dish with our tea and Ovaltine and biscuits before we went to bed. But the standard of cooking never improved, and I can still see and taste the lunch which was dished up every Wednesday and Saturday without fail, winter and summer: boiled mutton (which was christened 'Polly' after the ancient horse that drew the roller over the cricket pitches) and boiled greens (or 'laurel leaves', as we called them) followed by tapioca or sago.

What was saved on feeding us must, I assume, have been spent on the masters' salaries, because the standard of teaching was exceptional and the school's claim of a high scholarship rate was certainly justified. But our leisure activities were restricted and unimaginative: we were all obliged, unless ill or physically incapable, to play football, rugger or, in the summer, interminable games of cricket, every afternoon of the week, and on Sundays we were taken for long and tedious walks in crocodile formation, not through the fields and woods in the neighbourhood, but along the featureless arterial roads which surrounded Elstree. During the breaks between classes we were not allowed to choose our own form of relaxation; we had to go out into a gravelled yard adjoining the school buildings and kick a football about or appear to be engaged in some sort of physical exercise. On Saturday evenings there was occasionally a lantern lecture and, towards the end of my time, even a film; but the only activity organized by the staff was a club run for the senior boys by the music mistress, Miss Davis, the sole person who did anything creative for us outside school hours. Routine persisted even after bed-time: we had to undress and perform our ablutions in total silence, after which a bell was rung for ten minutes' talk or reading before lights out. This rule also applied to the first half of every meal, presumably so that our attention should not be diverted from the task of eating the food.

And always, no matter where we were or what we were doing, we were supervised and spied upon (which explained the absence of doors on the lavatories), with the result that the only place one ever achieved some privacy was in bed at night. The dormitories were all named after heroes of the 1914 War – Haig, French, Beatty, Jellicoe and so on – names which may have meant a great deal to the masters but had little significance for us. My first dormitory was called Horne and I never did discover who he was or what he did to justify being commemorated in this manner. It was at the end of a long passage which ran from one end of the school to the other, terminating in the sick-rooms, which were called Egypt (the home of the Ten Plagues). Being new boys, we were supervised by the housekeeper Miss Tate, a formidable woman with hefty thighs and a sloping shelf of bosom, who was nick-named 'Botta' from her idiosyncratic way of pronouncing 'butter', and punctually at eight o'clock she would appear in the door-way, jangling a bunch of keys, and say 'Settle down now, everybody!' We obediently did so, and with a brief 'Goodnight' she would switch off the light, leaving me to darkness and my private thoughts.

These usually took the form of fantasies in which I had the leading part. One night, after Miss Davis had played us a record of the Temple Choir Boy singing *Oh, For The Wings of a Dove*, I imagined I was dying of some incurable disease surrounded by my sorrowing family; at the last moment I rose up in my bed and sang, in a clear, pure treble, of the vision of heaven opening before me. Another night I flung myself in front of an on-coming car, thus saving the life of my current hero, Campbell, a fair-haired boy in an upper form. While I lay dying in the Sanatorium, he came to thank me and also offered to be my friend, whereupon I began to make a miraculous recovery.

But my favourite fantasy was set in the future. In it I wrote and composed a musical show which was a hit in the West End and then went to Broadway and repeated its success. The story of the show varied from night to night, but it consisted mostly of spectacular production numbers featuring several hundred singers and dancers. I even got as far as composing one of the songs: it was called *Love is Like a Pretty Maiden*, and most of the lyric consisted of 'Ah-ah-ah' or 'Ooh-ooh-ooh'. It was to be sung by a tenor with a voice like Dick Powell, while a huge chorus of Pretty Maidens, dressed in crinolines and picture hats, paraded round a set composed of trees covered with white blossom. The tune had to stay in my head, along with several others, because I still had no knowledge of how to put it on paper. But I decided that one day, somehow or other, I would learn to write music.

The rigours and repressions of life at Elstree, whatever their other effects upon me, certainly made me appreciate my home and my family more than ever. With the help of Cousin Willie, my father had obtained a job with the Gas, Light and Coke Company, whose emblem, Mr Therm, had been invented by the London Press Exchange, and which was later to become North Thames Gas. But it did not pay very well and my mother began to devise ways of supplementing the family income. During their summer holidays my sisters had started going to Germany on an 'exchange', a system by which they stayed with German families, who then sent their sons or daughters to stay with us. It worked pretty well: our first visitor, Fritz, was blond, handsome and charming, and caused a sensation at Wycombe Abbey, when he arrived to visit Noël. Herr Burzer was not so successful: he had the face of a thug, with several duelling scars, and boasted continually of the superiority of the German race. I had to share a room with him, and he was always admiring his own physique in the mirror. While he was staying with us, the death of Hindenburg was announced on the radio. As the German national anthem was played, he stood rigidly to attention, an alarming expression of satisfaction on his face, while our other 'exchange', Fräulein Schacht from Heidelberg, stood with her head bowed and her eyes full of apprehension. After Herr Burzer left, we were visited by the police: we had apparently been housing a suspected spy! The 'exchanges' gave Mother the idea of taking in other foreign boarders, or Paying Guests as they were euphemistically called, and she was so successful that for the next few years I was never sure which room I would be sleeping in when I came home for the holidays or who I might be sharing it with. The Denning Road maisonette soon became too small for our needs, and in 1934 we moved down the hill to Swiss Cottage where Mother had found a flat with six rooms, over a perambulator shop. It also had an attic and a flat roof, so that there was always space for one more P.G., and I remember several occasions when the place was so full that my father had to sleep on a camp bed in the hall.

Nevertheless, in spite of the inconveniences and discomforts, it was home, and I always dreaded saying goodbye to it when the holidays ended. Luckily I now had several close friends at school, in particular Charles Stromberg, the son of a Cambridgeshire parson, whose circumstances were similar in some respects to mine: 'I went to Elstree in 1931. I think there was a slight deduction for clergy's sons, and I was sent there with the idea of going on to a public school. I was senior to you, but you could be in different forms for different subjects, and I was very backward in maths. So you must have caught up with me somehow.' I had in fact caught up by a stroke of luck. During my last year at Godstowe I had been promoted from the kindergarten to the main school, where I even got as far as a Latin class presided over by the ferocious Mr Turner. On my first day at Elstree I was allocated to the bottom form, Seven B, along with the other new boys. The Form Master, Mr Burton, who had lost an eye playing squash, but had also captained Yorkshire and always wore a cricket blazer, asked anyone who knew 'amo' to put his hand up. I was the only one to do so. 'Do you know "mensa" too?' 'Yes, sir,' I replied truthfully. 'Then we don't want you here. Off you go to Seven A.' As a result of this I acquired a reputation for being 'brainy' and a likely candidate for a Harrow scholarship, and found myself progressing through the school at the rate of a form a term. I think Charles and I coincided round about the fifth form and began to lay the foundations of a friendship that has lasted ever since. We were both less well off than the other boys and we both detested games, but what really drew us together was our devotion to the Cinema. Having commenced my film-going at the age of four I did have what might be called a head-start on Charles: 'Living in the country, in the remote fens, I had hardly ever seen a film. But I was taken to something that was considered suitable for a child, in a double programme, and the other half was *Gold-Diggers of 1933*. That started me off.' But our interest in the Cinema was certainly not encouraged, and, thanks to the school regulations, even our holiday film-going was restricted. 'There was this daft rule that one couldn't go to a film for three weeks before the beginning of term, because cinemas were supposed to be full of infectious diseases. Most parents just ignored it, but my father was a parson and yours was a Presbyterian, so we had to observe it. I remember being furious in 1934, because *Queen Christina* was on at the Empress, Wisbech, and I had to miss it.' I had been luckier. *Queen Christina* came to the Hampstead Picture Playhouse before the prohibited period, and I decided to spend my entire week's pocket money of half a crown and take my sister Helen to see it, in the evening. It was a momentous occasion for me, and in preparation I bought *Picturegoer* magazine which carried a supplement entirely devoted to the film. Long before the great evening arrived I knew everything there was to know about it: the names of the supporting cast, the director, the designer, how long it had taken to make, and of course every detail of Garbo's life and career. Previous to *Queen Christina* I had gone to the cinema quite indiscriminately, without knowing or caring what I was going to see, provided it was a film; now I became a 'Fan' who bought two or three movie magazines a week and knew the particulars of every film on in Town or released to the locals. Another source of information was cigarette cards: Charles and I collected every Film Star series avidly, swapping with other boys at school and even conniving with the maids who smoked, in order to obtain a missing number. Owing to the three-week rule, we had to cram as many films as possible into the first part of the holidays, and at Christmas and Easter this gave us little more than a week, so the pace was furious. 'I remember coming to stay with you in 1935 at the beginning of the holidays, and we managed to see *The Thirty-Nine Steps*, *Jack of all Trades*, with Jack Hulbert, George Arliss in *Cardinal Richelieu* and *Becky Sharp*, the first Technicolor film. Cinemas in London opened at ten o'clock in the morning, and the Empire, Leicester Square, used to advertise One Thousand Seats at One and Six before One p.m. So things were made easier for us.' After *Queen Christina*, which more than lived up to what I had read about it, I became a devotee of Garbo's, while Charles, having seen *The Little Minister* (which I missed), gave his allegiance to Katherine Hepburn. Film magazines were of course banned at school, and during term we had to rely for information on one of the masters, Mr Walmsley. 'He used to go to the cinema once a week in Edgware and come back and tell us all about it. He was the only member of the staff who was at all sympathetic: he used to lend us his *Evening Standard*, and we read all the film reviews.'

Apart from having our particular idols, we were both rather partial to Madeleine Carroll, who, while no great shakes as an actress, was undoubtedly one of the most beautiful women on the screen, and this led indirectly to our forming a clandestine dramatic society. 'It really started on the cricket fields, where we used to spend hours waiting to go in and bat, as we were always sent in last. In the summer term we had to wear what were called "floppy hats" made of grey felt, and we used to amuse outselves modelling them into various styles, specially the "halo" style which Madeleine Carroll wore in *The Thirty-Nine Steps*.' Modelling hats led on to making up plays, in which I invariably took the lead, and by the following term we had formed a group which performed in the squash courts during the breaks when we should have been kicking footballs around. Inevitably we were discovered and banished from the squash courts but, rather surprisingly, given permission to use one of the class-rooms on Saturday afternoons for our dramatic activities. This concession may have been due to Mr Walmsley's intervention or it could have come about because the headmaster had retired and handed the school over to his son, Ian Sanderson. He was an ex-Naval Commander, with no academic training whatever; but he taught mathematics and French to the lower forms, and spent the rest of his time devising new time-tables or 'schedules', as he called them, which invariably caused confusion amongst the boys and dismay in the common-room. His wife was pretty and vivacious, and once confided to my mother that when school life became too much for her, she would retreat to their bedroom and tap-dance furiously. She made a change from her majestic mother-in-law, whose public functions had been confined to running the Wolf Cubs and appearing at evening prayers, dressed in a flowing dinner gown, to play the harmonium, and although life at Elstree continued to be austere, the atmosphere did become a little more relaxed.

Now that we lived in London, I was visiting the theatre fairly regularly, usually at matinées but sometimes in the evening. The success of the 1933 season was *Richard of Bordeaux* by Gordon Daviot at the New (now Albery) Theatre, in which John Gielgud played the King in a production beautifully designed by Motley. I was taken to see it and was very impressed, more perhaps by the décor than the play itself, since I particularly remember the men's shoes which had toes of such length that they had to be fastened to the knees with gold and silver chains. But I also admired John Gielgud, who from then on seemed to make his home at the New, either as director or actor. At the end of 1934 he played the lead in his own production of *Hamlet* and it too was a tremendous success, achieving the second longest run that the play has ever had. I was taken to an evening performance in the Christmas holidays and was so bowled over that I decided to present my own *Hamlet* the following term. Commander and Mrs Sanderson, Mr Walmsley and Miss Davis were officially invited, and we spent the whole term rehearsing it. To begin with, I reduced the text to forty-five minutes' playing time, while retaining most of Hamlet's soliloquies (I was playing the lead, naturally) and Polonius' speech to Laertes which we had already learnt in English class. My mother provided the costumes and props, including a skull of Yorick carved out of a large turnip; this shrank as the weeks went by, and finally had to be replaced by a fresh one. Helen typed the programmes and Charles was in charge of the lighting and music: 'The lighting consisted of switching the class-room lights on and off and slowly drawing a curtain on the line, "But see, the dawn in russet mantle clad . . .", and the music was the Pilgrims' Chorus from *Tannhäuser* played on the gramophone to cover scene changes.' On the day of the performance I woke up with a stomach ache which became more pronounced every hour. By the afternoon I was in a good deal of pain, but, true to tradition, the show went on and the Commander, probably against his better judgment, was so impressed that he made a short speech afterwards, inviting us all to tea the next day. But we never went, because after a night of agony I was rushed off to hospital in an ambulance and operated on for acute appendicitis. We did do another production the following term of a very feeble play which I had concocted; but though we were given our postponed tea-party, it was an unworthy successor to *Hamlet*.

1935 was Jubilee Year and my sisters and I watched the procession from a position by the parapet above Trafalgar Square which we had occupied since the early hours of the morning. It was enormously exciting and colourful and well worth the long hours of waiting. My mother, who had somehow got a seat in a window along the route, declared that the most moving moment of all was when she saw the toe of Queen Mary's pink shoe peeping from under her long, glittering dress. I had quite recovered from my operation, but in those days one was kept in hospital for a week or more and then sent to 'convalesce' for a fortnight. By the time I came home, since it was the Easter holidays, there was only one day to go before the dreaded three-week ban. I rushed off to Golders Green to see a double bill consisting of George Arliss in *The Iron Duke* and a version of *Lorna Doone* starring Victoria Hopper, which was small compensation for all the films I had missed. But the Jubilee occasioned a spate of documentaries about the reign of King George V, and one of these, entitled *Twenty-Five Glorious Years* or something of the sort, was playing at the Polytechnic Cinema in Regent Street, which, because it tended to show 'animal pictures' and films specifically made for children, was the only cinema my father would allow me to visit during the period of the ban. He agreed to take me to see it one Saturday afternoon, without realising, since he very rarely went to the cinema, that it was half of a double bill. At the end of *Twenty-Five Glorious Years* he rose to leave, but I pulled at his sleeve. 'There seems to be another film as well,' I observed innocently as the MGM lion began to roar. There was indeed: Joan Crawford, Clark Gable and Robert Montgomery in *Forsaking All Others*. It was a typical comedy of the period, in which Crawford, having been engaged to Gable, decides to marry Montgomery, who lets her down; she returns to Gable, deserts him again for Montgomery, and finally runs off with Gable on the eve of her marriage. At one point Clark put Joan over his knee and spanked her with a hairbrush, and I sensed that this was the only episode of which my father approved. When we left the cinema, I was fully expecting him to give me a severe ticking-off for having conned him into letting me see such a film; but all he said, as we walked down Regent Street, was, 'She seemed rather a silly sort of girl, didn't she?'

Noël had left Wycombe Abbey in 1934 and was studying medicine at University College, where she had obtained one of the few places open to women students. Christian now caused a certain amount of excitement by getting herself a job on *Vogue* as secretary to the Beauty Editress. She brought a free copy of the magazine home with her every fortnight and I became familiar with the photographs of Cecil Beaton, the fashion drawings of Eric and Christian Bérard, and the opinions of Lesley Blanch, who covered every cultural activity in London. But Helen created the greatest sensation when she applied for, and was given, a post in the Colonial Secretariat in Zanzibar. The very name, Zanzibar, seemed to be beyond belief glamorous and exotic, and we even called our new cat after it. Helen's departure was to take place during the summer holidays of 1935, but, to my distress, I was sent up to Stirling to stay with Aunt Christian a few days beforehand. I later discovered that Helen preferred to say goodbye to me rather than vice versa, and in any case I think my disappointment stemmed not so much from missing the leave-taking as from being absent when Helen took the whole family to see Cole Porter's *Anything Goes* at the Palace Theatre. A day or two later I was having the ritual breakfast at the vast dining-table in St Margaret's, when a letter arrived from my mother enclosing a cutting from the *Daily Express*. It was headed: ' "A ticket to the Arabian Nights" says Helen' and went on in the same vein. Without thinking, I passed it over to Aunt Christian. Adjusting her pince-nez, she read it, uttered one brief syllable, 'H'm!', passed the cutting back to me, and turned her attention to the *Scotsman*.

On Helen's departure Mother cleared out one of the larger rooms in the flat, which had been used as a double bedroom, and let it to a New Zealander, Terry Vaughan, who was studying music at the Royal Academy and who installed his own grand piano. Besides being a serious musician, Terry had written numbers for his University Revue Society, The Purple Patches, and he could also tap-dance. These accomplishments fascinated me, and my fantasy musicals began to take on a more detailed form. Lying awake in the school dormitory one summer night, I found myself trying to remember the music and words of the original Charleston, which for several years had been as dead as the Dodo. The tunes on our gramophone were now, more often than not, from the Astaire-Rogers films: *Smoke Gets in Your Eyes, Cheek to Cheek, Let's Face the Music, A Fine Romance.* At the beginning of the Christmas holidays in 1935 I went to the Empire and sat twice through the new *Broadway Melody* which introduced Eleanor Powell, a rather hearty girl with a wide grin and the ability to tap several hundred times to the minute, and an incredibly handsome leading man called Robert Taylor. The hit number was *You are My Lucky Star* and that too was played continually on our gramophone. Christian, who had more sophisticated tastes than the rest of us, was addicted to *You're the Top* and later to the songs from Rodgers and Hart's *On Your Toes*, which was a hit on Broadway but flopped in London. She also had an unaccountable yen for a number called *She Wore a Little Jacket of Blue*, but I have a feeling that this was connected with a current romance.

As if song-writing and tap-dancing were not enough, Terry now revealed that he had a distant relative who worked at Boreham Wood film studios. These lay down the other side of the hill from Elstree School, and were regarded by the authorities as all the Cities of the Plain rolled into one, but naturally for Charles and me their proximity was endlessly tantalising. Terry now proposed that he and I should pay his relative a visit and, permission having been reluctantly granted by my father, we set out one morning for Elstree in a high state of excitement; but when we arrived at the studio gates and Terry gave his relative's name, the guard said no such person worked there. However I must have looked woefully crestfallen, for after Terry had explained that he was a Colonial and I was a movie-crazy schoolboy from up the hill, we were let in and taken on a brief tour. It was a depressing experience and I have only two memories of it: watching Cary Grant doing interminable retakes of a fight scene for *The Amazing Quest of Ernest Bliss*, and being shown plaster miniatures of sheep which were to appear in the background of a film version of *As You Like It* which starred Elisabeth Bergner. We left rather sadly to catch the bus back to Edgware, and I have never again felt the slightest desire to visit a film studio, preferring just to watch the end product from a seat in the cinema.

Charles left Elstree at the end of 1935 to go to a public school in Canterbury, and our dramatic society ceased its activities, because I had to get down to the job of winning that essential scholarship. During my visit to Scotland I had announced in front of a gathering of relatives that I would be going to Harrow in 1937, which led to a cry of shocked disbelief from Aunt Dizzy. 'Ooh, Alexander!' she breathed – my Scots relations refused to call me Sandy – 'And how do you think you're going to manage that?' I disdained to reply, but made a firm resolve that, if only to show them all, I would fulfil my father's ambition of sending me to his old school.

I was one of three candidates from Elstree. The other two were James Collier and John Royde-Smith, who was a nephew of Naomi Royde-Smith, the novelist, and, to use a contemporary expression, the 'brainiest' person I have ever known. He was a frail boy, with glasses and a huge forehead, the archetype of the scholastic genius, and his academic knowledge seemed limitless. He also had a fund of knowledge on a subject which had so far been neglected in my education – Sex – and began initiating me one evening by asking me if I knew what the initials 'B.B.' stood for. I didn't.

'Bloody Bastard,' he told me, and then asked me if I knew what 'Bastard' meant. I said that I thought it was some sort of medieval serving-man. He laughed rather patronisingly and explained its true meaning, and then went on to ask me if I knew the meaning of 'B.F.'. When he had explained that too, I was a good deal wiser, and during the ensuing months, when we had time off from learning Latin and Greek, he continued to enlighten me on every aspect of the ever-interesting topic. He had read both the Claudius books by Robert Graves, which were published at about this time, and the excesses of Caligula and Messalina made ideal illustrations for his discourses. Perhaps this rendered my view of sex a little recherché, but at least I was no longer in total ignorance of how it functioned.

1936 began gloomily with the death of King George just a day before we returned to school for the spring term. One minor effect of this was that overnight a film starring Sidney Howard, called *Where's George?* (a title borrowed from the famous advertisement, in which the reply was 'Gone to Lyonch'), became *The Hope of his Side*. This must have entailed quite a feat of organisation, as the film was on release to all the local Odeons. Like most women at that time, my mother and my sister Christian were admirers of the Prince of Wales and felt that, as Edward the Eighth, he would bring a breath of fresh air to the Monarchy. He was considered very 'modern', which was the contemporary way of saying 'with it', and this was exemplified for me in the design of the new stamps: a photograph instead of a drawing, against a completely plain background. Of course other aspects of his 'modernity' were carefully concealed from most of us, although everyone speculated about whom he would marry. Mr Walmsley was heard to remark casually that he thought it would be a good idea if the King were to have an American wife, which drew mysteriously mixed reactions when I reported it to my family.

We were also beginning to worry about the increasing power of the Dictators in Europe, particularly of Mussolini who was actually making war on Abyssinia and defying the League of Nations. He and Hitler seemed to be turning into villains, when heretofore they had been regarded rather as clowns. There had even been a brief craze at school for making the Nazi salute and shouting 'Heil Hitler!': when your opposite number responded, you gave him a jab in the ribs and ran off. But now things were changing, and I began to understand why the lady from Heidelberg had looked so apprehensive. On the first day of the Easter holidays Mr Walmsley, who was on friendly terms with my family, took me to the Leicester Square Theatre to see Korda's new film, *Things to Come*, adapted from a book by H. G. Wells. It had caused a sensation with its elaborate futuristic sets and a spectacular climax where Raymond Massey, defying a mob of disapproving workers, sends his daughter, the beautiful ballet-dancer, Pearl Argyle, in a rocket to the moon, accompanied by her boy-friend, all to the music of Arthur Bliss; but the image that remained with me came in the opening sequence of the picture, when a crowd of West End revellers wave mockingly at the enemy planes which then proceed to bomb London to smithereens.

Our flat was positively bulging with P.G.s of various nationalities and my mother, deciding that a safety valve was necessary, found a farm labourer's cottage to let near Bolney in Sussex for a few shillings a week. She announced that if Noël would buy a car, she would rent the cottage. The car Noël found was a 1928 Morris, costing £15, which would probably fetch a fancy price today on the vintage car market: it was a two-seater saloon with a 'dickey', a kind of boot which opened to take two more passengers. The cottage had no electricity or mains water; we used oil lamps and drew our water from a well, and the lavatory was a shed at the bottom of the garden. But it could accommodate all the family and a P.G. or two, and the garden gave us vegetables and masses of apples and pears. Nearly every week-end a party of us would travel down there, either in Noël's car or on the Southdown bus, and the cottage would echo to the tune of *There's a Small Hotel* or *September in the Rain*, played on our newly-acquired portable gramophone. But I cannot pretend I was immediately converted to the Country Life; in fact I was sometimes despatched to Bolney against my will. One week-end I even wrote in the Visitors' Book 'Would have gone to *Careless Rapture*, if I hadn't had to come here.'

The theatrical sensation of 1935 had been a musical extravaganza called *Glamorous Night*, 'devised, written and produced', as the programme had it, by Ivor Novello, at Drury Lane. It was a gigantic Ruritanian spectacle, which included the shipwreck of a cruise liner in full view of the audience. *Careless Rapture* opened in 1936 and was even bigger and better, the finale of the second act being the destruction by earthquake and fire of an entire Chinese town. I had seen *Glamorous Night* and was panting to see its successor. Even Commander Sanderson had been and admitted that, having been out East himself, he was impressed by the way the sky had changed colour just before the earthquake. A friend of mine from school had asked me to go with him and his mother to a Saturday matinée, in the stalls, where we could never afford to sit, but my mother told me I would have to refuse, as we were going down to the cottage. But I did get to see the show eventually, from the gallery, and revelled in it. The earthquake was sensational and, having recently seen Jeanette MacDonald in *San Francisco*, I became fixated on earthquakes, and still am, although no doubt my first experience of a real one would immediately cure me. The earthquake in *Careless Rapture* was followed by a kind of dream ballet in front of a huge idol, in which both Dorothy Dickson and Ivor Novello, temporarily disguised as a Chinese Princess and her Lover, appeared with fashionably bare midriffs. I had seen Dorothy Dickson earlier that year in a revue called *Spread it Abroad* written by Herbert Farjeon: she and Walter Crisham had sung and danced a new number called *These Foolish Things*, and a member of the supporting cast had contributed a caricature of the Prime Minister's daughter, Ishbel MacDonald. Her name was Hermione Gingold.

My interest in the theatre was taking such a serious turn that my parents felt it necessary to consult the Commander, and one day during the following term I was summoned to his study.

'I believe you're thinking of taking up the Theatre, Wilson?'

'Yes, sir.'

'Well, I'd like to tell you a little story. A week or so ago an old boy came to see me. Walked up the drive, shabby clothes, holes in his socks and so on. Turned out he'd gone on the Stage. I asked him in here and we had a chat. D'you know why he'd come to see me?'

'No, sir.'

'Wanted to borrow some money. That's an actor for you. Now you'd do much better to go in for the Law or try for the Foreign Office. And you'd make your parents a lot happier. D'you understand?'

'Yes, sir.'

'Right then. Cut along.'

The whole interview only irritated me. Surely he realised that if I went into the Theatre, I would be successful? And even if I did run short of cash, the last person in the world I would try to borrow it from would be the Commander. As for making my parents happy, I felt certain they would change their minds when I had that hit show running in London and New York. Perhaps even the Commander would change his.

But for the time being I had to concentrate on the scholarship, and I have never worked as hard as I did then. In fact I believe I am inclined to be lazy as a result of it, because ever since the freedom of working when I feel like it has been such a luxury. The three of us, Collier, Royde-Smith and myself, were closeted with the Senior Classics Master, Mr Stainton, in a room at the other end of the building from the rest of the school, and there we slogged away at Virgil, Livy and Herodotus, until in the end we thought nothing of translating a *Times* leader into Latin or a page of hexameters into blank verse. Most of the time I did it all willingly, conscious of what was at stake; but occasionally my attention wandered, and once Mr Stainton, who himself had the profile and coiffure of an Ancient Greek, barked at me, 'The trouble with you, Wilson, is that you're too busy thinking about Ronald Colman and Greta Garbo!' 'Garbo, yes,' I wanted to reply, 'but not Colman. James Stewart perhaps or Charles Boyer.' But of course I didn't.

One evening after prayers, towards the end of the Christmas term, the Commander told the school to remain seated, as he had an important announcement to make. There was, he told us, a constitutional crisis in the country, due to the King's intention of marrying someone of whom the Church and the Government did not approve.

'I am not going to make any further comment,' he went on, in his best quarter-deck manner, his arms braced stiffly on the harmonium, 'but I have to warn you that when you go home for the holidays, you may find the country divided. If so, you will no doubt be told by your family which side they are on, and it is of course your duty to give them your loyalty. But here at Elstree, in the meanwhile, the subject will not be discussed and the school will remain neutral.'

It was a stirring speech, and I went up to Haig or Beatty, or whichever dormitory I was then assigned to, musing excitedly on the possibilities of Civil War. Mother and Christian would, I felt sure, be Cavaliers, while my father and Noël, in their serious-minded way, would no doubt be Cromwellians. Which side would I be on? Unfortunately I never had the chance to choose, as the crisis was resolved within a few days by the King's deciding to abdicate and marry Mrs Simpson. Predictably Mother and Christian were heartbroken, and I was rather sorry myself. Whatever other virtues the Duke and Duchess of York may have had, they could hardly be described as 'modern'.

By the time we reassembled for the spring term of 1937, the whole affair had been settled and the Coronation was announced to take place, as originally planned, in May, but with a different leading character. At the beginning of March, a few weeks before I was due to sit for the scholarship examination, I was again summoned to the Commander's study.

'I'm afraid I have some bad news for you, Wilson.'

'Yes, sir?'

'Your father has been taken rather seriously ill. He's gone into hospital, and I'm giving you the afternoon off to go and see him.'

'Thank you, sir.'

According to my father's diary, he had been suffering from a pain in his back for several weeks. Noël had arranged for him to be examined at the Regent's Park Clinic and he was admitted to University College Hospital with a diagnosis of pleurisy. This was the beginning of a long and exceedingly painful illness from which he was never to recover.

Our family circumstances were now so straitened that it became essential for me to obtain the best scholarship possible to Harrow, and my prospects were suddenly improved by the illness of Royde-Smith and his withdrawal from the examination. He had confidently, and with reason, been tipped as top scholar, and now all the school's hopes rested on Collier and me. Our work schedule was intensified and we were segregated from the rest of the school in a small dormitory for two, so that we could take our Latin and Greek to bed with us. What we actually did was to stay awake half the night discussing Sex, and I am astonished to this day that either of us had the energy, when the time came, to take the exams.

We were driven over to Harrow in a large limousine, with the Commander, and deposited at the Old Schools together with the other candidates. After the morning's exams the Commander collected Collier and me and took us to lunch at the King's Head. This was an unexpected treat, and I remember tucking into chicken livers and scrambled eggs, smug in the knowledge that back at Elstree everyone else was facing another helping of Polly and laurel leaves. In the afternoon there were more exams, and then we were driven back to Elstree in time for tea at six o'clock. This went on for three days, after which we returned to the normal school routine and waited anxiously for the results.

When they came through, they could not have been more satis-factory: I had won top scholarship, and Collier had been awarded second. So I had done what was expected of me, and could now give my full attention to more important things such as the Theatre and the Cinema. The three-week ban had been lifted, because the Commander had finally realised that it was being honoured more in the breach than in the observance; so I had a full month's film-going to look forward to. Charles came to stay the night at Elstree on his way back home from Canterbury, but our reunion was slightly soured by his having been to see our beloved Madeleine Carroll in *On the Avenue* that afternoon. 'You were furiously jealous,' he reminded me, 'because it was her first American film and you were anxious about what Hollywood had done to her.' A few days later my anxiety was allayed, when I saw the film for myself: Madeleine was more beautiful than ever and still spoke pure English.

But the big excitement of the holidays was of course the Coronation, and we had been given a week extra on account of it. According to *Vogue*, there was to be a Revival of Pageantry in Fashion and Every Day Living, and certainly the London decorations were a remarkable sight, each street competing with the next in colour and lavishness. Bond Street, where the *Vogue* office then was, had decided on plain white banners, which after a few days made it look, according to a wit in Christian's office, as if it were hanging out its dirty linen. She and my mother decided to boycott the Coronation, as a gesture of loyalty to Edward VIII, now Duke of Windsor, and went instead to visit my father, who was still in hospital; but Noël and I set out at the crack of dawn and found a place in Oxford Street along with some other students from University College. It was a very long wait, and to pass the time someone started a community sing-song. The hit of the moment was Bing Crosby's *Pennies From Heaven*, and when the crowds sang it, the people sitting in the stands threw down coins. It may not have been exactly a Revival of Pageantry, but it was all good fun.

The next day, after fitting in a matinée of the new Astaire-Rogers film, *Shall We Dance?*, I was driven back to school by Noël. We were greeted with surprise by the butler: we were a day early. I jumped into the car, and we drove back to town at top speed, arriving in time for me to catch Charles Laughton in *Rembrandt* at the local Odeon. The next day Charles Boyer and Jean Arthur opened in the West End in *History is Made at Night*. I saw that too, and then reported for my last term at Elstree. I had been made a prefect the previous year, and had progressed to second-in-command to Collier, the head boy, which was as far as I expected to go. But Collier's parents had decided to send him on to Harrow a term early, and so, to my surprise and the Commander's embarrassment, I was now Head of School. It must have been

exceedingly painful for him, since I imagine I was the first head boy of
Elstree who did not play for the School; I was scorer to the cricket
team, but that was hardly the same thing. Still, there was nothing for
either of us to do but put a good face on it and hope for the best. I and
a few others like me, who had proved themselves utterly hopeless at
cricket, were permitted to spend our half holidays working in the
garden instead. One afternoon the Commander was showing some
prospective parents round the school. I shall never forget his look of
abject shame, when, coming across me unexpectedly, crouched over a
flower bed, he was forced to introduce me: 'This is Wilson, the – the
Head of the School.'

But apart from my official duties I was having an easy time, and
Royde-Smith had now returned, to complete my sex-education. His
school work had been sent to Harrow and had created such an impression
that he was invited to sit for an examination on his own and was
awarded a special scholarship. He had the bed next to mine in the
senior dormitory and we discussed late into the night what it would be
like at Harrow. We imagined it as a cross between Narkover and
Dotheboys Hall, where our lives would be made hell by huge moustached
bullies and decadent aristocratic monitors, who would cane us relent-
lessly and destroy our innocence. We managed to treat the whole thing
as a joke, but I did have a few uneasy premonitions, which were
confirmed by the talk the Commander gave to each leaver on the last
Sunday of the term. 'You'll see some fellows doing things,' he warned
us, 'which will shock and disgust you. They will ask you to join in too,
and this you must on no account do.' Apart from this there was little in
his homily which I had not already learned in much greater detail and
variations from Royde-Smith.

Having failed conspicuously at athletics for my entire time at Elstree,
I suddenly blossomed briefly into a runner at the end of term sports
and won every event I had entered for. After tea in the garden my
mother and sisters sought out Mrs Sanderson to say their goodbyes.
'Thank you so much,' said my mother. 'It's been a lovely day.' 'It's
been the most ghastly day for me,' she replied, on the verge of tears.
'All the prizes have gone to the wrong people.' She then disappeared
upstairs, presumably for a strenuous session of tap-dancing.

The doctor in charge of my father's case had suggested that he might
benefit from leaving hospital for a time and going down to the country.
It was arranged that he should be taken by ambulance to Bolney,
where Noël, who was studying for an exam, would look after him. And
so it happened that in the end she did go away with him to a cottage in

the country. His condition was very much worse and his diary for these months is a chronicle of suffering: 'Restless night . . . more pain in the forenoon . . . very uncomfortable after lunch . . . a good deal of pain all evening . . . managed to get to sleep about one a.m. . . . weird nightmares . . .' But when the weather was fine, and it often was that summer, he spent most of the day in the garden, lying under an apple tree. Every week-end some or all of us went down to the cottage and, ill as he was, he enjoyed for the first time in many years leisure and peace, with his family around him. Helen was due back on leave in September, and this was something to look forward to, despite the fact that she had become engaged to a man who, when he came and visited my parents the previous year, had been considered 'unsuitable'. I never did discover why, but guessed later that it might have been on the grounds of 'class'. Poor as they were and driven to keep their heads above water by taking in a stream of boarders, my parents were still abiding by the social code that had ruled their lives in British India.

For me Helen's return brought a particular excitement: my first visit abroad. The 1937 Exposition was on in Paris and, fascinated by photographs of it in newspapers and magazines, I rather boldly wrote to her and suggested that I meet her in Paris on her way home from Zanzibar. She generously fell in with my suggestion, provided my fare could be raised – which it was, and I was seen off on the train to Dover at the beginning of September, in charge of an American lady in the same carriage who reminded me of Eleanor Powell. We had a wonderful week in Paris, visiting the historic buildings and museums, as well of course as the Exhibition. Like everyone else who went to it, I shall always remember the gigantic pavilions of Germany and the USSR confronting each other across the main avenue; in comparison, Great Britain's pavilion was very insignificant. We loyally went there for tea one afternoon, and shared an absurdly expensive muffin, which was brought to us with a flourish under a huge silver cover. In the evenings we dined in out-of-the-way little restaurants and I tasted wine for the first time. It was all a marvellous adventure, and I hope I showed as much gratitude as I felt.

One morning we paid a call on Uncle Frank, Mother's elder brother, who was living in a flat on the Quai de Béthune, on the Ile St Louis, with his second wife, Virginia. Until a few years previously they had also had a flat in London, affectionately called the Attic, where they entertained a great deal. But their career as West End producers had been brought to an end by an unfortunate lawsuit. In 1931 they presented a play called *Little Catherine* with Madeleine Carroll playing the lead, as the young Catherine the Great, and Harold Huth as the

Tsarevitch Peter. It was a failure and Madeleine Carroll, so I was told to my distress, behaved rather badly. A few years later Alexander Korda, fresh from his tremendous success with *The Private Life of Henry the Eighth*, made a film on the same subject, with Elisabeth Bergner and Douglas Fairbanks Junior. When it appeared, Frank and Virginia claimed to recognise a good deal of *Little Catherine* in the script. They sued Korda and lost. The whole affair practically bankrupted them, and they decided to retire to Paris, where Virginia made a reasonable living translating English plays into French. One of her greatest successes was Noël Coward's *Private Lives*, and she continued to adapt his plays until the beginning of the War.

These were the first professional theatre people I had met, apart from one or two visits backstage during the run of *Love on the Dole* at the Garrick, in which a school-friend of Christian's, Ruth Dunning, was understudying Wendy Hiller. Their talk, their behaviour, their whole attitude to life seemed to me totally different from anything I had previously experienced, and I was fascinated. Uncle Frank's theatrical career was more or less over by this time, and he had turned to novel-writing; but he still took a great interest in all that was going on, and I longed to tell him of my own aspirations. Virginia had also been an actress briefly in her youth, and had even been in a Broadway musical, *Sinbad*, with Al Jolson. Between them they had a fund of experience, and I felt I could hardly wait to begin accumulating some of my own. I was in the middle of writing my first play, a comedy called *Enter Aunt Edith*, about a girl called Perry (short for Peregrine, which I discovered later was a boy's name), who lived in a flat in Mayfair and had a crowd of friends who were always drinking cocktails and going to nightclubs. Her Puritanical Aunt Edith comes to stay and Perry has to warn her friends off. But they invade her flat one night and have a party: Aunt Edith is woken up, and, to everyone's amazement, asks to join in. Happy ending in a sea of cocktails. I wrote the part of Perry for Nora Swinburne, whom I had seen recently in a play called *Wise Tomorrow* with Diana Churchill and Martita Hunt. It was considered rather daring, because Miss Hunt's affection for Diana Churchill appeared to have Lesbian overtones; but these passed me by, and I was much more impressed by the charm and good sense displayed by Miss Swinburne.

Shortly after we returned from Paris, the farmers who owned the cottage at Bolney sold up and we had to move out. My father came back to London by ambulance and was readmitted to University College Hospital. That evening he wrote in his diary: 'A lovely day: everything looking at its best. So sorry to leave our little cottage, where Noël and

I spent so many happy days, and happy times with the family. Suffered a great deal of pain on the journey up, but everything so bright and beautiful.' A few days later I went in to say goodbye to him, as I was about to begin my first term at Harrow. He must have been sorely disappointed at not being able to take me there himself, but perhaps he still hoped that one day he would be well enough to come and visit me on the Hill.

After Elstree, Harrow seemed incredibly free. It was wonderful to be able to go out into the street whenever one felt like it, visit a shop or have a meal in a café. Instead of sleeping in a dormitory, I shared a whole room with one other boy, in which we could have our own furniture, pictures and books, and where we slept, in beds which folded up behind a curtain by day, so that one had the feeling of a grown-up sitting-room. We had to play football, but only if we were picked for a team; other afternoons, provided we were out of the house for an hour or so, we could take what exercise we pleased. I soon discovered that the easiest was a 'run'; this in fact meant donning shorts and a sweater, trotting down the Hill and for the next hour walking at my leisure round the streets of Harrow and Sudbury, dropping into a shop from time to time to buy a newspaper or some sweets, and of course examining the photographs outside every cinema. I had only been at Harrow two weeks when I had a stroke of luck and broke my wrist playing Rugger. It was painful for a while, but it meant that for the rest of the term I was excused all games and exercise – or 'eccer' as it was called. So while everyone else was rushing about on the football fields, I used to purchase a chocolate bar or two at the school tuck-shop and retire to my room to read *Gone with the Wind* which had just come into the House Library.

Another improvement was that I did not have to work so hard: indeed for my first year at Harrow I was ahead of the curriculum, owing to the intensity of Mr Stainton's classes at Elstree. In any case the time-table was not nearly so demanding: we did have to do Early Morning School for an hour before breakfast, but we had three half holidays a week, as opposed to Elstree's two, and instead of classes in the evening we only had preparation in the house. During our ample leisure we were free to do as we pleased, without being spied upon, and there were numerous clubs and societies to join. I naturally became a member of the Film Society and also joined the Chamber Music Club, more for its social cachet than any interest in Chamber Music, which then, as now, bored me to tears. I went to the Art School and found that I could draw and paint quite well, and for a brief period, due to the influence of *Vogue*, I contemplated becoming a fashion artist.

I had little opportunity to compare notes with Royde-Smith about the contrast between life at Harrow as it really was and as we imagined it would be, since we were in different houses, he at the Park and I at the Head Master's, and he had been put straight into the Lower Classical Fifth while I was in the Remove. There was a certain amount of bullying and 'ragging', and some of the monitors made 'fagging' for them an unpleasant chore; but on the whole, for most of the time I was there, I found Harrow a tolerant and easy-going place, where individuality was rarely discouraged and where, provided you did not flagrantly break the rules, you could live life pretty much as you pleased. As in any institution of such age, there were some absurd traditions, particularly in respect of dress, and a complicated system of privileges for seniority; but as such things seem to persist in many walks of life in this country, I suppose that could be taken as being part of our education. As regards the whole ethic of Public Schools, I still find it difficult to come to a satisfactory conclusion, and naturally, at the time, I had no feelings one way or the other: I was a scholarship boy, I had worked extremely hard to get there, and it was what my family wanted for me, so that was that.

It was now Christian's turn to enlarge her horizons, and she decided to try New York, which was, in those days, almost as remote as Zanzibar, but at the same time familiar, because of seeing it so frequently on the screen. She sailed there in October of 1937, without a job to go to, but with a few letters of introduction, and before long was taken on by American *Vogue*. There was a girl in her office called Edith Johnston, who was eager to correspond with someone in London: Christian told her to write to me, and for the next few years, until Edith got married, we were conscientious pen-friends. The Head Master's House Library – referred to as 'Reader' in the Harrow manner – subscribed to *Life Magazine*, and I read it with particular interest, paying great attention to the 'Show Business' section and the photographs of Broadway musicals. Rodgers and Hart's latest was called *Babes in Arms* and *Life* carried a full page colour photograph of Mitzi Green singing *The Lady is a Tramp*. At that time very few American musicals reached London, and then usually in Anglicised versions; I yearned to see one of the genuine articles on its home ground.

Another advantage of Harrow was the Exeat, or week-end holiday, which we were granted in the Winter and Summer terms. The Winter Exeat fell in the first week in November and lasted from Saturday morning to Monday evening. I fitted in a couple of films and a visit to the Old Vic, where Emlyn Williams was playing Richard the Third. I also of course went to see my father and told him as much as I could about my life at Harrow: he was a good deal weaker, and I had a feeling I might not see him again. One morning at the beginning of December I woke up to go to Early School with an inexplicable depression hanging over me. That evening I was called in to see the House Master, Mr Gorse.

'I'm afraid I have some bad news for you, Wilson,' he began, 'which I gather is not altogether unexpected.'

The last entry in my father's diary, on November 12th, read: 'Feeling *very* ill . . . I don't know what is wrong with me. Do the Family? Do the Doctors?' He had been suffering from a cancer which originated in an injury he had sustained playing football many years before. My mother, Helen, Noël and I travelled up to Stirling with his coffin on December 2nd and the following day he was buried in the churchyard at Logie. 'One of my husband's favourite walks was to Bridge of Alan,' wrote my mother, 'and from there to Sherrifmuir, which was a high hill at the beginning of the Ochils, and it was just under the Ochils that he was finally put to rest.'

Thanks to my father's careful accounting my mother was left sufficiently well off to be able to give up taking in P.G.s. As both Christian and Helen had left home, we no longer needed so many rooms and in the spring of 1938 she moved into a new block opposite where we were living, called Northways. It was my first experience of a modern flat and it all seemed very chic and 'streamlined', which was the fashionable accolade. My mother told Noël and me that we could choose the colour schemes for our rooms: she chose pink and I, very unwisely, chose apple green. The most important piece of furniture in my room was a new piano, bought in part exchange for our old school-room upright. It was an apple green Mini, flecked with gold, and decked with chromium bands and two electric candlesticks, with a stool to match. Minipianos had only recently come on the market and were, I think, the first articles to be saddled with that unfortunate prefix: I still have mine, stripped of its green and gold paint, its chrome and its candelabra, and I have composed all my shows on it. But at that time I was only just learning to play it, thanks to Helen, who, before she returned to Zanzibar, arranged for me to have lessons from her old singing teacher, Mrs Pestle, who lived in Willesden. I travelled there on the tube twice a week and came home to practise scales, arpeggios and the Minuet in G. I never expected to be anything more than a competent pianist; but soon, I hoped, I would be able to write music.

I was also reading avidly anything that I could get hold of on the subject of Theatre, and one of the books I acquired was Noël Coward's first volume of autobiography, *Present Indicative*. I had only seen him once, in an American film called *The Scoundrel*, but I knew a great deal about him and my mother had seen several of his shows. I remembered her coming home from *Cavalcade* and relating how convincingly Mary Clare had fallen in a dead faint on hearing of her son's death in the Great War. And of course Frank and Virginia knew him well, and he had visited the Attic. I was amazed and envious to read how early he had started his career, and how soon he had been successful. *The Vortex*, the play that made his name, had been produced in 1924, the year that I was born, at the Everyman in Hampstead, which I knew well as a cinema. He acted, wrote plays, composed songs – all the things I wanted to do. If I was to follow in his footsteps, there was no time to be lost! I now embarked on the first volume of his plays, which included *Private Lives*, *Hay Fever* and *The Vortex* itself. The latter fascinated me: so this was what the Twenties were like – cocktail-drinking society people dabbling in illicit sex, country-house parties where adulterous mothers danced to feverish jazz played on the piano by their drug-addict sons! It was all so reckless and romantic: could it really have been happening while I was a baby in Sale? At about the same time I came across a copy of *Gentlemen Prefer Blondes* in the local bookshop. Who were these marvellous, madcap girls who chased around Europe in search of diamonds and 'education'? Where had they disappeared to? The picture of a Lost World was beginning to take shape in my mind, and the figments of Coward's and Anita Loos' imaginations were given a framework of fact when I discovered Frederick Lewis Allen's *Only Yesterday* in the House Library. Here was the history of a decade which had ended only eight years ago and yet was already as remote as the Renaissance. If only I could return to it!

Meanwhile, back in 1938, the current decade was having its troubles. As the year progressed there was a growing realisation that the Next War, which had been discussed so freely but which most people refused to believe could actually happen, might break out at any moment. In the spring Christian returned unexpectedly from New York: her visa had run out and she had been advised, erroneously, to re-enter the States from Canada. The authorities now told her that if she wished to continue working in New York, she must go back to England and try and get on the British immigration quota. My mother suggested that in the meanwhile they should both take a trip to Zanzibar where Helen was about to be married in the autumn. Their passages were booked, but it looked as if the course of events might overtake us before they sailed. The summer was nerve-racking, as tension mounted to what came to be known as the Munich Crisis. Harrow had already announced that in the event of war the school would be evacuated to Cheltenham, and all the necessary arrangements had been made. I was about to join the Lower Fifth and start working for my School Certificate, the equivalent of the present day O-Levels. When the school reassembled, the crisis had still not been resolved. Our form master was Ronald Watkins, an authority on Shakespeare and a fanatical advocate of the Elizabethan open stage. The set play was *Macbeth* and, preoccupied as we were with what was happening at Munich, from the moment he began reading the opening scene with us what had been just a text-book became a living drama, which I still know almost line for line. Unlike most teachers at that time, Ronnie believed in emphasising the importance of Shakespeare as a dramatist and made us continually aware of the theatrical effect of his writing.

One afternoon soon after the beginning of term we were sitting in our class-room, waiting for him to arrive. Suddenly we heard a sound of cheering from the other rooms in the building. The door flew open and Ronnie burst in. 'Chamberlain has signed a pact with Hitler and Mussolini,' he announced jubilantly. 'He says it's Peace in Our Time!' The feeling of relief was indescribable. We all joined in the cheering.

Looking back on it in the light of what happened subsequently, it seemed strange to me that someone as informed as Ronnie Watkins could have greeted the news of Munich with such enthusiasm. I mentioned this to a friend of mine, Brian Stratton-Ferrier, who sat for the scholarship exam at the same time as I did, and who was also there that afternoon in the Lower Fifth Form Room.

'But you must remember we all thought we were going to be obliterated by air-raids at any minute. We thought that if there was a war, it would all be over in six months and three-quarters of the world's population would be dead. I remember reading a poem of Auden's at the time: "As the clever hopes expire of a low, dishonest decade . . ." But one wasn't ashamed of it until afterwards. We'd all been brought up to be Christians, we believed in peace at any price, and we were just relieved there wasn't going to be slaughter.'

This confirms what I have always felt about that time: we were all of us thoroughly scared. We had seen newsreels of aerial bombing in Spain and China and we were terrified that it might soon happen here. Of course there were political reasons: there was betrayal, conspiracy, compromise and sheer muddle. But the over-riding motive was plain, abject fear.

*   *   *

We settled down to *Macbeth* after a while, and the school term resumed its normal course. A week or so later Mother and Christian sailed for Africa. Christian was not to return until more than ten years later. On the voyage out she met her future husband, Michael Vigne, a Rhodesian. Helen's wedding was postponed, because of the illness of her fiancé, Cecil Haylett; instead Mother saw Christian married to Michael in Bulawayo and sailed back to London in the spring of 1939. During the school holidays we spent a week in Eastbourne: it had changed very little since we were last there, but the model shipwreck had disappeared from the life-boat house.

At the beginning of the Summer term, during which we would be sitting for the School Certificate, Ronnie staggered us by announcing that we were to put on a production of *The Medea*, the play we were studying for the exam. What was more, we were to make our own translation, into blank verse. He then proceeded to allot each of us a section of the play. 'I'll never forget it,' Brian told me. 'You'd get about fifty brilliant lines by Mortimer (John Mortimer, the future playwright) and then suddenly you'd get me.' We were also given parts to play: as well as being one of the Chorus, I was assigned the job of mask-maker, as it was to be an authentic Greek production. For Medea I found a joke mask of Mussolini which I repainted and decorated with green crepe paper hair: it was very effective. The production was staged in the garden of Kennet House, where several masters lived. The back lawn was arena-shaped and formed a natural auditorium: the scene was the house itself, the main entrance being from the French windows, above which was a balcony for Medea's final appearance in a fiery chariot. Brian played the Messenger, who brings the news of the death of Jason's new wife: 'And then I remember crouching down behind the parapet of the balcony, waving pieces of orange chiffon, which were supposed to be the flames of Medea's chariot.' The play was given one performance only, on the last Sunday of the Summer term, and was a great success, despite the fact that some of our deathless verse was rendered inaudible by the RAF fighter planes from Northolt manoeuvring above us.

The Summer Exeat was given for the Eton and Harrow cricket match at Lord's, which was memorable in 1939 because Harrow won for the first time in many years. When stumps were drawn, a fight broke out between Harrovians and Etonians outside the Pavilion. Noël urged me to join in, but I had no intention of doing so. Top hats were bashed and swagger canes broken in two: one elderly gentleman was 'debagged' and advertised in the paper next day for the contents of his trouser pockets. After the fighting died down, my mother picked up an umbrella handle and later had an umbrella fitted to it. The whole business was deplored by the more proletarian Sunday papers – quite rightly, I dare say. A year later many of the participants would be fighting elsewhere.

That evening, according to tradition, we went to a show, to see Herbert Farjeon's *Little Revue* at the Little Theatre, which no longer exists. The year before we had been to its predecessor, *Nine Sharp*. The leads were the same, Hermione Baddeley and Cyril Ritchard, and in the supporting cast were George Benson, Betty Ann Davies, Joan Sterndale Bennett and a rather plump girl called Vida Hope. It was the perfect intimate revue – witty, charming and delicious – and I promptly decided to write a revue myself one day. After the show we were invited by Frank and Virginia, who were on a visit from Paris, to join them at the Players' Theatre Club, which was then in an upstairs room in King Street, Covent Garden. Then, as now, the entertainment was the Victorian Late Joys: Leonard Sachs was Chairman and Peter Ustinov and Robert Eddison were in the cast. We had beer and sandwiches and joined in the choruses: I was wearing my first dinner jacket, with a stiff shirt, and I felt peerlessly adult.

In my search for plays to read I had come across the Gollancz Plays of the Year series in the Vaughan Library at Harrow. I read solidly through each one, and in the volume for 1937 I found an American play which enraptured me with its brittle, cynical exposé of Park Avenue society. It was *The Women* by Clare Booth Luce, and because of censorship problems it had not as yet been produced in London. But that summer Jack Buchanan announced that he would present it at the Lyric Theatre. Mother booked two rows of back stalls for the first evening of the holidays, and I took all my friends from Harrow. The play had a cast of forty, all female, and most of them had been imported from New York. The story was set in a No-Man's-Land of beauty-parlours, boudoirs, bathrooms and dress salons, through which scurried the Women of the title in pursuit of scandal, dressed and undressed in gorgeous gowns and negligées, chattering like birds and monkeys in a never-ending stream of cracks both wise, witty and wicked. Of all the plays I had seen and read up to that time, *The Women*, I thought, was the one I would like most to have written.

After the show a few of us walked part of the way back to Swiss Cottage through the summer night. The streets north of Oxford Circus were almost empty, and we amused ourselves by jumping on the rubber pads which made the traffic lights change. At Baker Street Station we said goodbye to each other. When we met again, the streets would be blacked out and the theatres would be closed. Already a new crisis was brewing, and this time people were beginning to feel that even war would be preferable to the demoralising uncertainty. Towards the end of August my mother got in touch with an old school-friend who lived with her husband outside Winchester and asked her if she could have me to stay.

The last show we went to before I left London was a matinée at the Ambassadors Theatre. Mother had made friends with a padre on the boat coming back from Africa, and she wanted to give him an outing before his leave ended. I often wonder what he thought of her choice of entertainment: *The Gate Revue* with Hermione Gingold. Previous Gate Revues had been produced at a theatre club, where censorship did not apply; but this one must have given the Lord Chamberlain a few head-aches. I could not make up my mind which of the two Hermiones, Baddeley and Gingold, was the funnier, and on the way out of the Ambassadors I bought a copy of Gabrielle Brune's number in the show, *Transatlantic Lullaby*, which had a seductive melody by Geoffrey Wright.

My mother's friend, Mrs Stewart, had a large garden where I sat in the August sunshine and wrote a social drama called *Only the Brave*. It was about a young couple, Don and Lena, who marry during the 1914 War. They are reunited at the Armistice, but their marriage nearly goes on the rocks during the 1920s. This occupied the second act, which consisted of a long party scene lifted straight from *The Vortex* by way of *Hay Fever* and embellished with wise-cracks in the style of *The Women*. At the end of it Don decides to save his marriage by taking Lena to Africa. The third act was set in the present when they return, with a nauseating small daughter, to find to their horror that war is about to break out again. But having already faced so much, they decide bravely to face this too.

Before I could finish the play, war did indeed break out. Mrs Stewart's son was a master at Winchester College and on the morning of Sunday, September 3rd, I and some friends were helping him to dig an air-raid shelter in his garden. His wife called us in to hear the Prime Minister on the radio. At the end of that melancholy little speech we had a glass of sherry and drank to Victory. I felt depressed and confused: what on earth was going to happen to us all now? The man who drove me home for lunch was in the Territorials and had to report to his unit that evening.

'It's absolutely bloody,' he said. 'I don't want to have to go and fight the bloody Germans.'

'No, I don't either,' I said.

'Oh, you're all right. It'll be over long before you have to go.' He changed gear angrily. 'But what the hell am *I* going to do?'

To everyone's surprise the massive air-raids did not happen – at least not that year. In fact very little happened. Noël came down for the week-end: she was unofficially engaged to a surgeon from U.C.H., David Wallace, who had joined the Air Force Reserve and was already in uniform. I told her that I thought the outbreak of war meant the end of civilisation; she cheered me up by saying that the Theatre was sure to flourish at a time like this, because people needed entertainment. Certainly life seemed to be rapidly returning to normal after the first flurry of excitement. The cinemas outside the London area were permitted to reopen and we went to see a rather futile comedy with Rosalind Russell and Robert Montgomery. After a week or so my mother thought it would be safe for me to return to London.

Harrow had decided to stay put this time, and we reassembled there as usual for the Winter term. Because of the black-out Early School was cancelled for the Duration and our evening activities drastically curtailed; otherwise life went on much as before. Most of the clubs and societies had temporarily ceased to function, and we were encouraged to entertain ourselves at week-ends. I decided to put on a House play for the end of term, and chose to do my own version of *Frankenstein*, based on Mary Shelley's novel which I had found in the Vaughan Library. I played the Monster – or the Man, as she called him – and the big scene occurred when I visited Frankenstein in his laboratory to check on progress in the creation of my mate. As in the original novel, Frankenstein suddenly realises that he will be responsible for a race of monsters and destroys the half-finished Bride. To simulate her innards we had filled a lot of balloons with red ink and fastened them into suitable shapes with rubber bands. At the climax Frankenstein swept the whole lot on to the floor, while I staggered about bellowing with frustration. The mess was indescribable and the audience adored it.

The Christmas attraction at the Empire, Leicester Square, was the film version of *The Women*, and my mother and I were there on the first day at ten a.m. to occupy two of the One Thousand Seats for One and Six. MGM had done it up proud, with an all-star cast and a fashion show in Technicolor. As Norma Shearer, having finally vanquished her foes in the Powder Room, ran upstairs to reclaim her husband and the music swelled, it seemed a fitting farewell to the Thirties. My mother and I reeled out into the daylight of war-time London, while the world advanced, with trepidation, into another decade.

The
Nineteen
Forties

DESPITE – or possibly because of – my involvement with Ronnie's production of *The Medea*, I did well in the School Certificate and won eight credits, which led to my being awarded the Fifth Form Scholarship. This meant a considerable reduction in my fees, and as a result I could now afford to have regular piano lessons at school. My teacher was a Mr Ebden, and at the end of the class he used to spend a few minutes going through the latest pop song, which I had brought along surreptitiously amongst my classical music. Bing Crosby, Bob Hope and Dorothy Lamour had just made the first in their 'Road' series, *The Road to Singapore*, and I wonder if Henry Havergal, the Head of Music, ever heard the strains of *Too Romantic* or *The Moon and the Willow Tree* filtering through the corridors of the Music Schools.

At the beginning of Summer Term 1940, the School assembled in the Speech Room one afternoon to hear a talk by a member of the staff, Mr Gannon, a slightly farouche character, with the air of an old sea dog and, unusually for that time, a beard. I think he was employed in a part-time capacity by the Foreign Office and as a result had recently spent a short while in Paris. The object of his talk was to tell us all, in a chatty and informative manner, how admirably the French were backing the War Effort and what a lot we could learn from them. Taxi drivers, for example, who had been called to the colours, spent their leaves driving their taxis in order to make a little extra money for their wives and children. And as for rationing – well of course we all knew how much the Frenchman liked his food. But he was being very sensible about it. Take baba au rhum – and I suppose a handful of us might have done so. The bakers were allowed to bake babas on Tuesday and Friday; but rum could be sold only on Wednesday and Saturday. Very well then. The Frenchman bought his baba on a Tuesday, took it home and put it in the larder, and on Wednesday he went and bought his rum, and on Wednesday evening – voilà! Baba au Rhum! Wasn't that

C

brilliant, and so typically French? We all laughed dutifully and agreed
that it was. Within a matter of weeks the French were in headlong
flight, and Paris – taxis, babas au rhum and all – was in the hands of
the Germans. In the meanwhile Mr Gannon had luckily been taken on
full time by the Foreign Office.

It was a dizzying summer. Suddenly the Phoney War had turned
into the real thing and was there, only a matter of miles away, across
the Channel. I tried to imagine Paris, as I had seen it for the first time
only three years before with Helen, occupied by the Nazis, and I could
not; it was unimaginable. But it had happened, and, who could tell, it
might happen in London before the summer ended. Nevertheless our
lives went on as usual: mornings in the classroom, afternoons of
cricket or swimming in Ducker, evenings of prep. and, now that the
days were longer, the clubs and societies were meeting again. At the
end of term I devised an intimate revue with three other boys which
was put on in my room at the Head Master's House. Brian was the
only member of the audience: 'I sat in your room and watched this
revue – song after song and sketch after sketch. It was the only time
in my life that I've been the only person in the audience for a two hour
show.' For the finale I wrote my first complete song, called, with total
lack of originality, *The Party's Over Now*.

London that August was busy and crowded – much more so than in
peace-time, when many of the theatres used to close and the cinemas
often showed revivals. In the first few days of the holidays I saw
Hitchcock's *Rebecca*, John Ford's *The Grapes of Wrath* and Thorold
Dickinson's immaculate version of *Gaslight* with Anton Walbrook and
Diana Wynyard. *Gone with the Wind* had come on in the spring and
was still attracting long queues in Leicester Square, as it was to do
throughout the War. The Theatre, as Noël had foretold, was flourishing:
Michael Redgrave was having an enormous success in Robert Ardrey's
Thunder Rock; a new play by Clare Booth Luce opened, *Margin for
Error*, and my mother and I went to the first night; there was a revue
called *New Faces* at the Comedy, in which a dark and beautiful actress,
Judy Campbell, sang, with almost no voice at all, *A Nightingale Sang
in Berkeley Square*, en evocation of pre-war Mayfair, totally irrelevant
to the present, and yet it was the hit of the moment. One afternoon I
went with a friend to the Dominion to see a new Ginger Rogers film,
Primrose Path. She had broken off her association with Astaire and was
beginning to make a name for herself as a straight actress. There was a
second feature and then the film itself, an effective and, for those days,
fairly strong drama about prostitution. At the end of it we rose to go;
but, as with my father at the Polytechnic, there seemed to be another

film. It turned out to be a 'sneak' preview and we decided to stay, out of curiosity more than anything. Suddenly I sat up: we were watching a film version of *The Boys from Syracuse*, a musical by Rodgers and Hart which had been featured in *Life* magazine a couple of years before. The show was based on Shakespeare's *Comedy of Errors* and the idea of Ancient Greeks singing and dancing in the modern idiom had very much intrigued me. The film had a tremendous advantage in that, through trick photography, both the Antipholi and the Dromios could be played by the same person, Allan Jones and Joe Penner respectively; Martha Raye was in splendid form as Luce, the maid, and Eric Blore and Alan Mowbray, as the jeweller and tailor who are dunning Antipholus of Ephesus, displayed what would nowadays be called the height of camp. The film was also amusing visually: the taxis in the streets of Ephesus were chariots with meters, and the newsboys sold chunks of stone carved with Greek hieroglyphics. But what really bowled me over was the songs: *Falling in Love with Love, Sing for your Supper, This Can't Be Love* – I had never heard melodies quite like this before, and the lyrics had a matching originality of thought and phrasing. I discovered later that at least half the score had been discarded, as was the habit in Hollywood musicals at that time; but there was more than enough left to make me want desperately to emulate it. I wrote off to Edith in New York and asked her to send me the sheet music. When it arrived, it turned out to be from the stage version: I now possessed my first numbers from a Broadway musical!

At the end of August I went to stay with a friend of Christian's, Thelma Ullmann, in the country near East Grinstead. She and her husband lived in the village of West Hoathly, in a rambling cottage which had a terraced garden at the back, with paths leading down to a lawn. I recruited her small son and some neighbours' children and concocted a show in aid of a local charity: a jazzed-up version of Theseus and the Minotaur. The audience sat on the lawn, while we performed in the garden, using the cottage as the Labyrinth. I played Dionysus, who appeared to Ariadne on Naxos accompanied by a portable gramophone playing an old 1920s number called *My Canary's got Circles under his Eyes*. Every now and then, while we rehearsed, a squadron of fighter planes would head towards the coast, and sometimes in the distance we heard gunfire. A day or two after I returned to London the air-raids, which everyone had dreaded for so long, finally began.

And now our lives did change. All the London theatres closed and the cinemas were only allowed to open during the day. Mother and I stayed on at Northways until the end of the holidays. Noël was living in at a hospital in Watford: she had married David Wallace in the spring, just before he went overseas with the RAF. My cousin, Joan Galbraith, took her room, but she and Mother slept on mattresses in the passage. We were on the ground floor and felt reasonably safe; in fact for a time it was almost enjoyable. The three of us stayed in every evening, listening to the radio, playing games and having cups of tea; when the warning sounded, we bedded down for the night and usually managed to sleep in spite of the noise. After a time one even got used to it and ceased to worry about the danger. But one night a house opposite received a direct hit: my mother saw the result and was badly shaken. When I went back to Harrow, she let our flat to the Admiralty who needed quarters for Wrens, and took a room near the school. By Christmas she had found a furnished flat in Pinner where we lived for the next three years.

There was again talk of Harrow evacuating, but the Governors decided against it: it was Churchill's school and its leaving London might look like a gesture of submission to the Germans. All the houses had ample cellars and we slept down there in bunks. Being up on the Hill, we also had a grand-stand view of what was going on in London. From his room in the Park Brian could see St Paul's: 'I remember watching the City blazing one night. It was extraordinarily beautiful, because the guns were firing tracer bullets, and the barrage balloons were reflected in the searchlights – like a brilliant fire-work display.' Every now and then bombs fell nearby and one night the Speech Room caught fire from incendiaries. The newspapers claimed that the Luftwaffe were attacking Harrow to revenge themselves on the school that nurtured Churchill; considering he hated his time there, they were wasting their bombs. 'One evening at prayers the whole house rocked as something landed on the playing-fields. Venny (the house master of the Park, the Rev. E. M. Venables) was in the middle of one of those long, long prayers he went in for. He only paused for a second and then continued as if nothing had happened.' But not everyone could face Harrow's dangerous situation with such sang-froid. Many parents were unwilling to expose their children to the risk, and before long the School's historic Five Hundred Faces shrank to under three hundred. Some houses had to be closed and their occupants were shared out among the ones remaining open. Later Malvern College, whose buildings had been requisitioned by the Government, moved into them. At Harrow's bleakest hour Churchill himself paid us a visit and put on a brave show of nostalgic emotion while we stood and sang the School songs at him in the repaired Speech Room.

Along with Brian, I had moved up into the Classical Sixth at the end of 1940, and if I had ever had any doubts about the advantages of being at Harrow, they would have vanished now. Our form master was E. V. C. Plumptre, known naturally as Plum, a delicately urbane personage, blessed with taste, knowledge and, above all, humour, who spoke with an endearing lisp and who could turn the most prosaic exercise into an entertainment of the highest order. The Sixth Form Room itself was unlike any other class-room in the School: there were no desks, just a long table round which we all sat in comfortable chairs. Sometimes when we were doing 'construe' (oral translation of a Latin or Greek author), we would take our chairs and sit in a circle round the fire. The room had a view of the School terraces and was pleasantly decorated: on the walls hung reproductions of famous paintings which were changed periodically. 'Life in the Sixth Form Room,' as Brian remembers it, 'was a constant delight. Every scurrilous undertone and innuendo would be picked out of Horace and Juvenal and everything was turned into a joke. It was all so informal, and it seems incredible now how much fun it must have been. I still have a letter from Plum: it must have twenty classical references, all of which were common jokes amongst us – and they were all out of Horace. Of course it benefited us, but the sad thing is that one expected life always to have the enormous pleasures that come out of a shared culture, shared references. We talked a common language then; but I've never found it since with anybody.'

Outside the Sixth Form Room life was less harmonious. It was now obvious that, contrary to what my Territorial friend had prophesied, the War would be far from over by the time I was due to be conscripted. Indeed, with most of Europe in the hands of the Dictators and the Far East over-run by the Japanese, it was difficult to see when it would ever end. I would soon be seventeen and the call-up age was eighteen. I was chafing to get away from school and into the Theatre: if I did not do it now, I might not survive to do it at all. Now that I could write music, I embarked on my first show, inspired partly by Plum but mostly by *The Boys from Syracuse*, a musical version of *The Birds* of Aristophanes. I was now learning piano from Henry Havergal himself and I showed him one of the songs, a ballad entitled *You are the Birdy for Me*. He was less than encouraging and advised me to try something more serious. I felt frustrated and misunderstood and resolved again to make a break from Harrow.

As a result of my 'Theseus and the Minotaur' epic I was invited down to West Hoathly in the Christmas holidays to take part in a pantomime which was being put on to raise money for a Forces canteen. The whole thing was organised by an American, Mabel Hopkins, from her large period house on the outskirts of the village, which she seemed to run as a kind of refuge and community centre for theatre people who happened to find themselves in the area. I jumped at the chance to stay there, even though the part I was offered was hardly memorable: the back half of the cow in *Jack and the Beanstalk*. Our director was Basil Coleman, a young actor who, being a conscientious objector, was working locally as a farm labourer. Another member of the cast was Stuart Burge, stationed nearby in the Army. Mabel herself played Jack, and the Principal Girl was Lulu Dukes, the daughter of Ashley Dukes and Marie Rambert. Lulu fascinated me: she was black-haired and jolie laide, with large eyes, a prominent nose and a huge mouth. She had been sent down from London to stay with Mabel, suffering from blitz exhaustion; but she was also in the process of breaking away from the enveloping background of her mother's ballet company and starting a career of her own. In view of Madame Rambert's formidable character, this was a courageous undertaking and Lulu had chosen to go to extremes: she was learning to tap-dance. Every day she travelled up to Town for a class at Buddy Bradley's and in the afternoons we could hear her practising hard on the balcony. She was also mad about Charles Trenet, and we used to sit on the floor in Mabel's huge drawing room listening to records of *Boum!* and *Pigeon Vole*, interspersed with Dietrich's original versions of *Blonde Women* and *Falling in Love Again*. Within a day or two I was vaguely in love with both Lulu and the whole set-up, and when I suddenly realised that the pantomime was due to open after the beginning of term, I had no hesitation in telephoning my mother and informing her that I would have to return to school a week late. When she remonstrated, I said firmly that I could not possibly let the show down; besides it was all part of the War Effort. This, I told myself, was the thin end of the wedge: my next move would be to leave Harrow entirely and devote my remaining time to the Theatre.

In the event I only played the first night of *Jack and the Beanstalk* – with a raving temperature – and then retired to bed at Mabel's with influenza. I lay and worked off my frustration by imagining how I would come back there in the spring and stage a large scale musical with Lulu and Basil and Stuart, which would probably transfer to the West End and be a smash hit. I finally returned to Harrow in the third week of term and on my first evening the house master, now a Mr Stevenson, took me aside. He was a remarkable man: a Scot, a historian and a Rugby International, who concealed beneath a rough-hewn appearance tremendous tolerance and kindness. He was very brief: 'Your mother tells me you're unsettled, Sandy. She's a wee bit unhappy about it. I think you should consider things very carefully before you make any decision.'

I remembered how determined my father had been that I should go to Harrow and to what lengths my mother had gone to raise the money for my school fees; but they had not known that there would be a War. I was supposed to be going up to Oxford when I left Harrow, but one could only get a year's deferment for University. What was the point of that? There was one other person I could consult: Virginia was now living in London. She had been working for ENSA since the outbreak of war. In the winter of 1939 Uncle Frank had died of pneumonia, while visiting her in Northern France, and when the Germans invaded, she escaped with the B.E.F., arriving in London with only the clothes she stood up in. Now she was Head of Welfare, with an office backstage at the Theatre Royal, Drury Lane. It was exciting to go and visit her, to enter the theatre where I had seen *Glamorous Night* and *Careless Rapture* by the Stage Door. Sometimes I would catch a glimpse of an audition, with Elsie April, who arranged all Noël Coward's music, pounding away at the piano. Once there was a knock on the door while I was in Virginia's office, formerly a dressing-room, and there was Lilian Braithwaite, who had played Florence Lancaster in *The Vortex*! She was also working for Welfare and always dressed elaborately for the job. Virginia told me how she had arrived one morning, during the Blitz, in a large hat on which there appeared to be an alien object. 'What have you got on your hat, Lilian?' Virginia asked her. Miss Braithwaite removed the object and examined it. 'Oh, that – it's a piece of the bedroom ceiling.'

Sometimes Virginia took me to lunch at Rules in Maiden Lane, where we would eat the specialty of the house, jugged hare. Other times I stayed the night in her flat in St James' Court, and we went to a play or a film and had dinner afterwards at the Ivy, which was then the favourite rendezvous of theatre people. Virginia had known the proprietor, Monsieur Abel, since the days when the Ivy was a small corner café with saw-dust on the floor, and he always kissed her hand and sat down with us for a chat. One evening during dinner I told her my dilemma. 'Well, my dear Sandy,' she said after a moment's thought, in her deliberate way. Although born an American, she had lived in Europe since her childhood and cultivated an almost exaggeratedly correct accent both in French and English. 'I know exactly how you feel and I sympathise utterly. But darling Elsie (my mother) has set her heart on your having a proper education, and in my opinion she is right. You want to write for the Theatre, you want to compose for the Theatre: you will do both much better if you complete your education.

I can't tell you how often your Uncle Frank used to say to me, "Virginia, I'd have given anything to have gone to University." And there are many, many people in the Theatre who would say the same.' She turned out to be absolutely right.

At the time however I still had misgivings, but I decided to stay on at Harrow and was entered for the scholarship examination at Oriel College, Oxford, at the beginning of 1942. In the meanwhile I heard from Lulu: she had begun her new career and was going into a revue with a repertory company at Southport in Lancashire. Would I write a song for her? She wanted to appear as Little Lulu, a cartoon character in the *Saturday Evening Post*, who was later used to advertise Kleenex. Luckily I followed the cartoon and was able to produce what she wanted. I was determined to travel up to Southport to see the show, and my mother wrote to some friends in Liverpool to ask if I could stay with them for the week-end. I arrived in Southport in the middle of the afternoon several hours before the performance was due to begin. In a northern sea-side resort, out of season, in war-time, there was nothing to do except wander round the shops and have a long cup of tea; but I was in such a state of excitement that I could have been in Venice and it would have made no difference. Finally it was time to go to the theatre, and the curtain rose. I can remember nothing of the rest of the show except a ballet featuring the leading lady, Lally Bowers, to the music of *Claire de Lune*. My song came in the second half, and as the circulation of the *Saturday Evening Post* in Southport must have been vestigial, I doubt if anybody in the audience knew who Lulu was meant to be. Fortunately the number ended with a frenzied tap-dance which earned Lulu a good round of applause, and I was convinced that the whole thing was an enormous success. We met briefly after the show, as I had to catch the last train back to Liverpool, and she told me that she was auditioning for a revue in London. I came home feeling certain that she and I were going to be the new Gertrude Lawrence and Noël Coward.

In the summer of 1941 Ronnie Watkins directed the first of many Elizabethan-style productions of Shakespeare in the Speech Room at Harrow. The play was *Twelfth Night* and I was cast as Olivia. In later years a special stage was constructed, but we had to make do with the existing platform and played in daylight, partly because the Speech Room was not blacked out and partly because of Ronnie's insisting on the same conditions as in Shakespeare's time. We all enjoyed working with him and, as usual, he illuminated the text for us; but I felt then, and still feel, that Olivia is a dreary character and apparently I gave a pretty dreary account of her. 'Olivia enounces her lines clearly,' said

the *Harrovian*'s critic, 'but it is a pity that she looks so elderly.'
Ronnie's next Shakespearian production was *Henry V* and he cast me,
much more sensibly, as Mistress Quickly; but, as things turned out, I
never played her.

Lulu had got into the revue, which was called *Rise Above It* and was
to open at the Comedy. The stars were both the Hermiones, Gingold
and Baddeley, partnered by Henry Kendall and Walter Crisham. I
immediately set about writing a number for Hermione Gingold and
sent it off to her; she replied saying that she had all the material she
needed, but she would like to meet me. On the first evening of the
summer holidays I invited all my friends from Harrow to see the show.
We occupied a whole row of the circle, and in the middle of a number
called *How's About?* in which he appeared as an American sailor
propositioning a Panama Hattie-style Gingold, Wally Crisham slipped
in a reference to 'those terrible Harrow boys' which must have mystified
the rest of the audience. Afterwards I took everyone backstage to meet
Lulu; but they somehow seemed to be deflected into Hermione
Baddeley's dressing-room. Through the open door I had a glimpse of
her pouring drinks for a mob of adoring Harrovians; Gingold had the
adjoining dressing-room and the door was closed. I knocked on it and
that unmistakable voice said, 'Come in!' She was alone with a woman
friend, and appeared to be in a gloomy mood. After greeting me she
continued the conversation. 'Quite honestly, darling,' she said, 'I feel
I should give it all up and become a WAAF.' If she had not been so
serious about it, I would have laughed out loud. When her friend left,
she told me she had an idea for a number. 'I want to be one of those
ladies who sit in a shop window and do invisible mending. Nobody
notices what she looks like, so she begins to feel invisible herself. Do
you think you could write it for me? Good. That'll be lovely.' She
addressed herself to her mirror and I felt the interview was at an end.
Next door I could hear Miss Baddeley insisting on everyone having
another drink. I said goodbye and left. Gingold, I am happy to say,
never made good her threat to join the Air Force, and I never wrote
that number about the Invisible Mender.

In January 1942 I sat for the Oriel Scholarship. Oxford struck me as
bleak and over-crowded. I felt I had probably done badly, and at the
end of the week, when I took the train back to London, I doubted if I
would ever see the place again and I did not particularly care. The
results came through at the beginning of the Spring term: I had not
even won an exhibition. Now there seemed to be nothing for it but to
finish out my time at Harrow and wait to be called up. At least the
War situation was improving: America had joined in, the German

Army was being rebuffed by the Russians, and we seemed to be winning in the Middle East. There was even talk of opening a Second Front in Europe. Perhaps after all I would survive to see the end of it.

The War Office was looking ahead to the re-opening of the Far East campaign and discovered that the Services, not surprisingly, had very few officers who could speak Chinese or Japanese. They circularised all the public schools and asked them to supply candidates for a two-year course at the School of Oriental Studies in London. It seemed to me a more interesting prospect than joining the Army as a private soldier, and I applied, despite the fact that I have never been much of a linguist. There was no kind of exam, just an interview which seemed to consist of questions about one's sporting abilities. I said I enjoyed playing squash, which was more or less true, and everyone looked relieved: they were obviously anxious to bag at least one Harrovian.

Harrow seemed just as anxious that I should eventually reach Oxford. I had to sit for a School Scholarship at the end of term, and to my amazement I won it. I knew quite well that I had done badly in the examinations; I had really ceased to care about my academic future. But somebody must have decided that I deserved the chance of going to University, and I was literally given a Classical Scholarship to Oriel, because I certainly had not earned it. In my current frame of mind I did not even feel particularly grateful. I was sorry in a way to leave Harrow early and miss that supposedly idyllic last Summer term, which would have included Ronnie's production of *Henry V*; but the time was out of joint in more ways than one. Harrow itself was in the throes of a sort of civil war, owing to the appointment of one of the masters, A. P. Boissier, to the Head Mastership. Brian was now Head Boy of the Park, and was in the thick of it all: 'If you were at all involved in the politics, Harrow was a very unhappy place just then. When "Tin-Bim" Vellacott – he was known as that because he was supposed to have been shot in the bottom in the 1914 War – resigned the Head Mastership to be Master of Peterhouse, it was difficult to get anyone to take on the job. The Governors were all preoccupied with the War, and when Boissier applied, they gave it to him. You were never aware of how badly he behaved. He sacked five house masters, including mine. For a whole year I was Leader of the Opposition: I had only to lift my little finger and we would have had the first revolution at Harrow since Byron.'

I was a School Monitor myself and vaguely aware of what was going on. But it had no interest for me any more, and in any case seemed pretty pointless when set against the conflict that was in progress beyond Harrow. But leaving when I did had a deeper effect on me than I realised. Even now, when things go wrong, I dream that I am back on the Hill, sitting in the Sixth Form Room and joining in the classical repartee with Plum.

I forget if we had a choice of which Oriental language to learn, but I found that I had been assigned to the Japanese course. It began in the Summer term and for some reason we were all billeted at Dulwich College and had to commute daily by train to the School of Oriental Studies in Bloomsbury. The Head Master of Dulwich, whose name was Gilkes, made it quite clear from the start that we would have to conform to all the school rules: we were all of leaving age or over, and such petty restrictions as not being allowed to smoke and having to go to bed at a certain time were more than we could stomach. To show that I was adult I grew a rather nasty moustache which I kept for the next four years. After a time Gilkes saw reason and treated us more leniently, but it got the whole project off to a very bad start.

We were allowed home at week-ends, and once we were up in Town, provided we attended our classes at the School, the rest of our time was our own, which meant that I could go to the theatre and the cinema as much as I chose and could afford, usually in the company of Guy de Moubray, a tall and emaciated Old Lorettonian who was as movie-crazy as myself. The air-raids on London had more or less ceased for the time being, and all the theatres were open again and thriving. Noël Coward brought two new plays to the Haymarket, *Present Laughter* and *This Happy Breed*, with Judy Campbell as leading lady, and I was lucky enough to see both first nights. In *Present Laughter* an unknown actor called James Donald had a wild success as the intense young playwright, Roland Maule; the next night, on his first entrance in *This Happy Breed*, he was applauded, which must be a unique incident in Theatre history. Every now and then an American musical would appear, but usually in an anaemic version which had been tailored to the English cast. I had seen several photographs of Cole Porter's *Dubarry Was a Lady* in *Life Magazine*, but when it opened in London half the score was missing, as it had been used in a Flanagan and Allen show the previous year, and the star, Frances Day, although fetching in her way, was no Ethel Merman. The English musicals tended to be mixtures of revue and variety with comedians such as Leslie Henson, Sydney Howard and the Hulberts, and with scores which were a hotch-potch of Charing Cross Road and pinches from Broadway successes. Film musicals were in general more rewarding, and we were all devoted fans of Betty Grable, Alice Faye and Carmen Miranda, who were presented in various combinations and permutations, and in glaring Technicolor, throughout the Duration. Rita Hayworth was also coming into her own, and Guy and I spent hours learning to play the Jerome Kern songs from *You Were Never Lovelier* in which she danced with Fred Astaire. I was also writing and composing, whenever I had the opportunity, and just before the Christmas holiday we presented a revue in the canteen at Dulwich College, to which I contributed most of the songs and several sketches.

It was a success, as even Mr Gilkes conceded, but my Japanese studies were suffering and by the next term I realised that I had been insane to imagine that I could ever become proficient in such a complex and alien language. My speech was passable, but my writing was lamentable, since, although the Japanese script is simpler than the Chinese, it employs several hundred characters and I simply could not memorise them. But we had all signed a contract with the War Office and in theory we were obliged to finish the course and be conscripted as interpreters into whichever branch of the Forces needed us. I knew that however hard I worked I would never reach the required standard, but if I tried to leave the course I would be virtually liable to prosecution. So I decided to appeal to the Head of the School, Professor Edwards, who was a woman and seemed to be sympathetic. She listened to what I had to say and agreed to put my case to the War Office. A few days later I was called in to see Mr Gilkes, who told me I had been released from my contract owing to my inability to learn Japanese. 'Perhaps if you'd spent less time on that revue . . .?' he suggested, and I wondered guiltily if he could be right.

When I told my mother the news, she decided to dramatise the whole affair and treated me for a while as if I was a traitor to my King and Country. I tried to point out to her that I was now bound to be called up into the Army at any moment and was fully prepared to go, but she refused to listen to me. To fill in the time, and to try to make myself as independent as possible, I took a job as a tutor in a crammer's in the Cromwell Road. For a couple of months I taught a class of six boys of different ages and capabilities in every subject from French to Mathematics in a room the size of a pantry. What with one thing and another, I was relieved when my call-up papers arrived.

Joining the Army was like going back to prep. school: the officers were the Masters, and the NCOs were the Prefects. The conditions were a little more primitive than at Elstree, but the food was rather better, and we could do what we liked with our free time. The work was usually boring and often seemed pointless, but it left one's mind free to pursue more interesting subjects. I spent three years in uniform and, while there were periods of discomfort and depression, on the whole I disliked it much less than I expected.

To begin with I had to report to Beverly, in Yorkshire, for pre-liminary training. This consisted of 'square-bashing', which I had already experienced in the OTC at Harrow, and learning how to use a rifle, a bren-gun and a hand-grenade. A lot of the remaining time seemed to be taken up in looking after one's 'equipment': applying blanco to the webbing, dubbin to the boots and polish to the brass, as well as cleaning one's rifle with a 'pull-through', and then learning how to arrange the whole lot in a symmetrical pile on one's bunk. I found this side of it tedious and irritating, but to my surprise the other members of the platoon took it very seriously and strongly disapproved of my attitude.

We were also given various aptitude and intelligence tests to help the authorities decide what to do with us at the end of the six weeks, and every now and then someone from the War Office would arrive to propagandise on behalf of a particular branch of the Service. I had not the least idea what I wanted to do. The others all seemed to fancy themselves as Paratroopers or Commandos but that did not appeal to me at all. One day we were summoned to hear a talk from an officer in the Catering Corps. He told us that there was a crying need for Front Line Cooks: their job was to drive up and down the Front Line taking hot meals to the fighting men; it fulfilled a basic need and we should all seriously consider offering ourselves for it. This struck me as an excellent idea: one would see a certain amount of action, one would meet a great many people, but above all one would be independent, whizzing up and down the trenches dishing out food to the hungry troops.

The day came when we all had to see the P.S.O. (Personnel Selection Officer). He had detailed information about each of us: our family backgrounds, our education, as well as the results of all those tests. After shuffling through my data, he asked me if I had any preference about my future role in the Army.

'Yes, sir,' I said promptly. 'I want to be a Front Line Cook.'

'A Front Line Cook?' He gazed at me in amazement, and then referred to a form, just to make sure he had the right person in front of him. 'But – but you went to Harrow!'

'I don't see what that's got to do with it, sir.' And I really did not. His attitude changed: he now regarded me with suspicion.

'You are serious about this?'

'Yes, sir, definitely. We were told the other day that Front Line Cooks are needed, and I want to be one.'

'I see.' He shuffled my papers again, and then a new thought struck him. 'Do you like cooking?'

'I haven't really done very much, but yes, I do rather.'

'I see . . .' He had clearly come to some decision, but it turned out to be a totally unexpected one: the next day I was told to report to the psychiatrist.

I was asked all the usual questions, including several about my sex life, which up to that time had been fairly uneventful. I waited in trepidation for the outcome. For what particular duty, I wondered, did my being an Old Harrovian qualify me? The Intelligence Corps perhaps, or Army Education? Or were they by any marvellous chance considering transferring me to ENSA? I imagined Virginia's face when I reported for duty to Drury Lane . . .

A day or two before our training ended the news came through: I was assigned as a clerk to the Ordnance Corps. I had no notion what the Ordnance Corps was or what it did, but this gap in my knowledge was filled during the next month when I was trained in my clerical duties at a school in Saltburn, a seaside resort on the north-east coast. We sat in a class-room for day after day and filled several note-books with information about the complicated processes whereby the Army receives its supplies of equipment. None of the notes I made seemed to have much bearing on any of the jobs I was subsequently given to do, but Saltburn was quite a pleasant little place, and one day when we were forming up outside our billet to march to the class-room, the corporal told us that the Allies had invaded Sicily. It was thrilling news and we gave a spontaneous cheer: after four years the tide was turning at last.

At the end of the course we were designated as Clerks Technical Class Three, our pay was increased by a shilling or two, and we were given our first leave. When my mother saw me lurching out of the Underground at Pinner Station, weighed down with full pack, tin helmet and a rifle, her attitude changed on the spot: she became the proud mother of a Soldier Son. I think she was probably as puzzled about my metamorphosis into a Clerk Technical as I was, but we did not discuss it and devoted ourselves instead to a week of intensive theatre- and cinema-going. At the end of it I had to report to Birmingham where I spent two days in transit on a race-course, waiting to be told my next posting. In a curious way I enjoyed the feeling of being completely in the dark about where I was going or what would happen when I arrived there. I have never been very good at making practical decisions, and the fact that for three years they were all made for me was a kind of luxury.

The next six weeks I spent in Cardiff, billeted in a church hall and working in a small and rather happy-go-lucky supply depot. There were plenty of cinemas to go to, and I was just about to start evening classes at Cardiff Art School, when somebody made another decision and I found myself back on the race-track at Birmingham. This time my destination was Bicester, or rather Arncott, the huge Ordnance Depot on its outskirts, where I was to spend the next year. It was a dismal place: several square miles of sheds, store-houses and offices, built in the middle of nowhere and surrounded by desolate fields dotted with the tin-roofed Nissen huts in which we lived. I shall never forget my feeling of despondency when I arrived there late at night in November and trudged through the mud and the darkness to my billet. What made me even more depressed was the news that my mother had decided to go out to Rhodesia and visit Christian, who now had two small daughters and an invalid husband: the flat at Pinner had been given up and Mother was staying with friends in Harrow until she should receive instructions about her embarkation. This meant that for the first time in my life I had no home: I was lonely and lost and thoroughly sorry for myself.

I was put to work in the filing department in the main office building under a corporal whose favourite topic of conversation was the inevitability of war with Russia as soon as the present conflict was ended. The filing system was complicated and incomprehensible: it consisted of innumerable strips of card which had to be inserted into slots on metal holders hung all round the room, like volumes of a tin book. Every consultation of the files or insertion of a new entry occasioned a burst of rattling and clattering accompanied by the corporal's muttered imprecations. After a few days of it I decided that, no matter what conclusion the Personnel Selection Officer and the Psychiatrist had come to between them, I was in the wrong job. I made an application to be transferred to the Educational Corps. In due course I received a summons to appear before my Company Officer, a beaky-nosed Major with an accusing manner who had already decided that I was up to no good.

'Can you give me one good reason,' he demanded, 'why I should consider this application of yours?'

I tried to explain why I felt I might be more usefully employed than in my present job, but he was not interested.

'What is an able-bodied fellow like you doing here in the first place?' he shouted. 'You ought to be over in France, fighting in the trenches!'

I wanted to point out to him that at present no-one was fighting in France, either in the trenches or elsewhere, but he was not prepared to listen.

'Application dismissed!' he announced with a thump on his desk. 'And if I hear any more of this sort of thing, I'll have you put on a charge for desertion.'

I felt enraged and insulted, but there was nothing I could do. As I left his office I took my feelings out on the door and slammed it hard. There was a yell from the Major and in a moment the Company Sergeant hauled me inside again. I was put on a charge for insolent behaviour, not quite as serious as desertion perhaps, but enough to get me seven days 'C.B.' – Confined to Barracks – which involved reporting to the Guard Room first thing in the morning and last thing at night, wearing full kit. At the end of the week I was again summoned in front of the Major. His manner had changed completely.

'I understand that your mother is going overseas, Wilson,' he said solicitously. 'I am granting you seven days compassionate leave.'

Reduced to a mild state of shock by this sudden reversal in my fortunes, I went off to London for a final fling of cinema-going. One day we saw Laurence Olivier in *Demi-Paradise* in the morning and Ingrid Bergman and Gary Cooper in *For Whom the Bell Tolls* in the afternoon. I stayed at Harrow with the Stevensons and must have driven them mad playing the songs from Gershwin's *Girl Crazy* which had just reappeared in a new film version starring Judy Garland and Mickey Rooney. On Sunday evening my mother saw me off on the Underground to Paddington, where I caught a train back to Bicester. A few days later she sailed for Africa.

It was the low spot of my time in the Army: whichever way I looked boredom and depression appeared inevitable. There was of course one other avenue of escape. It had been suggested to me once or twice that I should apply to be sent to OCTU, to train as an officer: I was after all an Old Harrovian and, unlike many of my fellow clerks, I had nothing physically wrong with me. But I had various reasons for not doing so, the most obvious being that I never felt I was 'officer material'. I knew what sort of people made good officers: they had been heads of houses and captains of teams at school, and I simply was not the type. What was more I had spent most of my life so far with them and, admirable as many of them were, I had had enough of them. I felt a strong urge to try and find out what people of a different social order were like, how, to use a cliché, 'the other half lived'. My motives were a little muddled perhaps: to begin with I simply wanted to be accepted, because my having been at Elstree and Harrow seemed to have put me in a position of privilege which the War had made unreal and out of date. We were, to use another cliché, 'all in this together' and my education and social background had so far cut me off from full participation. To my surprise, during my whole time in the Army, neither was ever brought up against me, even in fun, and I found that I was accepted by my fellow-rankers far more readily than any of them would have been accepted into the milieu in which I had grown up.

In addition I had a feeling which, however spurious it may seem in retrospect, was quite genuine at the time, that I had been given a unique opportunity to investigate the tastes, opinions and affections of the people who, all being well, would form the bulk of the public whom I hoped eventually to entertain. I was, I imagined, on a kind of mission, which had both moral and practical value, and if I now decided to train as an officer, I would be abandoning it just when it was beginning to pay off. And then something happened which seemed to justify these sincere, if somewhat flabby, aspirations.

Up till now my friends in the Army had mostly been people like myself, who had found themselves in the Ordnance Corps because they did not fit in anywhere else. We had more or less the same sort of background and possessed several interests in common. I had not so far really got to know anybody completely different from the kind of person I had been meeting all my life. Now I had an experience, only to be met with, I think, in the ranks of the Services: I found a 'mate'. It is difficult to describe this relationship without making it sound comic or suspect, but the bond between you and your 'mate' is very real and very strong, and, what is more, it is recognised and respected by the other men and even protected, where possible, when it is threatened by chance circumstances such as a change of job or a posting to another unit. No-one questions it or derides it, and no-one, unless he is very foolhardy, attempts to disrupt it.

Tony, like many other men in the Ordnance Corps, had a disability, and for someone of his age it was a particularly trying one: he was deaf, or 'Mutt and Jeff' as he used to call it. He came from Dagenham and had worked, of course, in the Ford Factory. When I met him he was in a state of panic because he thought he had 'caught something' off an ATS girl with whom he was walking out. He was worried by what his family would think and even more concerned about how it might affect his cricket, which was the most important thing in his life. When he told me the circumstances, I realised that it was unlikely, if not impossible, and told him so; but he would not be convinced until he had had a clearance from the hospital in Oxford. Nevertheless he had taken me into his confidence about something very personal; we had broken through each other's defences, and from now on we would share everything.

I had met Tony through being transferred to another department where the job I had to do was, if anything, more tedious than the previous one. Every article despatched from an Ordnance Depot was accompanied by a sheaf of different coloured vouchers; on the completion of the transaction these had to be sorted out according to colour and then filed. For hour after hour we sat in front of an arrangement of cubby-holes, stuffing them with slips of paper, took them out when they were full, filed them, and then started the whole process over again. If any job called for automation, that one did.

It was by now generally assumed that the Invasion of Europe would take place some time in the summer, and the Depot was working flat out twenty-four hours a day shipping supplies to the invasion army. Someone had advised me that if I could manage to get myself assigned to the night shift, I would find life more agreeable: there was less regimentation and supervision, and, if one could face the loss of sleep, it was possible to have the odd day off and go into Oxford. My application was successful and before long I had quite adjusted to the topsy-turvy existence of the night-worker. The atmosphere in the office was certainly much more free and easy than by day, and I made friends with an ATS corporal called Dot, who supervised the typing pool next door. We would while away the small hours by singing the latest song-hits to each other, and sometimes on a Saturday afternoon we would go into Oxford and hire a piano studio at Taphouses, the music shop. I now had quite a respectable collection of sheet music and had discovered Chappell's Piano Selections from old shows and films. Together Dot and I would run through our favourite numbers, from Astaire and Rogers to *Showboat* and *Lady, Be Good*, interspersing them with something new such as *Mairzy Doats* or *Long Ago and Far Away*.

Basil Coleman had joined the company at the Oxford Playhouse and on matinée days I would finish work in the morning, thumb a lift into Oxford, and go to his digs for a sleep. He would wake me at lunch-time and after lunch I would go to see the show at the New – usually a pre-West End tour – and then hitch-hike back to Bicester. I often had a hard time keeping awake the following night, but it was worth it. During one of my visits to Oxford I met an undergraduate from St John's and he invited me to have dinner in Hall one week-end: the experience made me determined to go up to University after the War, and I set about investigating how long my scholarship would be available.

One day in June I was woken up at lunch-time by the men in my hut and told that the Invasion had begun. The feeling of relief was tremendous and, as the summer progressed and the Allies penetrated further and further into Europe, hopes grew that the War would be over by

Christmas. The older men began to reckon how soon they would be de-mobbed and back in 'civvy street'. I knew that even when the War ended I would have to stay in the Army for quite a while longer and probably go overseas, but at least the end of it all seemed to be in sight. One evening Tony began to discuss the effect of 'class' on our friendship and said that once the War was over it would be impossible for us to know each other. I told him he was being absurd, that nothing could come between us, but he remained unconvinced.

Now that Peace in Europe seemed imminent, my mother began to grow restive in Bulawayo and, on hearing that my sister Noël was expecting a baby in November, decided that her presence was needed in London. Much as I looked forward to seeing her again, I felt it was foolish for her to return before the War was really over, and just at that time the first of the flying bombs began to land in London. But this only seemed to strengthen her resolve to come home, and she contrived to book herself a passage in the autumn. Meanwhile Paris had been liberated and I was astonished by the scenes on the newsreels: shots of cheering crowds and processions, then a burst of firing from German snipers; everyone took cover, the snipers were eliminated, and the cheering started again. Virginia was back in Europe from the Middle East and had gone over to France with ENSA in the early days of the Invasion. I wondered how she would feel on returning to Paris, where she had last been when Uncle Frank was still alive.

In September the black-out was lifted and it was announced that the last 'buzz-bomb' had fallen on London. I went up to Town on leave and found the Theatre booming: Peter Ustinov had a big success with *The Banbury Nose*, as had Terence Rattigan with *While the Sun Shines*; the Old Vic was enjoying a triumphant season at the New Theatre, and I saw Olivier's memorable Richard III. I managed to arrange a meeting with Charles Stromberg, who was also on leave, and together we went to see Billy Wilder's film, *Double Indemnity*, which had caused something of a sensation and was later considered the first of Hollywood's 'films noirs'.

My mother returned towards the end of October, in good time for the arrival of Noël's daughter, Carolyn, who was born on November 4th. Now that the pressure of work had relaxed, I was able to get up to London nearly every week-end, and in November my mother moved back into our flat in Northways and we now had a home again. Together with Noël, David and the new baby we celebrated Christmas there. The Germans were counter-attacking strongly and the hopes of an early end to the European war had temporarily faded; but we were together again, and the future began to take shape as a possibility instead of an uncertainty.

Tony met me on my return from Christmas leave with the news that I was to go on 'cadre', an arduous fortnight's course of infantry training which we were all expected to undergo once a year. I packed up my belongings and moved to the camp where the course took place. The next evening I went to meet Tony for a drink and just happened to look in at Company Office.

'Oh, Wilson,' the corporal called to me. 'You're on Overseas Draft. Report to the Orderly Room tomorrow at nine a.m. for kit inspection.'

Although I had half expected it, the news came as a shock and I knew that it would upset my mother, coming so soon after our reunion. But all the same the prospect of going abroad, wherever it might be, seemed tremendously exciting, and after those months of monotony and depression, it was very good to feel that at last I would really be *doing* something.

Three weeks later I sailed from Glasgow on a Dutch ship, the *Vollendam,* for destination unknown, although the concensus of opinion was that we were headed for the Middle East, as we had been issued with semi-tropical kit. My only regret at leaving Bicester was having to say goodbye to Tony. I had inevitably grown to feel responsible for him, and we had become wholly dependent on each other for companionship; but his deafness more or less precluded his being drafted overseas, and if it had not, the chances of our ending up in the same place were very remote. So there was nothing to be done but wish each other luck and hope to meet up again some time.

I had never travelled further by sea before than across the English Channel and boarding the *Vollendam* was an excitement in itself. We were directed deeper and deeper into the bowels of the ship and finally into what appeared to be a dining hall where we were each allotted a place at one of the many long tables. To my astonishment this turned out to be where we not only ate but slept and did everything else as well. At night hammocks were slung from the ceiling and, after the first struggle to get into one, I found it very comfortable. The crowded quarters took more getting used to, but there were the promenade decks to escape to and a recreation room and canteen in another part of the ship.

The first day out the weather was rough and continued to be so all through the Irish Sea. I had always been a bad sailor and expected to succumb at the first roll of the ship, and to make things worse I was put on garbage duty, which meant lugging bins of rubbish and swill from the galleys up on deck and throwing them overboard in the right direction, otherwise the wind blew it all back in your face. To my surprise the job was so arduous that I never had time to feel sick, although down below on our mess deck most of the other men were suffering abominably.

Once we had sailed through the Straits of Gibraltar, the weather changed and the voyage became more enjoyable. A ship's concert was organised and I had the colossal nerve to perform the whole of the Saga of Jenny from *Lady in the Dark* to a deservedly apathetic reception. We stopped at Malta, then still basking in its fame as the George Cross Island, but could only see it from the ship's rail, as there was no shore leave. A few days later Alexandria loomed up on the horizon. There was a burst of speculation: would we continue on to Port Said and the Suez Canal? But this, it turned out, was our port of disembarkation. We filed off the *Vollendam* and on to a train which took us down through Egypt to Tel el Kebir, where a huge Ordnance Depot had been built in the desert. But, in comparison with Bicester, this was a holiday camp. The huts we lived in were comfortable and spacious, and the NAAFI canteens, surrounded by palm trees and flower gardens, seemed more like night-clubs. There was a swimming pool and three cinemas, one of which, as if in anticipation of my arrival, was showing Jeanette MacDonald in *San Francisco*. The men all seemed unbelievably glamorous in their sun-tans and shorts; we, the new arrivals from England, in our crumpled battle-dress, looked at each other's pale faces in dazed disbelief. If ever there was a 'cushy posting', this was it.

The work unfortunately was no more interesting than it had been in England; only the destinations on the consignments sounded more exotic. I was put in charge of a corporal called Ron who instructed me in yet another totally incomprehensible procedure, and I also, for reasons which escape me now, had to learn to ride a motor-bike. As I had never even ridden a bicycle because of my father's anxiety over my survival, this was almost impossible; but no-one appeared to mind particularly. The corporal seemed much more interested in advising me how to get into Cairo and what to do when I got there. The sun shone by day; by night there were long sessions in the NAAFI, eating more fried eggs than I had seen for years and exotic cakes such as I had never seen, followed by a choice of the latest movies. One afternoon while I was lazing on my bunk the radio played a record of Frank Sinatra singing something called *People Will Say We're in Love*. I had heard reports in London of the tremendous success of *Oklahoma!* on Broadway: Richard Rodgers' partner, Lorenz Hart, had died and he had written the score with a new lyricist, Oscar Hammerstein. The song sounded a bit feeble to me. Where were the bounce and lilt of *The Boys from Syracuse*?

Now that I was on the same continent, I thought it might be feasible for me to spend my next leave with Helen and Cecil, who were now living in Dar-es-Salaam, and I got as far as investigating how long it would take to get there by air. But I should have known that the whole thing was too good to last. I had been at Tel el Kebir four weeks and had just about mastered the starting mechanism of the motor-bike when I was told to pack my kit in preparation for moving on again.

'Sounds as if you're going to Shaiba,' said Ron ominously.

'Where's that?' I asked.

'Paiforce.' I looked uncomprehending. 'Persia and Iraq. Shaiba's in Iraq, in the desert. In the RAF it's a punishment station.'

My heart sank. And I had never got to Cairo.

That night we set out on the first stage of our journey, by road and train, to Haifa where we spent a couple of days in transit. The spring flowers were blooming on Mount Carmel which a few of us climbed on our first evening. From Haifa we travelled by lorry for two days across the Syrian Desert on the long journey to Baghdad, which sounded an exciting destination. But by day it was a disappointment, squalid and ramshackle, far removed from the paintings of Edmund Dulac or even the films of Maria Montez; only by night, when the twinkling lights of the city were reflected in the River Tigris, did it possess a little of the glamour I had expected. Our transit camp was under the walls of the hideous Royal Palace, the home of the boy king Feisal, who would soon be going to Harrow. Even in March the whole place was hot and dusty, and I had my first taste of the East, that curious mixture of the intriguing and the repellant which is so alien to most Anglo-Saxons. From Baghdad we set out by train for Shaiba. We travelled overnight, sleeping on the floor of the third class carriages, and when the morning came there was nothing to be seen from the windows but miles and miles of grey waste-land. On the last stages of the journey we were accompanied by a swarm of locusts, like huge armour-plated grass-hoppers, which rattled and bumped on the glass in their headlong flight in search of vegetation. It was an alarming and fairly appropriate introduction to Shaiba.

It was here that I spent the next eighteen months of my life in the Army, in a Base Ordnance Depot which had been built originally to store supplies for onward shipment to Russia during the German invasion. At first it seemed even worse than Bicester. That was in the middle of nowhere; Shaiba was in the middle of nothing. Wherever one looked there was just the desert, flat, grey and endless. Basra was the nearest town, but that was out of bounds, except for a dreary suburb called Ashar which I only visited once. In winter the weather was cold and wet, and the camps were reduced to seas of mud and stagnant water. In summer the temperature rose to well over a hundred in the shade: there were sandflies, whose bite could cause a high fever, scorpions, centipedes and, naturally, flies – flies so persistent that they would sit on the nib of my pen, while I was writing, and drink the ink. In the Forces the Persian Gulf was referred to as the Arse-hole of the Middle East, and Shaiba was on the edge of it. And yet, in a strange way, it grew on me, and, for all its physical discomforts, it had certain advantages. In summer the weather was so hot that we were not allowed to work after mid-day; instead we had reveille at six in the morning so that we could work before breakfast, and, as most of us took our beds outside and slept in the open, I discovered the unique brilliance and freshness of dawn over the desert. After our dinner at mid-day we were supposed to have a siesta; but, for the first summer at least, I found the heat so stimulating that I spent the afternoons writing plays and composing songs on the NAAFI piano. There was a huge open-air cinema which was free and changed its programme twice a week, and at night I could lie under my sand-fly net and gaze up at the blazing eastern stars. It was a monotonous existence undoubtedly and if I had not been able to occupy my mind with reading, writing and music it might have been unbearable. But it was so removed in time and place and feeling from anything I had previously experienced that I felt suspended in a moral and mental vacuum, in which there were no responsibilities, no ties and no obligations; only the routine of the days and nights, the sun, the stars and the desert.

Another of Shaiba's amenities, and the only attractive building in the whole area, was the Church, called, a little whimsically, St Martin's in the Sands. I was still a practising Christian, albeit a slightly confused one, having been born into the Presbyterian Church and then obliged to turn Church of England during term-time at boarding school, while remaining Presbyterian during the holidays; I was confirmed at the age of twelve, while I was at Elstree, more because it was the done thing than from any feeling of conviction, and when my father died my mother reverted to the Church of England and I followed suit. Going to church while I was overseas was a link as much with home as with the Deity, and St Martin's in the Sands had a rather cosy padre who encouraged members of the congregation to stay behind after the service, for tea and biscuits in the vestry. It was thus that, on my first Sunday evening in Shaiba, I met Douglas Walch. Twenty-five years and two marriages later he reminded me how it happened: 'I arrived at the Church and found you sitting in my seat. So I sat behind you and tapped you on the shoulder and said, "That is my pew." I got to Shaiba in 1944, so I'd been there for a year before you, and that was why I was annoyed about your pinching my pew. Then we went through to the vestry for tea with the Vicar and you were awfully upset about sitting in my seat, and that's how it started. If you don't believe me,' he added characteristically, 'you must be wrong.'

Whereas I was at pains to live down my public school background and merge with the ranks, Doug, who had actually been at a secondary school, cultivated the air and appearance of a 'gentleman' and was known as 'The Duke'. We made an odd pair: my battle-dress was ill-fitting and unpressed, the pockets bulging with pens and note-books, and I never took much trouble about blanco-ing my puttees or polishing my brass; Doug, who had the faultless good looks of a 1930s matinée idol, was always immaculate from top to toe, every crease in place, his hair carefully brushed and his nails manicured. We hardly saw eye to eye on anything, and once, when I felt he had insulted me beyond bearing, I went so far as to aim a strong right at his perfect jaw – and missed. But he was, and is, excellent company and was also far more aware than me of the absurdity of our situation in Shaiba:

'There was never any purpose in the place from the day we got there. The original conception was to use the over-land route to get supplies to Russia, but by that time the Russians were doing so well that they didn't need any help from us. So that dried up. We were just there to supply the Infantry; the Signals were there because the Infantry had to communicate; the Engineers were there to look after the Signals and the Infantry. If the Infantry had moved out, we could all have gone home. They were there to defend us, and we were there to supply them. They could have wound up that Depot and sent us all to Germany: we all had infantry training. It was a bloody waste of our time and of our youth.'

I pointed out that, though it may have been a waste, we did at least survive, which is more than a lot of men our age did.

'Oh yes, we survived – on corned beef and dehydrated potatoes. I take my hat off to the cooks. Our staple diet was water melon and dates: we had them hot and cold, in fritters and tarts, with custard and without. I didn't eat melon for twenty years after I left Shaiba.'

Doug's attitude may sound frivolous, but it concealed a deep bitterness and frustration which was felt by many of the men there, while the majority of the others just sank into a kind of sun-struck apathy which often affected them physically: 'In Shaiba we were completely sexless things – we had no feelings one way or the other. I suppose we all

masturbated, but more out of a feeling of boredom than from any kind
of lust. In any case at that time people didn't get terribly hung up about
sex; I don't think we even discussed it. But isn't it a god-dam shame?
There we were – nineteen and twenty – not a wrinkle on our faces,
wasting away in the wilderness. Look at what boys of our age are
doing now. But we were caught up in the War and we were just
waiting for it to finish, and after the War we expected something
golden to happen. I remember seeing a pre-fab which the Labour Party
had erected somewhere in the Middle East: it was a super pre-fab,
like an American duplex, and there was a notice which said, "Every
Ex-Serviceman will get one of these." But all I really hoped for was
to get out and do my own thing again.'

When I had been at Shaiba two months, the War in Europe did end,
and on VE Day I wrote to my mother, who was again staying in
Stirling with Aunt Christian:

'How I wish we could be together in London today! The celebrations
must be terrific and I imagine everyone will go quite mad for a day or
two. Out here it's very difficult to work up much enthusiasm: I can only
feel very thankful that we've beaten the Germans at last. I just hope the
War with Japan doesn't last too long, and most of all I hope I shall be
home again soon and then we can have a *real* celebration. There are
various festivities being carried on here, and we are having two days
off from work, but there is little to do except get drunk – and then only
on rather inferior beer. I felt a bit hazy this morning after four brandies
and ginger beer in the office – the Colonel gave us drinks all round.
This afternoon he made a speech – not a very good one – and tomorrow
evening we are having a grand dinner.'

Two days later I wrote again:

'While you were revisiting the ancestral domain, I was distinguishing
myself by getting well and truly blotto, two nights running, although
the second night wasn't so bad. I said in my last letter that that was the
only way of celebrating out here, and so – I celebrated! It looks as
though I shall be the same next Saturday, as I'm having a large party
for my twenty-first birthday, and out here they don't come to parties
to play charades! Still it only happens once in a life-time and it's just
rather unfortunate that it comes so soon after V-Day. Our celebrations
weren't bad, but if I hadn't been tight, I don't think I would have had
much fun. As it was, I met quite a number of new people, with the
result that my guests next Saturday will run into the twenties.'

On the day following my birthday I wrote:

'I had a simply marvellous party last night, which went on until the
early hours. There were about twenty people crammed into our small

bunk, all drinking and singing and thoroughly enjoying themselves. I
do wish you could have seen it. A number of them clubbed together
and gave me a fountain pen – I was so overcome I didn't know what
to say. Wasn't it terribly kind of them? Then someone had made a
large key, with which I was presented, and I got them all to sign their
names on it and I will bring it back as a souvenir. In the course of the
evening I sang *Don't Let's be Beastly to the Germans* and Frank Sinatra's
song, *Come Out Wherever You Are.* I felt a bit groggy this morning and
could eat no breakfast, but that has passed off and now I am quite
all right again. Incidentally someone procured a bottle of vino from the
Italian prisoners, which helped things along.'

At the end of the letter I wrote:

'You will probably have to vote for me at the Election, so I will send
instructions later.'

Until a few months before it had never occurred to me that, when
the time came, I would vote anything but Conservative. My family
were Conservatives: Helen and Christian had even taken part in a
Pageant of Parliament at the Albert Hall in 1935 which was organised
by the Young Conservatives. My education had been in the Conservative tradition – a private preparatory school followed by one of the
oldest public schools, where Churchill himself had been a pupil. In
those surroundings Socialism had seemed little better than Communism,
a code of behaviour for conspirators and revolutionaries, whose adher-
ents, such as Stafford Cripps and James Maxton, talked a lot of
inflammatory nonsense. All my life I had benefited from Conservative
institutions; the least I could do in return, so I thought, was to vote
for the Tories.

But a few months in Shaiba changed my feelings completely. I had
already learned to live with and like the sort of people whom, previous
to joining the Army, I would have regarded as a lower order of beings,
only likely to be encountered in a master-servant relationship. The fact
that we had not had any servants for years made no difference: the old
class distinctions had been preserved, and I subscribed to them instinctively. But now, due to the chances of War, I had become one of
'Them'. I had even formed a friendship with one of the 'working class'
which was closer and warmer than any I had ever had with my so-called
equals. And in Shaiba I began to realise, with a growing certainty, that
the class to which I aspired had for years and years been treating these
people who were now my friends with a cold-hearted arrogance and a
total indifference to their true needs and feelings. The very fact that
we were all of us in that obsolete place, doing futile and unnecessary
jobs in deplorable conditions, was a testament to the callously auto-

cratic attitude of the majority of the people who ruled our lives. Even our own officers, who were far from being members of the ruling class, coming for the most part from the ranks of small-time businessmen, shop-walkers and the like, behaved with the same aloofness, as if the acquisition of a few pips had somehow elevated them into the upper echelons of society. If I had followed the path prescribed for someone of my background, I would have been one of them, looking down my nose at my inferiors and treating them like idiots and peasants. But now I had broken away from all that, and I resolved that never again would I align myself with the party who stood for the preservation of these barriers and these attitudes. I decided to vote Labour.

But for the moment, it seemed, my trip to Damascus was all in vain. When the General Election resulted in a Labour landslide, I was delighted, and it was only later that I realised, to my distress, that I had failed to contribute to it. The letter with my voting instructions reached my mother too late and she naturally cast my vote for the Tories. However there were to be other elections, and my change of heart, I am happy to say, turned out to be permanent.

Now that the War in Europe was over, most of us expected to be posted to the Far East. According to my 'demob.' group, which was 54, I was likely to remain in the Army at least another year. When I arrived in Shaiba, I had been asked if I could type, and on admitting that I could, a little, I was sent to the Headquarters Office as a typist. It was marginally less monotonous than in the jobs I had done elsewhere, but I still yearned to do something more productive. One evening I was summoned to my Company Office. There was a telephone call for me from Basra. It was Virginia.

'Sandy darling,' she cried, and her voice was like a message from another planet. 'I'm here for one night, between planes, and I've got to see you. I've spoken to your C.O. and it's all right. They're sending a jeep for you and we'll dine together. A tout à l'heure!'

I could hardly believe my ears, but it was all true, and within the hour I was sitting opposite Virginia in the restaurant of the Airport Hotel, Basra, eating the sort of food I had not laid eyes on for months. She was on her way to India, to organise more entertainment for the Forces, and tired as she must have been, she seemed nevertheless to be bursting with energy and enthusiasm, literally as well as metaphorically, since her battle-blouse could scarcely contain her buxom bosom. As clearly as I could, between mouthfuls, I tried to outline to her all my post-war ambitions, and received her assurance that she, Virginia, would personally see to their realisation. But in the meanwhile, I told her, I was bored to tears in a job that any fool could do. Was there a chance that she could arrange for my transfer to ENSA? She promised to do what she could, and a little while later my time was up. Feeling dazed and delighted, I was driven back through the night to Shaiba.

A week or so after our rendezvous in Basra I was told to proceed to Baghdad for an interview with the officer in charge of Forces Entertainment. The interview turned out to be an audition, and it took place in a small room mostly occupied by an upright piano. With the officer sitting almost at my elbow, I launched into a verse and two choruses of Cole Porter's *Don't Fence Me In* which was currently at the top of the hit parade. For a moment after I had finished he gazed at me with what I hoped was admiration but which I fear was probably utter bewilderment. How, he must have been asking himself, was he supposed to employ this totally untalented nephew of Madame Vernon's who could only play the piano rather badly and could not sing at all?

Nevertheless a few days after my return to Shaiba I was informed that an application had been made for my transfer to ENSA; I was also informed that, owing to the importance of my present job and the lack of anyone to replace me, the application had been refused. It was my last attempt to improve my lot in the Army. From now on, I realised, there was nothing to do but sit it out until my group was demobbed. With the dropping of the Atom Bomb and the capitulation of the Japanese even the prospect of a Far East posting was removed. Not that we were not all tremendously relieved that the War was finally over: we were, and whatever any of us might have felt subsequently, after six years of it we were far too hardened to take in the enormity of what had been done to Hiroshima or to regard the Bomb as anything but a God-send. Once again we were granted two days off and the whole depot was given over to boozing. Now I knew that I would have to work out the rest of my time here in Shaiba; my mother had made tentative suggestions in her letters that I might apply for an early release because of my scholarship to Oriel, but in my new role as a member of the masses I decided firmly against it. I was not going to be guilty of exercising such an obvious class privilege, even if it meant being bored to death for another year or more.

Luckily I became due for local leave in September, which meant a fortnight in Beirut, with the chance of spending some of the time in Palestine, if I wished. The leave camp at Beirut was on the beach and had its own canteen and cinema. I spent a week there during which I visited the Roman ruins of Baalbek, and then travelled by train to Jerusalem, which was then, as it now is once again, an undivided city. I stayed in a Catholic hostel, where I had the luxury of a room to myself, and spent the days exploring the Old City and the supposed sites of the New Testament. The high-spot, I had been told, was the Holy Sepulchre, where the atmosphere of sanctity was so powerful that one was compelled to fall on one's knees; but, try as I would, I could not feel it, and when I knelt it was only from a sense of duty. In the evenings the modern city offered all the pleasures I had not enjoyed since leaving England. Bette Davis' latest film, *Mr Skeffington*, was playing at one of the several luxurious super-cinemas: on the way home from seeing it I bought a copy of *Vogue*, and in my room at the hostel I pored over the photographs and sketches of the new fashions. Somehow they brought home to me more powerfully than anything else the fact that the War was over.

When I returned to Shaiba, there was a sense of change in the air. It had at last filtered through to the authorities that conditions there were not all they should be and a new Commanding Officer had been sent out with orders to do everything in his power to improve our welfare. His name was Colonel Tarrant and he was the only man I met in my three years in the Army who had the presence and authority one is led to expect of an officer. But he arrived too late. Most of the men had been in Shaiba two years or more and were justifiably cynical about promises of improvements in their condition, and in any case all they cared about at this stage was how soon they would be sent home. But Colonel Tarrant had an ambitious scheme which he was determined to carry through, and shortly after I came back off leave I discovered that I was going to be part of it. Someone had told him that I could draw and paint, and one day he called me into his office and asked me for a picture to hang in his bungalow. I was installed in a room at HQ and given a set of water-colours and some cartridge paper, and for a week I spent my afternoons painting a huge surrealist vision which I called *The Red Glove*. The Colonel expressed himself delighted with it, and then proceeded to outline to me his plans for the improvement of Shaiba. He was going to build a huge sports arena which would be called the Victory Stadium, and in another part of the depot there was to be a vast new canteen and theatre, which, since Shaiba was situated near the traditional site, was to be called the Garden of Eden, and, although nothing would grow, it was to be surrounded by a garden. To publicise all this and to raise everybody's morale, there was to be a Unit Magazine, and this was where I came in: I was offered the job of editing it. Without hesitation I accepted, and suggested as my Art Editor a fellow typist, Fred Wilde, who in civilian life designed textiles. Fred, who was as bored with his job as I was, jumped at the idea, and we were soon installed in our own office with all the equipment necessary to produce a magazine. The Colonel also decided that there should be a competition, open to the whole depot, for suggestions for a title: he would judge the result and the prize would be a pound. I think there were five printable entries, and the winning one – *Ahead* – was, I regret to say, mine. I set about designing a cover of the utmost banality: a hand holding a flaming torch from the smoke of which emerged the lettering of the title. Now that we had a cover, Fred and I were faced with the task of finding something to put inside it. Notices were posted in every Company Office inviting contributions of any kind – articles, short stories, drawings, jokes, anything. For the next few days we sat in the Editorial Office awaiting a flood of material. Nothing whatsoever arrived. With difficulty Fred persuaded one or two NCOs in charge of Company Sports to submit articles on the prospects for the coming football season. Apart from that our only contribution was Colonel Tarrant's inspiring foreword to the magazine, in which he hailed it as the Voice of Shaiba which would utter all our feelings about the Present and all our hopes for the Future.

After a week of waiting Fred and I looked at each other and realised that if the first issue of *Ahead* was to appear, we would just have to write it all ourselves. He contributed a short story, an article on textile designing and innumerable vignettes, page headings and other decorations. I wrote a humorous column, which borrowed heavily from Beachcomber, some reviews of films soon to appear at the Depot Cinema, an article about long runs and short runs in the West End Theatre, which might have interested three other people besides myself, and the first of a series of caricatures entitled Camp Characters, Number One being 'The Duke', for which I doubt if Doug has ever forgiven me. We then had to type and draw all the stencils and, with the help of a Sikh and an Arab boy, roneo all the sheets, fold them and staple them, ready for dispatch to our waiting public.

To say that the supply exceeded the demand would be the kindest understatement: of our first issue of five hundred I think we sold about fifty. We included another appeal for contributions at the end of the number, which had no more effect than before; but Colonel Tarrant was not discouraged and congratulated us on a fine beginning. So Fred and I retired to our office and began to rack our brains for material for the second issue. In the meanwhile the Colonel's other plans were going ahead: the Victory Stadium was taking shape, and so was the new canteen. A friend of mine called Bob, who was a keen horticulturist, had been given the job of creating the Garden of Eden: with an ingenuity born of desperation, he devised trees from telegraph poles hung with green camouflage netting, which were erected round an artificial oasis. The Iraquis who were working for him thought he had gone 'meknoun' (insane) and punctuated their labours with fits of incredulous laughter; but the Garden was eventually completed and from a distance looked almost real. When the interior of the canteen was finished, I was commissioned to decorate the theatre proscenium, and for several days I sat on top of a ladder painting two huge pin-up girls, one blonde, the other brunette, who reclined on either side of the arch supporting at its centre the masks of Comedy and Tragedy. Since there had been only one visiting entertainment, a South African concert party called the Springboks, in the last year, it seemed unlikely that the theatre would be over-booked; but the Colonel's enthusiasm was unflagging. Indeed there was something almost heroic about it, and I found myself championing all his projects in the face of scathing comments from all sides. The officers were just as critical as the men: Colonel Tarrant's obsession with welfare seemed to reflect on their own record, and they were delighted by the Other Ranks' lack of response.

At Christmas time the whole depot got drunk once again, and on Christmas night, emboldened by alcohol, I made my way to the Colonel's bungalow through the darkness to wish him the compliments of the season. There was no-one at home and I collapsed into insensibility on the door-step, where he found me a little while later. He asked me in for a drink and began to tell me about his marital problems; in the middle of the conversation there was a knock on the door and a bunch of officers arrived intent on making the Colonel join them in the mess, which he was clearly reluctant to do. Without considering the possible consequences, I suddenly turned on them and began to upbraid them for their disloyalty and hypocrisy. Their mouths fell open in shocked amazement, and Colonel Tarrant, hurriedly stepping into the breach, thanked them for their invitation but said he was tired and about to go to bed. They shuffled out with malevolent glances in my direction, and when they were gone the Colonel said very firmly:

'And now I'm going to drive you back to your Camp, Wilson, otherwise God knows what they'll think.'

Whatever they did think, there were no repercussions, presumably because it was the Season of Good Will. Soon after that there was a change of policy on the part of the authorities or else the bills for Shaiba's improvements came in, and Colonel Tarrant was recalled to England. In a valedictory message in the final issue of *Ahead* he thanked everyone for their enthusiasm and co-operation and gave an address at the War Office where anyone who wished to do so would be welcome to get in touch with him when they reached home. He departed as suddenly as he had arrived, leaving behind him the Victory Stadium and the Garden of Eden Canteen as extravagant monuments to his wasted efforts.

Now that the War was over, my mother began casting around for something to occupy herself, and one day I received a letter from her announcing that she had the chance to buy a small hotel in Brooke Market, a square behind the Prudential Building in Holborn, on the borders of the City of London. It had come to her attention through her youngest brother, Harold, who had spent most of his life in Australia but had returned to England after the break-up of his marriage and was living at Brooke House until he could find a new home of his own. I was appalled at the idea; Mother was sixty-five and had, in my opinion, reached an age when she should retire gracefully and enjoy her grandchildren and, of course, my impending triumphs in the Theatre. I wrote back and told her so, but once again the letter arrived too late: she had already bought Brooke House and embarked on her new career as a hotelier, something which, she now maintained, she had fancied being since her youth. The flat at Northways was let and I was again without a home of my own, although Mother assured me that there would always be a room available for me at Brooke House whenever I needed it. The whole business only made me more determined to go my own way: not only would I refuse to go to Oxford, I would set up in a place of my own, an attic, a hovel, anywhere, and, free from all my previous ties, devote myself to my theatrical destiny. I began composing feverishly, an operetta based on Charlotte Brontë's *Villette* which I had just read for the first time. I was also writing a play, a revelation of life at a public school in war-time, at whose climax the lead, a neurotic trouble-maker, commits suicide after admitting to an unnatural passion for the head of the house. It was not based remotely on anything that I had ever experienced at Harrow, where unnatural passions had as a rule been either gratified or ignored; but I felt I was doing for the Public School what Clare Booth Luce had done for New York Society. Unfortunately where *The Women* was scintillating and sophisticated, my play was turgid and naïve. I showed it to the Sergeant in charge of Education and he advised me to try writing something funny instead.

Charles and I continued to correspond, frequently and at great length. He was still stationed in England, in the Isle of Wight, and kept me up to date with the Theatre and the Cinema by posting cuttings from James Agate and Dilys Powell. C. B. Cochran announced a big new A. P. Herbert musical, *Big Ben*; Noël Coward was preparing a revue, to be called *Sigh No More*, and Ivor Novello had written

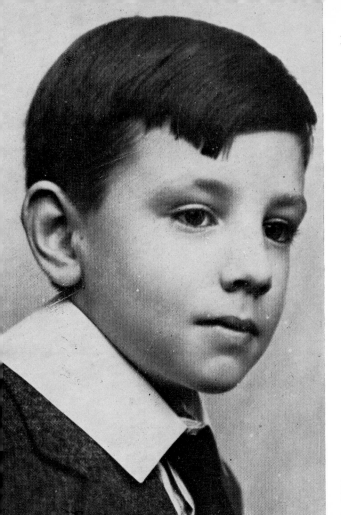

My first Eton collar

A visit from the family, Elstree
School: *L. to R.*: One of the
'P.G.s', Helen, my mother,
myself and my father

With my mother at a famil
wedding in the mid-thirtie

Love from Mummy Scudi

Below: In the garden at th
cottage, Bolney. *L. to R*
Noël, myself, my fathe
my mother, Christian

another successful operetta, *Perchance to Dream*, a song from which, *We'll Gather Lilacs in the Spring Again*, became a sort of theme tune for the forces overseas who hoped soon to be homeward-bound. It was reassuring to hear that they were all at it again, and made it seem in a way as if the War had never happened. Charles also went to see the latest edition of Hermione Gingold's revue at the Ambassadors Theatre, *Sweetest and Lowest*. She had recently published a very slim volume of autobiography, entitled *The World is Square*, and Charles, taking his courage in both hands, went round to see her afterwards and asked her to sign a copy for me. It eventually arrived in Shaiba and reading it made me long to be back in London again. The summer was approaching, and as the weather changed I found the heat was no longer stimulating; I was succumbing to the lassitude of all Shaiba veterans expressed in the Arab phrase, 'Allah keefiq' or 'I couldn't care less'. On top of that Colonel Tarrant's Welfare Scheme was being gradually run down and it looked as if I would be returned to the typing pool at any moment.

But then, to my surprise, I was told that I was due to go on leave. While the War was still on, home leave had been given on a ballot system, and many men stayed overseas for two or three years before their number came up; but now everyone was entitled to it after eighteen months. At the beginning of June a party of us set off down the railway line to Baghdad once more. This time the journey across the desert was far less gruelling: we travelled by Nairn Transport, air-conditioned buses with every amenity on board, including a refrigerator. When we reached Haifa, we were armed with rifles for our ride through the town to the transit camp: the Palestine troubles were beginning. From Haifa we went to another transit camp in Port Said, where I saw one of the few ENSA shows of my Army career – a production of an old Frederick Lonsdale play, *Canaries Sometimes Sing*. I also ran into Doug, travelling back to Shaiba from leave: I said I would see him again in a few weeks' time. The next day we set sail across the Mediterranean to Toulon in weather so warm that most of us slept on deck. The atmosphere was carefree and there were frequent sing-songs, which always seemed to end with the new Andrews Sisters number, *Rum and Coca Cola*. There was a night to wait in Toulon: Bette Davis was playing in *The Corn is Green* at the Transit Camp Cinema. The rail journey across France was uncomfortable and interminable, but by daylight we were on board the cross-channel steamer. Riding up to Victoria, we all glued our noses to the train windows, absorbing every stick and stone that passed by. Some of us shared a taxi from the station; I was the last to get off, after following Mother's slightly confusing directions. She was standing outside

Brooke House Hotel, wearing a curious black overall and looking considerably older. It was not the home-coming I had imagined, but it would certainly do.

In the last week of my leave, when I was preparing myself to face returning to Shaiba, a letter arrived from the War Office: I had been granted a 'B' Release from the Army in order to take up my scholarship at Oxford. At first I thought it must be a mistake, but soon I realised that my mother must have made the application without consulting me. For a few moments I was furious, and then I thought of what was awaiting me at the end of the long trail back to Shaiba – months of heat, boredom, frustration and discomfort: if I really thought I could forego Oxford for that, I must be kidding myself. Besides, three weeks in London, going to the theatre, seeing my friends and revisiting my old haunts, had brought home to me all too forcibly how much I missed it. In an alarmingly short while my new-found principles of equality and fraternity, my high resolve to stick it out with the other fellows, melted away into the past: I decided to go to Oxford.

On an evening in October I boarded the train at Paddington, wearing my new civvies: a pin-stripe suit and a pork-pie hat. I had no idea what to expect. Would it be like going back to school again? If so, how much would I remember after my time in the Army? But in any case I would only be there for two years: it was a means to an end, and it had got me out of uniform. After that, life could really begin.

Oxford

THERE is a song in the musical, *Cabin in the Sky*, that goes something like this: 'Do what you want to do, and you'll be what you want to be'. If someone were to ask me why my two years at Oxford meant so much to me, that is what I would reply: I was doing what I wanted to do, and, as a result, I became what I wanted to be. For the first time in my life I felt no responsibility to anyone or anything but myself. Until then I had done everything because it was expected of me – by my family, by the various schools I had been to, or by the Army; now I suddenly discovered that I need please nobody but myself.

There was of course a certain obligation to obtain a degree, but I felt fairly confident I could manage that, as, apart from a brief period towards the end of my time at Harrow, I had always been at my best in the examination room. Moreover I managed to make things easier for myself in that respect by obtaining permission to read English Literature instead of Greats (in other words, Latin and Greek) which, as a Classical Scholar, I was expected to do. When the Provost of Oriel pointed this out to me, I simply said, rather firmly, that three years in the Army had obliterated most of my knowledge of the Dead Languages and all I could manage was English. He was reluctant to make this concession but the University authorities had been instructed to be lenient with ex-service undergraduates and I was allowed to do as I wished.

We were also enabled to sit for our Finals after two years instead of the customary three, and, apart from the necessity of studying Anglo-Saxon for the first year, the English Literature course consisted, for the most part, of authors whom I had already studied at school and knew something about. I was assigned to Doctor Percy Sympson as my tutor – an aged authority on Ben Jonson, who was on the point of retirement and who tended to snooze off during tutorials – and instructed to attend various lectures which might be relevant to my subject. But I quickly discovered, to my amazement, that, apart from having to deliver an essay once a week to Dr Sympson and turn up at a lady professor's Anglo-Saxon classes, everything else was conducted on a voluntary basis and the amount of work I did was left entirely up to me. To begin with, I attended lectures conscientiously and took copious notes – particularly at those delivered by Lord David Cecil, who was the most popular lecturer in English at the time. But during my second term other activities began to claim my attention and the academic side of Oxford took a back seat. By dint of cramming a great deal of information into my head during the last few weeks before my Finals, I managed to obtain a second-class degree, which disappointed my mother, but which, considering how little work I had done, seemed to me quite an achievement. In any case that 'BA Oxon' has made not the slightest difference to my subsequent career; but everything else about Oxford had a profound influence on the rest of my life.

The first freedom I felt at Oxford was entirely physical. On the evening I arrived in College, the Porter directed me to my rooms, which were in the Rhodes Building, a rather ugly addition to Oriel which abuts on to the High. I was quite expecting to share them with at least one other undergraduate, but I found, to my astonishment, that, being a scholar, I had a bedroom and a large sitting-room to myself. After three years of inhabiting a hut, along with anything up to thirty other men, the sense of space was almost hallucinatory and I walked from room to room saying to myself, 'This is mine – *all* mine!'. Within a week or so I had grown used to it, but it was brought home to me again when Tony, who was still in the Army and stationed at Bicester, came over to see me one afternoon. I had been in touch with him when I was first home on leave and we had been out together – to the cinema, inevitably – a couple of times, and nothing in our relationship seemed to have altered. But when I took him into College, he was plainly over-awed, and when he saw my rooms, he gasped. 'Is this all yours?' he asked incredulously, just as I had asked myself when I first saw them. 'Blimey,' he went on, when I told him it was, 'they do you proud here, don't they?'. From that moment the barriers, which I had taken such credit for penetrating when we first met, began to descend again. We corresponded occasionally after that, and then gradually lost touch with each other altogether. Tony had, after all, proved right: our friendship could not survive the Peace.

A good deal has been written and said about Post-War Oxford by the many more or less celebrated people who were there, and not all of it has been complimentary; but, however one estimates its values, it was a unique place and a unique time, and even now I find it difficult to sum up the qualities that made it so, if only because they were so many and so varied. To begin with, we were not just from a great variety of backgrounds, we were of different ages. In normal times the average age of a freshman is eighteen or nineteen and he has recently left school; in 1946 the majority of freshmen were at least over twenty-one, and a good many of them were much older, some even married, with children. Many of us had had a year at University before being called up, others, like myself, were up there for the first time, after serving in the forces for anything up to six years, and still others, now that the War was over, were able to postpone their National Service and come to University from school. As a result, young men of widely varying age and experience were suddenly landed together, in statu pupillari, with almost unlimited freedom to express themselves, after years of a discipline which had been imposed both by School and by the War. It was a heady mixture, to say the least, and I found it totally intoxicating.

Along with the freedom of space and of expression, I was also discovering the freedom from fear. The War had in fact been over for more than a year, but it was not until I reached Oxford that I fully realised it. One day in the High I ran into Brian, whom I had scarcely seen or heard of since I left Harrow in 1942. For all I knew he could have been killed while serving in the Navy, but here he was again, alive and well and at Brasenose, just across the way. We had survived, and the dangers that had, to a greater or lesser extent, threatened our lives now no longer existed. One by one other faces from the past turned up, although of course some had gone for good, which only made me appreciate the more keenly how lucky I was to be here, still young and whole, and with most of my life still before me. And not only was the War over, but there had been a change of Government, so that it seemed possible that all those dreams of a Post-War Utopia on which we had nourished ourselves during the last six years might actually come true. Without doubt, to be at Oxford in 1946 induced in me a euphoria of release and a tingle of anticipation unlike anything I have ever experienced since, and it was all the more exhilarating in that I had gone there almost reluctantly, regarding it simply as a convenient stop-gap between one phase of my life and the next.

In the present-day atmosphere these probably sound rather specious sentiments and, wondering if I was again idealising the Past, as I had done with the 1920s, I decided to set my own feelings against those of three close friends from my time at Oxford. The first, Michael Godley, was ex-service like myself, but from a rather different background, and his reasons for wanting to go to Oxford in the first place were also different:

'It was partly linked with my father: his father was artisan working-class, and he himself had aspirations and he was self-educated. During the first World War he met the father of Harold Hobson (later to become Theatre Critic of the *Sunday Times*), who went to Oriel in the early Twenties. He was a cripple as a result of polio, and his parents had struggled and sacrificed, so that he could have a car to get around; but they needed someone to see him up to Oxford at the beginning of each term and my father used to go – just about the time I was born. On the first night of term he would be given a gown and go into Hall with Harold, and he used to sit there and think, "This is what I want for my son."

'It was certainly an escape for me, because I came from a northern provincial city, and I worked and worked at Grammar School for my Oxford entrance, and when I got it, this was the achievement – to get there and enjoy it. This was enough.'

Heather Couper met Michael at Oxford, where they fell in love, and they were married soon after graduating:

'It was the same with me. We were both only children and we knew that our parents would die happy if they could see us go to Oxford. It's made their lives in both cases. The first person who ever suggested it was my uncle, a vicar, who had been at Keble and said, "I think she should try for Oxford." I think all I knew about it was The Boat Race, Zuleika Dobson and Gaudy Night. It was a legendary city, like going to Katmandu now. But it was the attainment: once you were there, you became an Oxford Person.'

Heather, Michael and I all went up together in the Autumn of 1946. Penny Peters, now Penny Griffin, had already been there for two years:

'I went up while the War was still on and there were girls galore; the only men were medical students and a certain amount of chemists and physicists, who were reserved, and short course cadets and medical crocks. Then suddenly, in my third year, it was as if the flood gates opened and all these men rampaged into the University. Suddenly the Proctors no longer progged people. When I first came up, we used to drink in the Turf, because it had five different exits to escape by. I and another girl used to nip along to the Town Hall and jive with the GIs, and if we'd been caught, we could have been sent down. Then everything changed . . .'

'I'm in a slightly different category from the rest of you, because I had connections with Oxford. My godfather lived in the Woodstock Road, and I used to go and visit him, and one of my brothers was up at

Oxford before the War, and I spent a whole summer there when I was twelve. He was at Queen's, reading Classics, and he took me round almost everywhere with him and I used to sit curled up in a room in Balliol while he and all his friends put the world to rights. I know it sounds very sentimental, but I was taken up to the roof of the Radcliffe Camera – you could still go there – and in those days all the clocks of Oxford used to chime on the hour. It was a marvellous summer afternoon and I was looking out over Matthew Arnold's Dreaming Spires, and I said to myself, "I am going to come here."

'I was left at school virtually all the War, with my parents in India, and I had to have something to work for, as I didn't have a home. So I got my Matric at fourteen and I refused to take my Higher. I said, "If I can't get into Oxford, I'm not going into any other University." I just used to sit and read and dream of the time when I would be in the Bodleian. I didn't think of it in terms of a career or what I was going to do there. It was just a place.'

To Michael, the only let-down about Oxford was on the academic side:

'I was very, very keen on my subject, English Literature, and I expected to be tutored by brilliant people who would open up a wider cultural dimension for me. In fact, if anyone asks me if I have any complaints about Oxford, I say, "None, except the education was appalling." But the rest of it was everything I had hoped for, because one was able to be anything one wanted to be. The important thing was that this could only be for a limit of three years – and life isn't like that generally. If you become Prime Minister, you've got to face the next election; but if you become President of the Union, you are only allowed to be it for a term, which meant it had a special quality that can never be taken away from you. You never had any sense of failure or of growing old.'

Heather regarded going to Oxford as 'the supreme accolade – social, professional, cultural, everything. I thought that once having got there, I would be in a different class from everyone else and the world would be my oyster. The extraordinary thing is that every other word I knew has lost its meaning in some way, but "Oxford" hasn't. I think it's unfair in a way, but it's true. It's still the most difficult place to get into – with Cambridge – in the world, and I'm jolly grateful to it, because it hasn't devalued.'

'It also trained one to think for oneself,' was Penny's view. 'I immensely valued the fact that your tutor gave you a totally impossible assignment every week and just expected you to get on with it. It was discipline: no matter how terrible your hangover, you had to get it done. I value that, because now, no matter what intransigent material gets stuck in front of me, I know how to tackle it.'

It came down to this: whatever each of us sought when we came up to University, Oxford gave to us.

Early on in my first term I made it my business to get involved in any theatrical activity I could find, and I was amazed to discover how much there was. I had of course heard of the Oxford University Dramatic Society – the OUDS – and I joined it at once. They were planning a large-scale production of a deservedly forgotten Ibsen play, *The Pretenders*, to be presented at the Playhouse Theatre in the following term. It was an elaborate historical drama of such magnitude that it required two directors: Glynne Wickham, the President, was in charge of the principals, while the crowd scenes had been assigned to Anthony Besch, who was to make his name as an opera director in later life. I was cast as a member of the Birch-leg Faction, and we began rehearsals in November. I only had one line, 'The Birch-legs have won!', which I had to rush on and deliver in the middle of a banquet scene; otherwise we were just required to mill around as a mob or march about as soldiers, which was not very satisfying, but it was at least a start.

The OUDS was an institution of long standing and fine reputation, but the society that appealed to me was the Experimental Theatre Club, which had been started during the War when the OUDS was temporarily disbanded. I was introduced to it by Guy de Moubray, my fellow cinema-goer from the days of the Japanese Course at Dulwich, who had turned up at Trinity College. He was, I think, more interested in its social side than in its dramatic activities.

'They're giving a dance this term,' he told me excitedly, 'and it'll be a marvellous chance to meet some girls.'

So we duly went along to the first meeting, having enrolled as members through our college representatives, and listened while the President, John Hale, outlined the term's activities. The main production was to be a play by Pirandello. I forget which one, because it was never referred to by its title but only as 'The Pirandello'. There was also to be an Acting Competition, for which entries were invited, and a list of visiting speakers was read out, which included, I remember, Dame Sybil Thorndike. An appeal was then made for suggestions for next term's speakers, and, plucking up courage, I raised my hand.

'I think,' I said, banking heavily on our one meeting and my signed volume of her autobiography, 'that I can get Hermione Gingold.'

A murmur went round the room, and all eyes were turned on me. I wondered for a moment if I had made an idiotic gaffe: perhaps to a society that was planning to produce 'The Pirandello' a revue actress was anathema.

'Really?' said John Hale, with a quizzical smile. 'That sounds a very interesting idea.'

Without conscious calculation I had put myself in the way of killing two birds with one stone: the ETC members were now aware of my existence, and I had a valid pretext for getting in touch again with Hermione, which I hastened to do during the vacation. She professed herself delighted at the idea of coming down to Oxford to address a crowd of young undergraduates and asked me to come and see her in her little house in Kinnerton Street to talk about it.

'But couldn't I,' she suggested over a cup of tea, 'just meet them? Do I have to *say* anything?'

In the end she never did come to address the ETC, but we became friends from that moment on.

Guy was bowled over by my enterprise.

'That was terrific,' he told me after the meeting. 'Now we ought to go to the Playhouse Bar for coffee one morning. *Everyone* goes there, and perhaps we could get to meet Liz Zaiman.'

'Who's Liz Zaiman?'

'I'm not sure, but I know she's involved in absolutely *everything*.'

So a few days later we met after a lecture – I was still attending them – and made our first visit to the Playhouse Coffee Bar, which was situated on the first floor, at the back of the dress circle. In those days the Playhouse was not the University Theatre, but a commercial repertory house which allowed the OUDS the use of its stage once a year. But it had become the favourite rendezvous of the University's Theatrical Clique, and for the rest of my time at Oxford scarcely a morning went by that I did not drop into the Coffee Bar and sit there, usually on the floor, gossiping and discussing the Theatre until it was midday, when, as often as not, we would all move down the street to the Randolph Hotel Bar and continue the gossip and discussion until lunch-time, whereupon we repaired to the British Restaurant near the bus station, where one could have an unimaginative but substantial meal for two shillings and threepence.

On that first morning at the Playhouse we did indeed meet Elizabeth Zaiman, but only briefly, as she was going out and we were coming in. She had a pale, emaciated face with enormous, staring eyes, surrounded by a cloud of frizzy black hair, and she wore a long black cloak with a silver clasp. At first she seemed frightening, but then I noticed that she had, like Hermione Gingold, a gap between her two front teeth and this somehow made her less alarming. She was, as always, in a whirl of activity, organising the ETC Social and devising a cabaret to liven up the proceedings.

'You are coming, aren't you?' She fixed us with her huge eyes. 'Tickets are five bob, sandwiches included,' and she swept on her way, her cloak billowing behind her.

I make particular mention of that cloak, because at that time, in the winter of 1946, any unusual garment was not only a symbol of individuality, it was a precious possession. Clothes were severely rationed, and I had only my demob suit and an old sports jacket to serve for every occasion. I also had my army battle-dress and, following a current fashion among ex-service students, I had it dyed black and wore it nearly every day. Ex-naval men kept their duffle coats, and that too started a fashion. We all had to make do with what we had got or what we could invent, and the appearance of a scarlet neckerchief, a pair of green suede shoes or a gilt chain belt became the occasion for comment and discussion. Out of the uniform drabness of the War we were struggling to emerge into a life of colour and brilliance, but our means were limited both by Government restrictions and, in most cases, by lack of money. There was little of the flamboyance and extravagance which I associated with the Oxford of the Twenties and Thirties, but there was a continual striving to express one's individuality visually, which, while probably making us appear a pretty motley crowd to an outsider, gave us, for each other, a certain bizarre glamour. Unlike the students of today, we had no style to conform to; we had had enough of conforming during the War, and each of us now set out to create a style of his own.

Some were more successful than others, and this seems as appropriate a moment as any to introduce the Oxford character who, more than anyone else, provided a focus of attention, admiration and disapproval: Kenneth Peacock Tynan, the illegitimate son of a Birmingham department store tycoon and a lady's maid. Even in such a heterogeneous crowd as we were, Ken, with his death's head features and his attenuated body encased in the famous plum-coloured suit, was unmistakable. There were probably many more talented people up at Oxford at the time, perhaps several more original, but he was the leader and, whether one adored him or despised him, one could certainly not ignore him.

For Michael, Ken was all he expected from Oxford:

'He was wildly eccentric, conventionally brilliant, and with an outrageous confidence which I certainly didn't have, as a provincial boy – although in fact he was a provincial boy himself. One gradually realised that most of what he did was derivative: he was a magpie, and I was aware of the fact later that he hadn't acknowledged his sources. Nevertheless he did it extremely well, and I was very much drawn to him – though not as a person.'

Like Michael, I felt that Ken had an aura of brilliance and daring, but I never found that I could penetrate that aura to discover the person behind it. Indeed as a person I found him faintly inhuman and forbidding. Heather, probably because she was a girl, felt differently. Her first sight of Ken was at the same meeting of the ETC to which Guy had taken me:

'Liz made me come, and afterwards she said, "Well, what did you think of Ken?", and I said, "He's very *queer*, isn't he?" And she said, "He's *not* queer!", and I said, "I think he's *very* queer," and she said, "He's *not*!", and I said, "But he *looks* so queer". Then she said, "Do you know what queer means?", and I said, "No" – I was that innocent.

'But I was attracted to him as a person. In fact I was absolutely in his thrall, and I was very nervous of him, because he never stopped telling me that I shouldn't be a virgin. He had this great line of asking me to tea and saying, "When you come into the room, it's as though there's a portcullis between us." It's laughable now, but virginity was something very important in those days – something you valued enormously, and when it had gone, this was crossing the Rubicon. Yet he never actually made a pass. Mind you, I'm not at all sure that I wanted to go to bed with him in any case; but I might have done, just for the glory, because I venerated him.'

But Ken's spell eluded Penny altogether:

'I didn't venerate him a bit. I always thought he was terribly immature and terribly spoiled, and I was really rather sorry for him, having sat and listened to him saying endlessly how difficult it was for him to be illegitimate. I found him incredibly Pseud: I realised that he was very well read, but his thought processes were desperately meretricious and undisciplined, and he was subject to these wild enthusiasms. He was always out to shock – all that business of going about saying, "Of course I'm a hereditary syphilitic, just like Oswald" – and I didn't like him as a person. I thought there was something creepy about him, something malformed inside. But he *was* good entertainment: he was very lively, and, although I didn't like any of the things he did, I could see that at least he brought vitality.'

My first experience of Ken as a performer was at the ETC Social, when he was part of the cabaret, presenting a slightly scabrous mind-reading act which caused much laughter among the initiated. At the end of that term, 'The Pirandello' having fallen through, the ETC asked him to produce an entertainment at short notice. He concocted a treatment of *Hamlet* and called it *A Toy in Blood*: it was much the sort of thing, in embryo, which Charles Marowitz does in his versions of Shakespeare nowadays. The first half of the bill was a medieval morality play, *Nice Wanton*, in which I featured briefly as Daniel the Judge. The whole programme was unremarkable – and certainly under-rehearsed – but I had made my acting début at Oxford, and I belonged.

When I caught the train to Paddington at the end of term I felt, for the first time since we had moved there in 1932, reluctant to return to London. Contrary to what I had expected, Oxford had turned out to be such an exciting place that in a few weeks it had become the centre of my world.

During the vacation my mother and I went to Drury Lane to see Noël Coward's new operetta, *Pacific 1860*, a show that had been eagerly awaited, partly because it was to reopen the Lane after the War and also because it was the London début of a renowned American star, Mary Martin. It turned out to be a sad disappointment: Miss Martin, who had made her name singing Cole Porter's *My Heart Belongs to Daddy* and whom I had admired as the spirited heroine of several snappy Paramount musicals, was asked to appear as a femme fatale in a crinoline on a Caribbean island, where she seemed absurdly out of place and time. It closed in the New Year and Drury Lane announced that the next production would be *Oklahoma!*

That winter of 1947 was one of the longest and coldest in the country's history, and I don't imagine that anyone who lived through it has ever forgotten it. When I returned to Oxford, it was under deep snow and remained so for the whole term. The heating arrangements in College, never exactly opulent, were cut to a minimum, and each room was only allowed one small scuttle of coal per day. The coal bunker was just outside my door and I used to creep out at night and snaffle an extra lump or two, and I also, quite against the regulations, ran a small electric fire on which I used to heat milk and make toast to sustain me through the small hours on the nights when I had to churn out my weekly essay for Dr Sympson. Public lighting and heating was severely restricted, and – the worst blow of all – cinemas were only allowed to open for a few hours a day and, because there was an economic crisis as well, import of new American films was banned. We had to rely for our entertainment on what seemed like endless re-runs of old Margaret Lockwood and Phyllis Calvert melodramas from the Gainsborough Studios.

But, despite all the gloom, my life at Oxford became, if anything, even more exciting. There had been some talk the previous term of the ETC's producing a revue: rather an unorthodox project for a society which was dedicated to encouraging the avant-garde drama, but it was suggested as a possible means of supplementing the club's funds which were then, as they usually were, at a low ebb. The man behind the idea was an ex-naval student, Peter Bentley, and he had got in touch with me during the vacation, having heard that I wrote lyrics and sketches, and asked me to submit some material. I set to work at once and ended up writing about half the show as well as appearing in it.

The revue was called *Oxford Circus*, an appropriate title as it turned out, since the cast, which was forty strong, included a conjuror, a ballerina and an impersonator who gave lengthy imitations of well-known radio personalities. The music was provided by Donald Swann at the piano and a group called the Bandits, and Peter recruited all the prettiest girls he could find, including Heather, to act as chorus:

'It was like every 1930s film I had ever seen, that first rehearsal in a studio at Taphouse's, with all of us in our shorts and our blouses, and Donald at the piano thumping out the music. I thought, "I am going to be Ginger Rogers. Now I know that this is what I was born for. It's all coming true!" '

Penny also joined the cast, to sing and to act in several sketches:

'Having endured two years of the ETC, I can't tell you what a relief it was to be doing a revue, because we had been *so* heavy and cultural – Eugene O'Neill, Sartre, Pirandello, Maeterlinck; then suddenly on we came with those dance routines and those point numbers – it was a breath of fresh air!'

I had written a two-part sketch contrasting the glamour of pre-War Oxford with the drabness of the present, and Penny was cast as a vamp-ish actress being entertained in his rooms by a besotted undergraduate – me.

'It was the first piece you ever wrote about the 1920s. Peter Bentley wanted me to do a Gingold on it, and he also insisted that I use a three-foot long cigarette holder, and I wore a long string of beads round my neck and hanging down my back. At one stage I had to slip them to the front, twirl them round and catch them in my teeth, which I found very difficult, what with having to cope with the cigarette holder and assume alluring attitudes on the sofa. I wasn't really clued up on the 1920s, and the only thing that was familiar about it was the dress I was wearing – a genuine one, I believe – which was very similar to one my mother used to wear.'

The theme of nostalgia for pre-War Oxford recurred when Michael sang a song I had written:

'Oxford's not what it used to be
In the palmy days of Nineteen Thirty-eight,
When we never thought that one a.m. was late,
And we never drank a brandy
That didn't have a date . . .'

and the finale, *C'est la Paix*, performed, for some reason, by the girls in night-dresses and the boys in pyjamas, deplored the fact that peace-time austerity made life even drearier than during the War. But our general feeling about the present was summed up in a chorus number, *Back to Normal Again*, a waltz whose opening lines were:

'We're learning to be gay again,
Turning night into day again . . .'

and which, when we all sang it together at the first run-through, seemed for a few moments to epitomise the longings of a whole generation. We were performing the show in a gymnasium in Alfred Street, which had no stage and very few other facilities, the weather was bitterly cold, and we could only make an entrance from the back of the hall, which meant that we had to run round from the dressing-rooms through the snow. But we were suddenly carried away by an infectious elation, and when the number came to an end, we spontaneously sang it again, and then again, until Peter had to insist on our rehearsing something else.

The revue was only to be given one performance, but this had such an uproarious reception that we decided on the spot to give a second the following night. As we left the gymnasium after the show, on our way to a celebration party, I clutched hold of Penny and shouted, in the manner which I had learned from so many Hollywood films, 'We're a hit! We're a hit!' She looked at me a little sceptically, as if to say, 'Don't get carried away,' but there was no denying that I was ex-periencing for the first time the authentic taste of success. I had also, without knowing it, reached a milestone: although I continued to act whenever I was given the chance, from then on I spent more and more of my time writing words and music.

After having taken part in such frolics, it came as a surprise to read in one of the daily papers an article which described the post-War Oxford generation as excessively earnest hard-workers who had forgotten what it was like to have a good time. Certainly I saw very little of the kind of high living described by Evelyn Waugh in *Brideshead Revisited* and, even if it had existed, I could not have afforded it; but there seemed to be no shortage of parties of one sort or another, at which the drink was usually a concoction based on a bottle or two of gin poured into a bowl with whatever additions the guests might bring. Sometimes the style of party harked back to previous decades: there was a Surrealist Party, and a Cold Comfort Farm Party, to which everyone came dressed as a character from the book. And I, having read somewhere about the Bright Young Things and their Children's Parties, gave one in my rooms in Oriel: for two or three hours, over a tea of cakes and biscuits and dressed in shorts and rompers, we all behaved like demented infants, shouting and squabbling and playing games. Ken Tynan, who was present, wrote it up in a piece for *Vogue* in which he attempted to restore Oxford's reputation for gaiety and inventiveness; he could hardly know that I was simply taking another step towards recreating my favourite period.

The person who did most towards dispelling Oxford's drab post-War image was a plump Australian expatriate called Stanley Parker, who had made his name in the Thirties by drawing theatrical cartoons for the *Sporting and Dramatic Magazine*. He had a brother called Kenny, who was a talented photographer, and they occupied a flat over a shop in the Broad, where they gave a series of rowdy and notorious parties.

Penny thought Stanley was 'the wickedest man I'd ever met. I'll never forget my first party there, in that studio with the negress's head decorated with ostrich feathers, and drinks being poured out of jugs shaped like swans, and incense burning. I was so shattered, because in one corner there were two chaps in a clinch and in another two women, and over there was someone with her knickers off, and Stanley was getting a bit hot under the collar and saying, "Now, now, you can't go *that* far . . .!" '

This did indeed seem to be the depth of depravity, although the amount of active promiscuity that went on appeared to me to be negligible, and most of us were still bound by old-fashioned taboos where sex was concerned. Michael recalled an extraordinary scene in the men's dressing-room during the run of an OUDS production.

'There we were – Robert Hardy, Alan Cooke, Norman Painting and John Schlesinger – all undressing, and Alan suddenly got very sensitive and said, "You're all laughing at me, because I'm a virgin." So I said, "Well, I'm a virgin", and Tim Hardy said, "So am I", and so did Norman and John. We all said so, and we were about twenty-three or four and we'd all been in the Services. The reason why I was a virgin was partly because I was romantic and partly because I was conceited. After all, the objective of most of the girls there was to find a husband, and there weren't any around who were simply good-time girls. So I was terrified of committing myself. Nowadays, so I'm told, if a girl doesn't make herself available, she doesn't get a man; but it wasn't so in our day.'

The long, cold winter of 1947 finally ended, and when I took the train back to London for the vacation, the fields on either side of the railway line were flooded by the thaw. In April *Oklahoma!* opened at Drury Lane, to unanimously enthusiastic reviews, and I took my mother to see it the following month. Its impact was so astonishing and exhilarating that by the last curtain I was breathless and at the same time almost on the point of tears. The whole thing, with its primary colours, rousing dances and rustic characters, had a child-like simplicity, but was also brilliantly ingenious and entirely different from anything I had ever seen, and for weeks afterwards I could not get it out of my head. I bought the vocal score and played the songs over and over again on the piano I had installed in my rooms at Oriel, and during the summer vacation I used to walk down to Drury Lane from my mother's hotel after dinner at least once a week and pay three-and-six to stand at the back of the dress circle. I must have seen *Oklahoma!* about thirty times in all and, although I was never to write the same kind of show, it taught me more about the creation and construction of a musical than anything else I have seen in the Theatre.

Oxford Circus had been such a success, both artistically and financially, that the ETC asked Peter to produce another revue during the Summer term, and this time I was entrusted with the bulk of the writing and we tried to make it more of a piece and less of a variety show than its predecessor. Peter's landlady had a very pretty daughter called Corinne, nick-named Biddo, who had curly blonde hair and cheeks like Claudette Colbert's and was a trained dancer, and he invited her to appear in the revue and stage the numbers, which gave us a little of the professional gloss we were lacking. A friend of Biddo's, Jack Viner, who was in the rag-trade, lent us some play-suits and bathing costumes for the girls to wear in the chorus numbers, and, although we were again in the Alfred Street Gymnasium, this time a stage was installed and one side of the hall was curtained off, so that we no longer had to make our entrances through the audience. We ran for three nights, to packed houses, and Stanley and Kenny Parker, together with their mother, Cecilia, sat in the front row every night until they could almost join in the numbers. Biddo and I performed a deliberately Cole Porter-style duet, *Why Shouldn't We?*, dressed as teenagers, which was Stanley's favourite, and Penny, something of a femme fatale in private life, appeared as a water-front whore, complete with the regulation shoulder bag, breaking loose from importunate sailors – among them Michael Croft of the

Youth Theatre – to sing a mournful ballad entitled *The Trouble with Me*. Ken Tynan, making his début in revue, performed with great success a monologue, *Treasurer's Report*, for which he claimed authorship, but which I later discovered in a collection of pieces by Robert Benchley, while Donald Swann's contribution was a rousing male chorus number, *My Sister Ruth*, which later appeared in a West End revue. The bulk of the show, as its title, *High, Broad and Corny*, suggests, dealt with Oxford life and University characters, but every now and then we managed to insert a song or a sketch that would have a wider appeal.

The closing number was called *We've Gotta Keep Acting* and during the same term I also found myself taking the lead in the Oriel College play. This came about quite unexpectedly, because I had suggested to the College Dramatic Society that we should do Ben Jonson's *Bartholomew Fair* which I wanted to direct. A day or two later I had a visit from a freshman, Cyril Frankel, whom I had never met but who told me that he thought my idea was very dull and instead we should put on the French mime play, *L'Enfant Prodigue*. Before I had time to tell Cyril that I had never heard of it, he went on to inform me that he would direct it and I would play the leading part.

'But – but I've never done any mime in my life!' I protested, now thoroughly rattled.

'Then I'll teach you,' said Cyril, and his manner was so persuasive that the next thing I knew *Bartholomew Fair* was dropped and Heather and I and the other three members of the cast were doing barres in a studio in Taphouse's. The play was a nineteenth century version of the parable of the Prodigal, set to music by André Wormser, and I played Pierrot, the Son, to Heather's Columbine, and I think that in many ways it was one of the most extraordinary experiences of my life. By sheer force of personality Cyril turned us, in a matter of weeks, into accomplished pantomimists, and in a rôle which kept me on stage almost throughout the play I was able to acquit myself with distinction, something which I have never done again from that day to this and which still continues to astonish me. I think the College authorities were rather astonished by the whole affair as well, as Oriel in those days was hardly renowned for its cultural activities, and when our stage was erected in the middle quad several members of the rowing team got drunk the following night and demolished it. However it was repaired in time for the performance and, whether the rowing team liked it or not, we were a success. Cyril disappeared from Oxford as mysteriously as he had arrived, and the next time I saw him he had become, not surprisingly, a flourishing film director.

But the most sensational theatrical occasion of that eventful summer was undoubtedly Ken Tynan's production of *Samson Agonistes* which he staged in St Mary's Church in the High. None of my group of friends was in it, but we all went on the first night and sat together in a pew, and the first thing to assail our vision was Ken himself, as the Angel of Death, suspended above the altar, his hands clasped and his eyes closed. For Samson's cage he had hired a tram-line repair tower which was installed in the chancel: on top of it, wearing chains and little beside, was a magnificent-looking gentleman called James Lund. Delilah was played by Vicki Prensky, a voluptuous brunette from Lady Margaret Hall, whose costume was split to the waist to reveal fish-net tights and Carmen Miranda sandals, while on her head she wore a mass of feathers and spangles which had lately graced Robert Helpmann in *The Faery Princess* at Covent Garden. During her encounter with Samson Vicki was obliged to climb the tram-repair tower wearing this get-up, thus adding a spice of danger to an already thrill-packed evening. We were at the same time helpless with laughter and awed by the daring of it all, and the fact that it was taking place inside a church gave the whole event a frisson of sacrilege; but it was overwhelmingly theatrical and remains for me the high-spot among Ken's Oxford exploits. Indeed I feel it a matter for regret that he has never been able to perpetrate something equally astonishing in the professional theatre.

Summer is the time of Commems in Oxford, and I invited Heather to the Oriel Ball, for which I had been asked to compose a special waltz. Round about midnight we decided to go and join Michael at a party on a barge which was being given by the OUDS in honour of Terence Rattigan. To reach the river we had to climb over several walls, but Heather, like most of the girls that summer, was wearing a crinoline.

'So we decided that you should climb over the wall, and I would take off my crinoline and hand it to you. Then I would climb over the wall, in my bra and knickers, while you turned your back like a gentleman. Then I would put on my crinoline and we'd walk to the next wall and do the same thing again until we got to the barge.'

Like so much that happened at Oxford, it was both romantic and ridiculous. This time last year I had been sitting at a typewriter in an office in the middle of the desert; but life had turned a somersault, and I was still in mid-air, neither knowing nor caring where I was going to land.

In the Michaelmas Term the ETC announced that their Spring production would be Maxwell Anderson's *Winterset*, to be directed by Ken Tynan.

The play is a verse drama, which deals, in imaginary terms, with the aftermath of the Sacco and Vanzetti case, and seemed an odd choice for an Oxford dramatic society in 1947; but Ken's prestige was such that nobody questioned it, and we all set about preparing our auditions for Mio and Miriamne, the two leading roles. I knew a little about the piece, since I had read it in a collection of the Fifty Best American Plays, and I had seen the film version, with Burgess Meredith and Margo, in 1937: not only was the subject matter a little obscure, it also required an elaborate physical production since the action takes place in and around a basement apartment in a tenement building in the shadow of Brooklyn Bridge and the cast, which includes a plethora of walking-on parts besides the principals, runs to well over thirty. There was nowhere in the centre of Oxford large enough to house it, and it was decided to put it on in the hall of a social centre a mile or so up the Cowley Road.

The ETC also decided, perhaps by way of contrast, to present another revue, and, as Peter Bentley had gone down at the end of the Summer term, I took on the job of directing it, along with the indefatigable Liz Zaiman and Russell Enoch, who had appeared briefly in Ken's *Samson Agonistes* as one of the casualties from Gaza, and who later changed his name to William Russell, when he became a professional actor. We decided that this time the revue would really be intimate, with a cast of twelve and no extraneous turns or diversions; I was aiming in fact to approximate as nearly as possible to the format of the Farjeon and Ambassadors Theatre revues which I so much admired. We chose our cast with care: it naturally included Biddo and Heather, who was developing into a first-class comedienne, and Jennifer Ramage, the statuesque daughter of Cathleen Nesbitt, who had scored a triumph in *High, Broad and Corny* in a sketch in which two lady dons discuss their pupils and other matters over a cup of cocoa. Among the males were John Schlesinger, Alan Cooke, Anthony Schooling and, of course, Ken, who this time contributed a monologue that was entirely original: an amateur producer's notes to his company, which included several impressions of theatrical celebrities, the most memorable being of Robert Helpmann: 'God! There's an owl on my shoulder!'

Although rationing of everything, including clothes, was still in force, there was a noticeable lightening of the austerity which we had endured throughout the previous year, and the most obvious indication of this was the appearance of the New Look. During the Christmas holidays I was invited to Paris to stay with the son of Frank and Virginia's doctor, Bernard Hautant, who lived with his widowed mother in an apartment near the Rond Point. I was taken to the Folies Bergères for the first time and also to see Jean-Louis Barrault and Madeleine Renaud at the Marigny Theatre and Charles Trenet at the Olympia, and one afternoon we went to a film called *Les Jeux Sont Faits*, scripted by Jean-Paul Sartre, whose Existentialist philosophy was the talk of intellectual circles in London and whose play, *Huis Clos*, had inspired a sketch in the first ETC revue. Paris, which the War had scarcely touched, was a startling contrast to the shabbiness of London: the synthetic coffee was undrinkable and food seemed very expensive, but otherwise it was all as I remembered it from 1937 and now I was just the right age to appreciate it to the full. I was enthralled by everything, but the most amazing sight was the young girls with their voluminous skirts swirling round their ankles: after years of utility clothes, which used the bare minimum of material and hardly any trimming, these huge, flamboyant garments, containing yards of cloth and often bordered with fur or lace, seemed to be the height of extravagance and glamour. The older generation of Parisians, including Mme Hautant, regarded them with the same disapproval which they would later extend towards the mini-skirt, but Bernard and I were enraptured, and on my return to Oxford I propagandised incessantly for the new fashion and wrote a song, *The New Look*, which was used as the opening to the second half of the new revue, and which enabled all the girls to show off Jack Viner's latest creations.

After the success of *Oklahoma!* London was inundated with imported American musicals, and within a few months I had seen *Annie, Get Your Gun, Brigadoon, Finian's Rainbow* and *High Button Shoes*. I first heard the music of the latter at Hermione Gingold's house. She had been over to New York for a holiday and brought back the records (the long-playing album of a whole show had yet to appear).

'Listen to this,' she commanded everybody. 'I think it's rather special: every song in it is written in the style of the period.'

I dutifully listened, and when the show came to the London Hippodrome I went to see it twice and loved it, although the critical verdict had not been favourable. The songs of Jule Styne captured exactly the flavour of the early 1900s, as did the Mack Sennett bathing-belle ballet, one of Jerome Robbins' first ventures into musical comedy. I also saw the New York City Ballet at Covent Garden in a programme that included Robbins' *Fancy Free* which formed the basis for the musical, *On the Town*. Now at last, instead of Anglicised versions of American shows, we were getting the real thing and the effect was remarkable. Within a year or so the old conventions of musical comedy and operetta had been swept away, so that even C. B. Cochran's *Bless the*

Bride, successful as it was, seemed out of date and caused my mother to remark that 'it wasn't a patch on *Oklahoma!*'

Another high-spot of that theatrical season was the visit to London of Mae West in her own melodrama, *Diamond Lil*. I was fascinated to see her in real life, her corseted thighs rotating gently like a motor ticking over, as she ambled round the stage in a lilac spotlight delivering her renowned double-entendres. Stanley Parker was naturally in a fever about her and announced that he would be giving a party for her in his studio 'on Sexagesima Sunday'.

I had auditioned, along with many others, for the part of Mio in *Winterset* and failed to get it; but Ken asked me to play Garth, the heroine's brother, which meant that I was directing and appearing in the revue and rehearsing for *Winterset* simultaneously. However I knew that this would have to be my last fling on the theatrical scene because in the following term I was due to take my finals and would not be granted permission to do any more acting; so I decided to make the most of it. We called the new revue *Ritzy, Regal and Super*, after the three cinemas in Oxford, and it was staged in a church hall off the Woodstock Road. I had written one number, *Medusa*, specifically for Peter Wildeblood, who had appeared very successfully in both the previous revues, and although he had gone down from Oxford in the summer, he promised to return to appear in *Ritzy, Regal and Super*. But something interfered with his plans and I had to take over his material, including *Medusa*, in which the figure of Greek Legend lamented the fact that every man she met was turned to stone on the spot. It was of course inspired by Hermione Gingold and I nursed the hope that one day perhaps she might perform it. At least half of the numbers in this revue were about subjects unconnected with Oxford; but one serious ballad, which again borrowed the title, *The Party's Over Now*, dealt with something which was at the back of all our minds: what was life going to be like when we left Oxford for good?

The show had an even more enthusiastic reception than its predecessors, and I was amazed to read a rather derogatory review in the *Isis*, complaining that some of the numbers, particularly *Medusa* and a monologue by Jennifer Ramage as a factory worker exhorting her work-mates to 'hit their targets', were excessively dirty. This led to a visit from the Proctor the following night, when the hall was so full that he had to sit on the floor; despite his discomfort his verdict on the show was that, provided we went that far and no further, we could continue the run. The *Isis* review, far from interfering with our success, had added to it, so that on the last night people actually climbed into the hall through the windows when they found they could not get in through the door.

That performance was greeted with seemingly endless applause and cheers, and I was just about to thank the audience when Ken stepped forward out of the line-up and raised his hand for silence.

'Ladies and gentlemen,' he announced, 'I have the great pleasure and honour to inform you of the presence here in the audience tonight of that fantastic and fabulous Hollywood star, Miss Mae West!'

The audience gasped in unison and then went mad. At the back of the hall I could discern an undulating figure, glittering with sequins and diamanté and crowned with ostrich feathers, approaching the stage. As it came nearer it did indeed seem to be Mae West and I began to wonder what on earth she would find to say about the revue. But when Ken reached down to hand her over the footlights, I detected a muscularity about the outstretched arm and a swarthiness beneath the face powder, and the penny dropped: it was Stanley Parker in drag. For a moment I was furious with him, and even more so with Ken; it seemed so typical of him that, not content with his lion's share of the limelight, he had to interfere with my moment of glory. But on the other hand it was a jape in the best Oxford tradition and it certainly added the finishing touch to an amazing evening.

Meanwhile *Winterset* was going into production, and, despite my antipathy towards Ken as a personality, I found that rehearsing under his direction was both enjoyable and rewarding; in fact I felt much more at ease with him as an actor than I ever did in real life. I was also full of admiration for his ability to organise and co-ordinate such an elaborate production, and among many effects he created one was particularly stunning and, I think, the first of its kind. Every now and then in the course of the play a train is heard thundering across Brooklyn Bridge: Ken decided that the train should pass not only over the stage but over the audience as well, and for this he devised a primitive version of stereophonic sound. His sound man was an American – one of the few connected with this production of an American play – who had the unforgettable name of Jarvis Doctorow and who looked, with his glasses and heavy moustache, like a young version of Groucho Marx. Under Ken's direction Jarvis rigged up a series of loud-speakers across the ceiling of the hall in Cowley Road; these were connected to the panatrope (tape machines were still in the future) which played a record of train noises. I can still see Jarvis, like the mad scientist in a Universal horror film, twisting dial after dial with hieratic gestures as he passed the sound from one loudspeaker to the next. I believe that the effect on the audience, when they first heard it, was overwhelming.

Ken also played the part of Judge Gaunt, who has been responsible for passing the death sentence on Romagna, the character who represents Sacco and Vanzetti, and who now, driven crazy by guilt and uncertainty, wanders around the streets seeking reassurance from anybody who will talk to him. It was extraordinary to hear, at close quarters, how the stammer which would often render Ken speechless offstage vanished as soon as he was playing a rôle; I was also impressed by his strength as an actor, and have often regretted that he was only to have one chance to display it professionally, as the Player King in what turned out to be a totally disastrous production of *Hamlet*.

Winterset ran for a week and, although the play must have seemed rather irrelevant, the production made a tremendous sensation and the hall was filled every night. Halfway through the run we received a visit from some French students from the Sorbonne, who had come to Oxford to see the current OUDS production, with a view to taking it over to Paris during the vacation. But the OUDS were presenting *The Shoemaker's Holiday* and the French boys found it quite incomprehensible; someone advised them to have a look at *Winterset* and they decided on the spot to take that to Paris instead. They told us they had rented the Théâtre des Champs Elysées, and we were all – cast, stage-staff, everybody – invited to come over, together with the costumes, set and Jarvis Doctorow's sound effects, to perform *Winterset* for a week. We all agreed with alacrity, and I wrote off to Bernard Hautant asking if I could stay with him and his mother, since we had been asked, if possible, to find our own accommodation, in order to save money. Another difficulty arose over the Government's currency regulations: due to the economic crisis there was no allowance at all for going abroad, and the French sponsors had to arrange for us to be doled out a few francs pocket money every day of our visit.

I took advantage of being a principal to demand that I go to Paris by air because I was such a bad sailor. It was my first flight since the five shilling flip I had taken with my mother before the War and I was beside myself with excitement. A few days before we were due to leave, we were told that, owing to a misunderstanding, the theatre had only been engaged for one night; but the show was still on, and the whole massive production was being transported across the Channel just for one performance.

Everything went according to plan, at least initially, and the cast reached Paris safely and assembled for rehearsals. But the scenery was delayed in customs and had still not arrived on the day of the performance. Ken went into desperate consultation with the stage staff to try and devise a means of presenting the play on a bare stage, and the cast were told to break for lunch. Most of us went to a café across the street from the theatre and sat at the tables outside discussing anxiously what was to be done. Suddenly somebody gave a shout and pointed: a pantechnicon had turned the corner from the Champs Elysées. The scenery had arrived! We all set to and helped to unload it and within an hour or so the dress rehearsal started.

Although only a few of us spoke French at all well, the stage staff managed to supply all our needs with speed and efficiency. There was only one unfortunate incident. *Winterset* ends with most of the principals being wiped out by machine-gun fire and dying on stage in a welter of blood. Ken asked the prop man to supply 'du sang' for the dress rehearsal and it duly arrived; but it was the real thing, bull's blood from the abattoirs. It was too late to find a substitute and both then and for the performance the wretched victims had to smear themselves with the stuff, which then proceeded to clot and cause a hideous smell. I thanked God and Maxwell Anderson that Garth, the character I was playing, was one of the few survivors.

Even at the time it struck me as a little incongruous that a French audience should assemble for one night to see a drama society from Oxford perform a play in American, and our reception was polite rather than enthusiastic, although the reviews the next day hailed the whole thing as a hugely successful cultural exchange. We were all invited to a very grand reception where we were given quantities of champagne and flattery, and a group of us became rather carried away and decided to go to a night-club. Antoinette Watney, who had designed the sets, said that she knew of a marvellous little place in Montmartre, where the wine was cheap, and we all scrambled into taxis and set off. When we arrived, I did think the 'little place' seemed rather too smart to be as cheap as Antoinette claimed, but by then there was no turning back. It was only an hour or so later, when the bill arrived, that we realised that things had changed a little since her last visit, in 1938: between us we had just about enough money to pay for one glass of the champagne we had so recklessly ordered. Michael Croft, always inclined to be belligerent, began to accuse the management of overcharging us. In a moment several gendarmes appeared and we found ourselves being hustled into the street. I grabbed Heather's arm and tried desperately to explain to one of the policemen that she was 'ma femme, qui est enceinte'. Even had he believed me, which I doubt, it made no difference, and the next thing we knew we were all under lock and key in a large cell in the local gendarmerie, where we spent the night trying to tell the police, in French of varying intelligibility, who we were and why we should be released on the spot, to no effect whatsoever.

Eventually dawn broke, and I assume that some explanation had been made to the authorities, or perhaps they were just bored to death with us, because we were allowed to leave and I never did hear who paid our bill at the night-club. I arrived back at the Hautants' apartment as Bernard was having his breakfast and told him the whole story. When I met Mme Hautant at lunch-time, she merely said with a wry smile:

'J'ai entendu dire que vous avez passé une nuit blanche.'

Most of the cast left for England that day and as soon as he disembarked at Dover Michael Croft rang the *Daily Mirror* and gave them the whole story. It was thought for a time that the incident might damage Anglo-French cultural relations for years to come, but the fears proved unfounded. The only person who was really upset was Ken, who had stayed on at the reception and missed the whole thing.

During the same vacation Ken celebrated his twenty-first birthday and we were all invited to a party which was to take place on a river-boat on the Thames. As usual, everyone was asked to bring something to drink, and Michael Croft, Peter Wildeblood and I clubbed together to buy a bottle of gin. We also decided, as a joke, to come dressed as sailors, and Michael, who had been in the Navy during the War, procured the uniforms for us. He and Peter, along with one or two other guests, had taken rooms at my mother's hotel for the night, and in the afternoon the three of us went for a walk in Kew Gardens. It was a moment of calm in a period of intense activity, and as we strolled across the grass in the gentle spring sunlight I found myself assessing my present situation and speculating vaguely about the future. Next term I was due to sit for my Finals, which would mean concentrating very hard on work, if I was to get a degree. After that, what? Peter had already been down from Oxford for some months and was trying to establish himself in journalism; in the meanwhile there was talk of his taking on the job of manager at my mother's hotel. Michael, who at that time wanted to be a writer, had another year at University. As for me, I was still intent on going into the Theatre, but my precise aims had altered somewhat in the time I had been at Oxford. Originally I had wanted to follow Noël Coward's footsteps, to be an actor to begin with and then a playwright, composer and everything else in rapid succession. Now, having been able to try my hand as a performer, I did not really feel that I had it in me to make a success, and unless one is convinced of this there is no point in embarking on what is one of the most disheartening professions in the world. Besides, so many of my Oxford friends wanted to be actors that I felt there would not be much room for me. But as a writer, on the other hand, I might stand a chance. I had proved that my words and my music could entertain a critical audience: perhaps that was the line I should follow. As we walked towards the gates of the Gardens, I felt that I was reaching another turning point.

We had been instructed to be at Westminster Pier at seven o'clock, and after we had boarded the river-boat I deposited our bottle of gin under a chair in the lounge, intending to open it later on in the evening. We were to sail down-stream to Greenwich, then back to Westminster, to take on board the whole cast of an American play, *Anna Lucasta*, which had opened in Oxford and was now playing at His Majesty's. Then we would sail up-stream to Hampton Court where we were to disembark and be taken back to London by a fleet of buses. As the party progressed it gradually dawned on those of the guests who lived out of town that they would be arriving back in the West End at about four in the morning with no means of getting home. In an access of hospitality, induced by several drinks, I gave one or two people the address of my mother's hotel and told them they would be sure to find a room there. Stanley and Kenny Parker were also worried about where to leave their mother for the night, as they felt it would be best to off-load her on our return to Westminster since, much as she enjoyed parties, she might not last the course. So I gave them the address too, and Cecilia was led off the boat and into a taxi as the all-black cast of *Anna Lucasta* trooped aboard. There was a band on the boat and dancing commenced as we turned up-stream and headed towards Hampton Court. On going to the lounge to get our bottle of gin, I discovered that the chair I had put it under was occupied by the star of *Anna Lucasta*, the beautiful Hilda Sims, where she remained for the rest of the party, and I had not the nerve to start feeling around under her New Look skirts for my bottle. Fortunately by this time there was enough drink on board for our contribution not to be missed.

Meanwhile, back at the hotel, my mother was receiving what proved to be the harbinger of a wholesale invasion. She was shocked to discover on her doorstep a completely strange elderly lady in a state of semi-intoxication who was claiming to be a friend of mine. With the help of Frank, the only member of the staff who lived in and to whom she referred as 'the butler', she deposited Mrs Parker on the sofa in the lounge where she promptly passed out. My mother now began to have dire apprehensions about what was going on aboard our river-boat, but she was hardly prepared for what actually happened. I imagined that

I had only given the hotel's address to a few people, but they had of course passed it on to their friends, and by the time we reached Hampton Court about half the guests had decided that they were going to spend what was left of the night at Brooke House Hotel. Quite oblivious of what I had started, when we got back to London I went to Lyons Corner House in Coventry Street with one or two others to have breakfast. I finally arrived home at about six o'clock in the morning to find my mother waiting for me in a state about equally divided between rage and despair. Not only had she been faced with a procession of more or less inebriated students of both sexes, most of whom she had never met, all claiming that I had assured them they could find accommodation there; but none of them seemed to have any idea where I was or what had happened to me, and she was beginning to have visions of my having fallen overboard and sunk to the bottom of the Thames. However on my return, after she had given me a brisk dressing-down, her business sense reasserted itself and she instructed Frank to wake everybody promptly at eight o'clock and present each one with a bill. Frank was a Dickensian character, with a face like a Cruikshank drawing, and Heather remembers to this day waking up in a bed which she was sharing with two other girls to see him peering round the door, counting the heads and depositing three accounts on the carpet.

My mother was somewhat mollified when everybody not only paid their bills but clubbed together and bought her a large bunch of flowers, and in later years she was rather proud of the fact that she had for one night not only been Ken Tynan's landlady but had also turned on him and accused him of drowning her son.

During my last term at Oxford I was officially forbidden to take part in any theatrical activity whatsoever, but Oriel were putting on a production of Marlowe's play about the college's founder, *Edward II*, and I sneaked on in one or two scenes heavily disguised as a peasant. The play was directed by an intense young Pole, Andy Ciolkosz, whom I had got to know through our common interest in the Theatre. He told me that his girl friend was a professional actress who was at present with the Old Vic Company; he was very much in love and wanted to marry her immediately, but she was insisting that they wait until he had got his degree. Her name was Diana Maddox.

Another friend of mine in Oriel was Peter King, who had stage-managed Cyril Frankel's production of *L'Enfant Prodigue*. He was reading Law, but was fascinated by every form of Show Business, particularly the Cinema, as his father, Sam King, was a co-director of a chain of picture-houses. We used to go to films together and had also begun to collaborate on a musical about Shepherd's Market which never got further than a synopsis and a couple of songs. But in the middle of the Summer term Peter told me that, if I was interested, he could take the Playhouse Theatre in London (now a BBC studio) for one night at the end of the long vacation for me to put on a revue, using the best material and performers from the three shows we had done for the ETC. I jumped at the opportunity and, as soon as Schools were over, set about organising the production.

One afternoon a few days before *Edward II* opened Andy asked the cast to come to his rooms to try on their costumes which, through the good offices of Diana Maddox, were being provided by courtesy of the Old Vic. I arrived for my fitting to find a crowd of my fellow-students being ordered about by a rather bossy girl who had a perfect oval face, a short upper lip and a slight cast in one eye, a feature which I had first noticed in Norma Shearer and always find extremely attractive. She treated us all, including Andy, as if we were overgrown children, but she obviously knew what she was about and we were all fitted up in our medieval rig-outs in double quick time.

As the moment drew near for me to leave Oxford for good, my feelings were confused, to say the least. So much had happened in the two years that I had been up, and I was changed forever from the person I had been when I was a freshman. Among other things, I had had my first love affairs, and I had also ceased to believe in God. On the other hand I had had my first success and believed quite firmly in my own abilities. But I had no idea what I was going to do, what the next step in my career should be. At Oxford it had all fallen into my lap, just as and when I needed it, and for two years it seemed that I could not put a foot wrong. But perhaps I had been living in a charmed circle – not a fool's paradise, but certainly some sort of magic realm, where every-thing was as I wished it to be. I knew, because I had seen it, that life was not like that; but all the same I imagined that, if my luck would hold, there was no reason why I should not make it so. I was not particularly afraid of the future, in fact I was eager to get going, to move on; but there was the thought at the back of my mind that I could, if I had chosen to, have stayed on at Oxford for another year, as most of my contemporaries were doing. Still, it was too late now, and perhaps two years of this dream existence was enough; any more, and I might never be able to come to grips again with reality.

But in a sense, I suppose, I never did leave Oxford. The things I enjoyed most in life subsequently I enjoyed because they reminded me of my life there; the times that were the saddest and the emptiest were when I imagined that I was cut off from Oxford for ever.

Revues –
and a
Musical

Giving away my sister Noël,
at the Savoy Chapel, 1940

With Doug Walch in Shaiba,
1945

Above: The cast of Oxford University Experimental Theatre Club Revue *Ritzy, Regal and Super,* 1947. *L. to R.:* John Schlesinger, Anthony Schooling, Corinne Hunt, Jennifer Ramage, Heather Couper, myself, Guy de Moubray, Elizabeth Zaiman, Alan Cooke, Russell Enoch (William Russell), Pat Hackwood, June Weller, Kenneth Tynan

Below: Ken Tynan's production of *Winterset. L. to R.:* myself, Michael Smee, Barbara Carter

WHAT was Intimate Revue? And why did it vanish from the
Theatre? Its disappearance is usually associated with the
success, early in the 1960s, of *Beyond the Fringe*, and the
claim has been substantiated, not without a certain satisfaction, by
Dr Jonathan Miller. But I think that, as is sometimes his wont, the
celebrated polymath is taking a little too much upon himself. *Beyond
the Fringe* was basically just another intimate revue, and only differed
from its predecessors in that instead of a mixed cast it featured four
exceptionally gifted young men, and, whereas revue had tended to skirt
rather gingerly round politics, *Beyond the Fringe* dealt with them – and
particularly with politicians – head on. It brought about, I think, the
liberation of Revue rather than its demise; that can be laid, like so many
other things, at the door of Television. When shows like the exemplary
That Was the Week That Was began to deal with events that had
happened as recently as the previous day, and in a free-wheeling manner
totally unhampered by censorship, any stage revue, no matter how
daringly topical it may have seemed on opening night, was bound to
look a little out of date in comparison. And so, after one or two
unsuccessful attempts at resuscitation, Intimate Revue was quietly laid
to rest.

This seems to me a pity, because, at its best, it was a very satisfying
form of entertainment. It was born during the first World War and
flourished throughout the Twenties, Thirties and Forties. It had a final
blossoming in the Fifties, of which I was lucky to be a part, when
London spawned a crop of tiny theatres, which existed in the first place
to present plays that would otherwise, either because of censorship or
their uncommercial nature, never have been seen. When they lost
money, as they tended to, the club would recoup by putting on an
intimate revue. This sounds like a very simple procedure, but in fact
revue is one of the most difficult forms of theatre to succeed in. It
requires for a start a small but talented and versatile cast, since everyone

is called upon, in the course of the show, to do everything – act, sing and dance. Indeed this is one of the charms of revue, that the audience never knows what may happen next, who will appear, in what new guise, doing something quite different from his previous appearance. Perhaps it was this charade-like nature of revue that appealed to me, with its reminders of the interminable historical pageants we used to stage at home in my childhood, in which friends and family kept reappearing in fresh disguises. Revue is also a pot-pourri, in which there should be a little bit of something for everyone; or perhaps it can better be described as a banquet, where each course should contrast with, or offset the flavour of, its neighbours. Thus a satirical sketch may be followed by a romantic ballad, a dance interlude by a 'point' number. The 'running order', as I was to learn very early on, is all-important and may be changed a hundred times during rehearsal or on tour and even, on occasion, after the first night. And nothing – *nothing* – must go on too long. The finest lesson I learned from my experience with Revue was an old one: 'Brevity is the Soul of Wit', and as a result I have never, I hope, been unduly difficult about applying or accepting 'cuts', because they nearly always improve the show.

The other reason that I am very grateful to Intimate Revue is a very practical one: for five years from the time I went down from Oxford it made me a slender, but adequate, living. For a writer I was extraordinarily lucky in that I never had to take a job outside the Theatre to keep me going. Once or twice, during a lean period, I was on the point of contacting Gabbitas Thring to offer myself once more as a tutor, the only occupation for which I was remotely qualified. But at the last moment the phone would ring: could I do a number for so-and-so, such-and-such a revue needed a new sketch, had I any old material that could be used in a hurry? And Gabbitas Thring would have to do without me until the next emergency.

But initially I had pursued my intention of going into the Theatre in an active capacity, and with this in mind I asked my aunt, Virginia Vernon, to fulfil her promise, made to me when we met in the Airport Hotel in Basrah, that, when the time came and I had completed my education, she would arrange introductions to her various contacts in the business. Virginia had in the meanwhile decided to give up the Theatre in favour of Journalism, and was now Paris correspondent for the *Daily Mirror*; but she kept her word and during the autumn, while I was preparing the Oxford revue for the Playhouse Theatre, I had several interviews with theatrical managements. They were all polite, out of deference to Frank and Virginia, and they were all, with one exception, unhelpful. The exception was Bronson Albery, the manager of three of London's best theatres, the New (now called, in his honour, the Albery), the Criterion and Wyndhams. Bronny, as I learned to call him much, much later, had his office in the New, and as soon as we had got over the formalities he said, in a business-like manner, 'I think the best thing you can do is to go to the Old Vic School and learn the practical side of the Theatre. How does that strike you?'

It struck me as very sensible, and Bronny there and then rang the School, of which he was a Governor, and arranged an interview for me. Thanks to his sponsorship I was given a place on the Production Course, although the quota had already been filled, and was told to report to the School, which was at that time in the bomb-damaged Old Vic Theatre itself, at the beginning of the autumn term, a day or two after our Sunday night performance at the Playhouse.

The revue, which we called *Oxford Circus*, was taking shape very well. Apart from the title number, it was composed almost entirely of material that had proved successful at Oxford. Ken contributed his Producer Monologue and also did a number about a male ballet dancer, originated and written by Peter Wildeblood, of which the first line was, 'I wish my Mum 'ad never seen Pavlova.' Penny, who was now working on a magazine in London, came back to do her 1920s vamp, Musette Mallory:

'When we did it again at the Playhouse, I was very nervous, because I knew Gingold was going to be in the audience. I remember thinking how incredibly brash of me it was to take off this fabulous lady to her face.'

I was less bold: I decided it would be safer to perform *Medusa* in the manner of Beatrice Lillie, and on this occasion I wore a head-dress of realistically writhing snakes designed and made for me by Anthony Schooling's brother, Hugh. Penny also sang *The Trouble with Me* and the sad song of a girl who has left the joys of Oxford behind her, *The Party's Over Now*. Heather reappeared as Shirley, a monstrous tea-shop waitress, in a sketch from *High, Broad and Corny*, while Jennifer Ramage recreated her factory worker and her lady Don, in company with June Green, wife of the poet, Roger Lancelyn-Green. Biddo and I sang and danced *Why Shouldn't We?*, and Donald Swann, once more our pianist, contributed *My Sister Ruth*, which was to be sung by John Schlesinger. At the last minute John had to bow out and was replaced by Lindsay Anderson: thus one of this country's future film directors took over from another. Our stage manager was Geoffrey Sharp, who was later to forsake the Theatre to become one of London's most successful restaurateurs, and our wardrobe was in the hands of Ken Tynan's erstwhile Delilah, Vicki Prensky. Assisting me as director, as well as appearing throughout the show, was the irrepressible Liz Zaiman.

Of the performance itself I have rather hazy memories, since on the night and for several days beforehand I had been suffering from attacks of acute nausea. I only recall that it seemed to be a great success and we were all very happy. Hermione Gingold, who had indeed been present, came on to a party which my sister Noël gave for us in the flat in Chester Square where she and David Wallace were now living. *Sweetest and Lowest* had finally closed in the summer.

'I'm planning a new revue for November,' she told me, 'and I want to do *Medusa*.'

Also at the Playhouse Theatre that night was Laurier Lister, who had directed a revue called *Tuppence Coloured* at the Lyric Theatre, Hammersmith, during the previous year. I owed his presence to the composer of *Transatlantic Lullaby*, the song from the Gate Revue, Geoffrey Wright:

'A friend of mine, Tony Stansfeld, used to stay at your mother's hotel, and I was living at that time quite nearby in a flat in Great Ormond Street. Tony said to me at one moment, "The lady who runs my hotel has an undergraduate son who's passionately keen on doing musicals. Can I bring him round some time to talk to you?" '

Geoffrey turned out to be a character of great gentleness and charm. He was prematurely bald, with an individual wit and a habit of prefacing his announcements, whether humorous or tragic, with the words, 'My dear', enunciated with great emphasis, a form of speech common, I believe, amongst his group at Cambridge in the early Thirties. I asked him up to Oxford to see *High, Broad and Corny* and we met again during the vacation, when I was staying with Peter King in a house at Sandbanks which his family had rented for the summer. Geoffrey was musical director for the pre-London tour of *Tuppence Coloured* and when it came to the Bournemouth Pavilion, Peter and I went to see the show, which starred Max Adrian, Joyce Grenfell and Elisabeth Welch, and also featured, as a kind of running gag, a dancer called John Heawood, who covered scene changes by appearing as a pixillated stage-hand. It was an attempt, and on the whole a successful one, to present a highbrow revue: there were contributions by such people as Benjamin Britten, Christopher Fry and John Betjeman, and John Piper and the cartoonist, Emmett, had designed some of the décor.

Laurier Lister was now planning a follow-up, to be called *Oranges and Lemons*, which would repeat the format except for the replacement of Joyce Grenfell, who preferred to limit her stage appearances, by Diana Churchill. After seeing the revue at the Playhouse, Laurier contacted me and asked me to contribute some material. He invited me to tea on a Sunday afternoon at the house in Sanderstead that he shared with Max Adrian and which had been called by his mother, for some sentimental reason which I never discovered, Minnesota. I set out from Victoria, in a state of extreme nervousness, by the train he suggested, and when it reached Sanderstead I discovered, to my horror, that all the doors on the platform side of the carriage where I was sitting were locked. I dashed through to the next carriage just as the train began to leave the station, found a door that opened, and flung myself out on to the platform, landing at the feet of the astonished Laurier. He helped me up and bore me off to Minnesota in his car, where we were greeted by Max Adrian.

'What a dreadful, dreadful thing!' he cried, on being told by Laurier of my precipitate arrival. Turning his piercing blue eyes upon me, he suggested, in accents of deep concern, that I should have a large brandy. I refused, but such was the enveloping atmosphere of kindness created by Max that I quite forgot my nervousness and we all fell to discussing ideas for the show. They were looking for an opening number for the three stars and I came up with a suggestion. That summer there had been an open air exhibition of sculpture in London in which a group of three figures by Henry Moore had been the centre piece: my idea was that Max, Lis Welch and Diana Churchill should represent it, and the first lines of their number were:

> 'Three old ladies out for a lark,
> Spending the summer in Battersea Park.'

Max also expressed a desire to appear as an insomniac sheep: 'I'm a sheep who can't sleep, And I feel I could weep . . .' I wrote the number and it went into the show, but was taken out, not unexpectedly, in Birmingham. Solos in revue had a tendency to start off with the words, 'I'm a –', ('I'm a Botticelli Angel, and I'm bored,' is another example that comes to mind) and I learned later to avoid, if possible, what we all came to call an 'I'm-a' number.

Round about the same time I received a call from Andy Ciolkosz. Diana Maddox had been cast in Hermione's new revue, which was to be called *Slings and Arrows*, and wanted me to write a song for her. I invited her round to Brooke House Hotel and she described an idea she had had. At that time J. Arthur Rank was the most powerful figure in British films, and he had lately instituted the Rank Charm School which was designed to discover unknown girls and groom them for stardom. So far its product had been notably unimpressive, and Diana wanted to appear as a waitress who had been 'spotted', but after a year's training had failed to make the grade and was now back at her old job. I listened politely while she talked, illustrating her idea with a great deal of gesture and facial expression. It didn't strike me as a very good one, but I told her I would think about it. A few days later, while travelling on the top of a bus, the opening lines suddenly came to me:

'I want to thank
You, Mister Rank . . .'

and by the next day I had completed the lyric and the music. Over the next few years that was how Diana and I worked together: she would suggest something with enormous enthusiasm, which I would receive rather coolly; then I would mull it over and, like as not, find the idea worked. Once the number or sketch was written, I would give it to Diana to get on with, and invariably she performed it, down to the last inflection and nuance, exactly as I had envisaged it. And on top of that she would always endow it with something extra of her own.

On the first day of term at the Old Vic School I arrived, as instructed, at the Stage Door in Waterloo Road, still suffering from intermittent nausea. It was exciting and a little awe-inspiring to be working in a theatre where I had seen so many notable actors and actresses in the past: Charles Laughton and Flora Robson in *Macbeth*, John Gielgud as a controversially youthful *King Lear* and as Prospero in a *Tempest* designed by Oliver Messel, Laurence Olivier as *Henry V* and Vivien Leigh as Titania. The only part of the Old Vic that was seriously damaged was the upper circle; otherwise it was intact, which meant that we would be studying in a working theatre under the same conditions as professionals. The dressing-rooms and offices had been converted into class-rooms, and the stalls bar was equipped as a canteen. The stage was naturally occupied for most of the time by the Acting Course; but we, the Production Course, and the Designing Course had our allotted hours when we could use it to put our class-room knowledge into practice. The three Directors of the School were celebrated men of the Theatre: Michel St Denis, Glen Byam Shaw and George Devine. The head Instructor for the Production Course was Cecil Clarke who, in his correctness of dress and precision of manner, resembled a Government official rather than a stage-lighting expert; but this certainly reinforced his insistence on professional discipline at all times. Our other instructors were Margaret ('Percy') Harris, of the famous

Motley group, whose designs for *Richard of Bordeaux* had so impressed
me, and John Terry, who trained us in the basics of stage carpentry
and scene-shifting. We also received lectures from Richard Southern, a
somewhat fanatical figure, on Theatre Architecture and from the poet,
Christopher Hassall, who had been responsible for the lyrics of Ivor
Novello's operettas at Drury Lane. The latter attempted, in monthly
talks of an hour's length, to teach us the entire history of Drama from
the Ancient Greeks to the present day, an exercise which I, with the
superiority of a newly acquired BA Eng. Lit., considered a waste of
time. But he did it with a rather unctuous charm, which, allied to his
sensual appearance, made his lectures a great success with the girl
students. We also had occasional sessions with teachers from the
Acting Course, since it was impressed on us from the start that the
Actor must be considered before everything as he is the one who
finally has to go out onstage and do the job. I remember James Cairn-
cross making an astonishing entrance to deliver a talk on make-up:
one side of his face was a handsome young man's, the other the wrinkled
visage of an octogenarian. It was as if both Dorian Gray and his
Portrait were presenting themselves simultaneously.

On the first day of term, after Cecil Clarke had informed us about
our time-table and other practical matters, Glen Byam Shaw was
ushered in to give us a short address on theatrical conduct in general.
He laid particular emphasis on discipline and told us that we would be
expected to arrive on time whenever we were required and excuses
would not be accepted.

'Of course if you have a serious reason for being absent, that's
another matter. If you are really ill, with pneumonia or measles or
jaundice . . .'

As he said these words, his eyes fell on my face. He told me later
that he felt as if he had cast a spell, because I appeared to be bright
yellow. When I went back to the hotel that evening, my mother called
the doctor who diagnosed jaundice immediately.

Apart from this enforced absence, I was a reasonably diligent student
during my year at the Old Vic School, and, as Bronson Albery had
intended, I acquired a pretty thorough knowledge of the practical side
of the Theatre which has been invaluable to me ever since and which I
have always tried to bear in mind whatever I am writing. The School,
particularly during its occupation of the Old Vic Theatre, was eminently
equipped to give its pupils a total understanding of their subject, and
the staff were whole-heartedly dedicated to instilling into us an ideal
ethic of the Theatre; perhaps too ideal, since Theatre, as most of us

discovered later, very rarely measures up to one's highest expectations. But the Directors were, I think, trying to create some sort of continuity, by which they hoped to pass on the best of their students, via the Young Vic Company, into the Old Vic, in the hope of establishing a National Theatre whose participants would all be imbued with the same concept of perfection. Like so many other dreams, it was doomed to disappointment: within a few years internal and external politics would lead to dissension among the Governors of the Old Vic and the eventual closing-down of the School.

I realised later that I was very lucky to have been a student there at that time, and, to my surprise, I was even asked to join the Advanced Course, where the more promising students would have the opportunity of acting as assistant directors on productions for the Old Vic. But by then I was already established, albeit precariously, as a revue lyricist and writing had become a full-time occupation. When I went to say goodbye to George Devine, he expressed a hope that I might one day write a musical for him to produce at the Old Vic. He smiled as he said it, but I could tell that he meant it seriously.

Peter Bentley, who had initiated the series of revues for the ETC at Oxford, was now working professionally as a stage director for the Birmingham Rep. In the autumn of 1948 a season of provincial repertory was given at the St James' Theatre in London, and Peter invited me to see the Birmingham production of *The Rivals* in modern dress. After the performance I went round backstage and he insisted that I must meet the actress who was playing Lydia Languish. Her name was Gwen Cherrell and she had a very English quality of freshness, verging at times on the hearty, which was emphasised by her honey-coloured hair and slightly protruding teeth. Peter had told Gwen all about our Oxford revues, and one evening, while I was working on a new number, Gwen rang me to say that she was going to audition the next morning for *Slings and Arrows*.

'Peter described a number you wrote for Penny Peters called *Why Wasn't I Born Beautiful?* Do you think I could do it for my audition?'

'Of course,' I told her, and she arranged to come round immediately and collect the music. When she arrived, she asked me about the number I was working on.

'What's it about?'

I was, and still am, rather reluctant to talk about something until it is completed, but I told her. There had lately been a minor Red Scare in Whitehall, and a few civil servants had been sacked because of their suspected Communist affiliations. I was writing a song for a girl secretary who had, to her astonishment, in the expression then current, been 'purged'. I was going to call the number *Taken as Red*.

'You must finish it!' said Gwen.

'Well, I'm going to,' I replied rather haughtily.

'No, I mean you must finish it now, and I'll do it for the audition tomorrow.'

'But – but how can you? I haven't even composed the music!'

'Do it tonight. I'll take the lyric home with me, and I'll come and collect the music first thing in the morning.'

I was quite non-plussed, but, like Diana, Gwen had a knack of getting her own way, and I set to work and completed the whole thing in the small hours. Gwen collected the music, as arranged, the following morning and went off to audition for Hermione and the revue's director, Charles Hickman.

That evening, when I came back from the School, she rang me:

'Guess what! I've got the job!'

I congratulated her.

'And what's more, when I finished my audition, Gingold said, "You're in the show, and so is the number." '

I was amazed and delighted. Diana's song, *Thanks, Mr Rank*, had also been accepted, and Hermione had asked Geoffrey and me to write a number for herself and the boys, a turn-of-the-century bathing belle scena called *Come for a Bathe at Brighton*. *Medusa* was also in the programme, but in the course of rehearsal Hermione was sent a lyric about an elderly lady theatre-goer who was baffled by references in Intimate Revue to 'someone or something called Binkie' – Binkie being the soubriquet of Hugh Beaumont, the head of H. M. Tennents. It was rather an 'in' joke, but she had had a great success in the *Sweet and Low* series with a recurring sketch in which she and either Henry Kendall or Walter Crisham exchanged poisonous remarks about theatrical celebrities over dinner at the Ivy. *Medusa* was dropped in favour of *Binkie*.

I was naturally disappointed, but things in general were going so well that I felt no need to dwell on it. Laurier had taken a number from *Ritzy, Regal and Super* about the film critics of the *Sunday Times* and the *Observer*, Dilys Powell and C. A. Lejeune, for Diana Churchill and Daphne Oxenford. And, perhaps most rewarding of all, Elisabeth Welch was going to sing *Dress Nonsense*, a song I had written for her about the extraordinary new fashions from Paris.

Oranges and Lemons went into rehearsal ahead of *Slings and Arrows*, but was due to open at about the same time, at the Lyric, Hammersmith, since it was going on a pre-London tour, while *Slings and Arrows* was opening 'cold', at the Comedy. H. M. Tennents were presenting it, and when it came to the Theatre Royal, Brighton, Virginia, who was on a visit to London, suggested we should go down there for the Saturday night.

'I'm dying to see the show,' she told me breathlessly, 'and we can stay at the Royal Crescent. Binkie and John Perry (his partner) will be there too, and so will darling John G. (as she always referred to John Gielgud), because his new play opens there next week. We can have drinks with them and it will be very good for you.'

We were duly invited to Binkie and John's suite for a drink before the show, and John Gielgud joined us. I was quite happy to sit and listen while the others discussed the Theatre, and it was only when they got on to the subject of *Oranges and Lemons* that I raised my voice. I had already seen it once in Birmingham, where it had included a song about the Atom Bomb, with music by Geoffrey, which Lis Welch had performed with great feeling and effect. Binkie now announced that it had been taken out.

'Oh, but that was one of the best things in the show!' I protested.

'Really?' he said, turning his bland gaze upon me. 'Well, I couldn't understand a word of it. And in any case it was far too gloomy.'

I began to argue with him, but found that the conversation had already taken another turn. A few minutes after that Virginia and I took our leave. Some time later she told me that she feared my disagreement with Binkie had prejudiced him against me – something which I found hard to believe, but she could have been right.

After the show we found ourselves strolling back along the front to the hotel, in company with John Gielgud, who had made a kind mention of my contributions. Virginia told him that I also had some material in Hermione's new show.

'I do admire Toni Gingold,' he mused, with typically faultless modulations. 'She has suddenly turned herself into a professional.'

Oranges and Lemons opened successfully at the Lyric, Hammersmith, in November. My numbers, particularly *Dress Nonsense*, were well received, and Donald Swann, who had written much of the music, was also praised. The show transferred to the Globe in the New Year, where it had a respectable run, but on the whole I think it was considered to fall short of its predecessor, *Tuppence Coloured*. This was was partly due to the absence of Joyce Grenfell; Diana Churchill had great style and charm as an actress, but she lacked the trace of grotesquerie which a revue comedienne requires. And I felt personally that the show belied its title by being a little insipid – a fault it owed perhaps to Laurier whose over-riding criterion was one of 'good taste'.

Although I had contributed less to *Slings and Arrows*, I was somehow more involved with it, probably because of my devotion to Hermione. And of course I was intimately concerned with the success of Diana and Gwen, who were both relying on a number of mine to make their mark. The opening was awaited with excitement; it was Hermione's return to the West End after her huge success at the Ambassadors, and it was decided that the best way to accommodate her many admirers was to give two 'first nights', one, to be attended by the critics, at seven o'clock, and the other at midnight. This, in 1948, signalled an occasion of almost pre-War glamour and raised anticipation to dizzy heights.

For the first performance I had booked two stalls for my mother and a friend of hers, while I sat in the dress circle with my sister Noël. The opening number was called *Morning, Noon and Night* and was in the form of three elaborate tableaux in the mid-Victorian period, each one arranged in front of a painted cloth. When the second cloth rose to reveal 'Night' – Walter Crisham and Hermione, dressed in a vast hooped skirt, with their backs to the audience – the applause was thunderous. Hermione turned and gave an enormous wink : 'I've got the Dagenham Girl Pipers hidden under this.' A tremendous roar of laughter, and the show was away.

But, prejudiced as I was, even I could sense that by the end of it the audience were not as satisfied as they ought to be. There were marvellous moments : Hermione, in a wicked send-up of Eileen Herlie as Medea, draping herself round a pillar and declaiming, 'This is my Personal Column!'; Hermione as a bejewelled laundress, grown rich on excess charges : 'And I crush pyjama buttons into fragments, With these rather dainty Cartier casse-noisettes'; and, perhaps funniest of all, Hermione as a whey-faced masseuse, in Peter Myers' number, pummelling and otherwise maltreating Christopher Hewett. Gwen's song went well, largely thanks to her inherent guts, and Diana, to my delight, stopped the show with *Thanks, Mr Rank*. But much of the rest misfired and it did appear as if wit and topicality had been sacrificed in favour of prettiness and what I was learning to recognise as 'camp'. The finale somehow typified this : the scene was a decorative conservatory, with the boys as gardeners in green baize aprons, led by Walter Crisham. One by one the ladies of the cast were introduced, each dressed as a hot-house flower. Unfortunately most of them had bad legs – too thin, too fat, or in one case too short. Gwen was an exception and looked very pretty as a hydrangea, and Hermione, who has marvellous legs, made a splendiferous orchid. But the whole effect was of something out of the Ziegfeld Follies gone wrong, and left the audience in an embarrassed mood.

At the second house I sat in the same seats in the circle with Hugh Schooling, and because it was midnight and the audience was largely composed of Theatre people, the show went with a bang from start to finish and the reception was delirious. But it was of course the first house which the critics would review, and the notices both the next day and subsequently were luke-warm, and almost all of them complained of an excess of theatrical 'parish-pumpery' in the material, the number about Binkie coming in for particular disfavour. Hermione was persuaded to remove it almost at once and substituted her own disquisition on Bucalosi's Dance of the Grasshoppers from *Sweeter and Lower*, with its famous opening line: 'I have been arsed to talk to you this evening about Mewssick . . .' Business was reasonably good, and it was decided to run the show on over Christmas and in the New Year to present a Second Edition, with several new items, including, at last, *Medusa*. I was also approached to write a new number for Walter Crisham, who badly needed fresh material, and I produced a song called *What of the Night?*, about a Watchman in London in 1666. It began: 'Twelve o'clock and everything's ghastly' and proceeded to describe all the goings-on in town at that time. Hermione herself contributed a throw-away: 'Hush, hush, whisper who dares! Christopher Wren is designing some stairs', and the number ended: '. . . and now some darned fool's gone and started a Fire. Oh, what a terrible night!' But Wally didn't care for it, and it was given instead to Wallas Eaton who somehow made the whole thing seem rather sinister.

The Second Edition fared a little better than the first, and *Medusa* received one or two nice mentions in the Press. But the run petered out in the spring, and Hermione went off to New York. I was told later that she had made the mistake of taking too much control in the choice of material; when the *Sweet and Low* series was running so successfully at the Ambassadors, the management had made the final decisions and on one or two occasions she had even been obliged to do material against her will and had subsequently been proved wrong. Like many other actors and actresses, Hermione has always suffered from a sense of insecurity and a lack of confidence in her own enormous talent, and I believe that this had led her at times to listen to flattery rather than sound advice. Because of her innate kindness and generosity, but also because of her fear of loneliness, she likes to have company all the time, and while I was working for her I was constantly asked to Kinnerton Street for parties and gatherings. She preferred male company always, but there would sometimes be a favoured female friend, such as Ilena Sylva, the actress, or 'Pekoe' Schooling, a distant relative of my friend Hugh, or, most amusing of all, the bug-eyed agent and former night-club owner, Elma Warren, whose gaucheries kept us in fits of laughter. From being frightened of Hermione, on our first meeting, I grew to love her very much, and, although *Slings and Arrows* is generally accounted a failure, for me it provided a first foothold in the professional Theatre and this I owe entirely to her.

When, during the Spring Term, it was suggested that the Production and Design Courses at the Old Vic should stage an entertainment for the Acting Course, it seemed inevitable that we should decide to do a revue. Val May and I directed it, along with a Swedish girl called Eva Sköld who had the build of Anne Sheridan and a smoky vocal technique to match. My particular friend on the Production Course was a Scots girl, Anne Watson, who had a weakness for sweet things and shared with me a tendency towards laziness. We used to sit at the back of Lilian Baylis's box, munching chocolate and gossiping, when we should have been on the stage learning how to run flats or throw lines. She had a very sweet soprano and for her I wrote a sentimental ballad about a girl Stage Manager who is in love with a stage-hand, but they never meet because 'I'm always on the Prompt Side and he's always O.P.' We had a song about our three Directors, Devine, Byam Shaw and St Denis, who all had the mannerism of ending every sentence with the words 'You know' – a habit which seems to have become almost universal nowadays – and our most spectacular number was *Elsie Smith*, a song saga performed by Eva Sköld, while the rest of the company mimed the near-downfall of Elsie at the hands of a character called Nick the Spiv. At one point the Seven Deadly Sins appeared out of the orchestra pit, wearing grotesque masks, and poor Anne had a terrible time trying to writhe about in a convincing representation of Lust. The song was later performed by Elisabeth Welch in Laurier Lister's *Penny Plain* but without the lavish trappings we managed to give it at the Old Vic. Our finale began with the lines,

'Take me back to the Waterloo Road
Where the Theatre was fun,
And we never had to worry
If the show was going to run.'

At that time I had had scarcely enough experience of professional Theatre to know what I was talking about, but the words did, I'm afraid, turn out to be prophetic.

That summer I took over the rental of my mother's flat at Northways, Swiss Cottage, which had been let to my cousin, Joan Galbraith, and her widowed mother. I asked Hugh, who was hoping to get into the antique business and needed somewhere to live in London, to share with me, and on the day we moved in he brought me a house-warming present, a silver-grey kitten that he had found in a pet-shop in Wardour Street. I called her Sylvia, after Sylvia Fowler, the cattiest character in *The Women*, and she lived with me – or rather permitted me to live with her – for the next thirteen years, having kittens as and when she felt in the mood, fed on the best of everything, and generally running my life. In return she consented to allow me to ghost-write and illustrate her memoirs, which were later published, with some success, as *This is Sylvia*.

After achieving her ambition of being in a Gingold revue, Gwen reverted to straight acting and was now appearing with great success in Peter Ustinov's *Love of Four Colonels*. One day she came to have lunch with me in the Waterloo Road and told me she wanted me to meet two girl-friends of hers who had been fellow-students at the Webber-Douglas School of Drama. They were now working as student stage-staff at the Oxford Playhouse and had made a sensation in the pantomime with a turn as two horrendous girl-guides.

'Their names are Angela Lee and Celia Helda, and they're looking for some material to start a cabaret act. Celia is in London now. Can I tell her to get in touch with you?'

Coincidentally I received a letter from Stanley Parker, also recommending Angela and Celia to my attention. 'They are,' he wrote, 'like a young version of the Hermiones – Baddeley and Gingold.' I was naturally intrigued.

Celia came to see me one evening at Northways, and it was arranged that the two of them would give me an audition of their girl-guide act a few days later. When they appeared together, I realised that Stanley's description had not been far off the mark: Celia was slim, blonde and acid, while Angela was plump, brunette and rorty. They were neither of them exactly expert in singing or dancing, as they would be the first to admit, but they had the makings of a hilarious comedy team. All they needed was an idea or, as it later came to be called, a 'gimmick'.

Very tentatively I suggested the Nineteen Twenties, and then, as Celia tells it:

'That immediately sparked something off in us. I thought, "I'll be able to make the costumes. They're so easy – straight up and down . . ." Later on you and I went to the British Museum Newspaper Library to look at the fashion magazines of the period, and we laughed so much that we were practically asked to leave.'

'We reacted in a very positive way,' Angela says, 'and I ran to my mother who instantly said, "*I* shall teach you to Charleston." '

Celia got busy with her sewing machine and made two sets of costumes: 'One was tennis frocks – white, with a green sash and matching cloche hats – and the other was evening dresses in blue and red crêpe with fringing from John Lewis, and we sewed sequins on the shoulder-straps.' I produced an opening number – my first song in the 1920s idiom – a dance 'novelty', called *The Yoo-Hoo Bounce.*

'The act got under way at the Proscenium Club in Dover Street, which opened once a week to give aspiring amateurs a chance. Our claque, headed by John Moffatt and Robert Brown (the actors, who had also been working at the Oxford Playhouse) were forced to come and applaud. In fact we didn't really need them, because the audience, to our astonishment, reacted quite involuntarily with shrieks of laughter. The Twenties had caught on.'

I was delighted, but regarded the whole business as a very enjoyable self-indulgence on my part. I was continuing to write revue material, and in the same summer Geoffrey Wright asked me if I would like to collaborate with him on a musical: he suggested that we should do an adaptation of *The Rivals.* I was very flattered and agreed at once, and when Hugh and I went for a holiday to his parents' house in the Isle of Wight I started work on the book. Geoffrey and I proceeded with our collaboration intermittently over the next few months and found that we worked very satisfactorily together: we would meet at his flat in Great Ormond Street to discuss ideas for new lyrics and to try out the settings Geoffrey had composed for ones I had written, after which he would make lunch and we would discuss the current musical theatre. *Oklahoma!* had ended its run at Drury Lane, to be replaced by Rodgers and Hammerstein's equally successful *Carousel.* The latest musical hit on Broadway was Cole Porter's *Kiss Me, Kate* and this was due to open shortly at the Coliseum; at home I kept a Haig Whisky bottle which I filled with sixpences in order to pay for two stall seats when I had saved up enough. Geoffrey shared my admiration for Rodgers and Hart and introduced me to the scores of some of their musicals which had never been produced in London, such as *I Married an Angel, Babes in Arms* and *Pal Joey.*

During my last term at the Old Vic School Ken Tynan suddenly rang me out of the blue and told me he had some news of great importance to all of us.

'Two ladies called Elizabeth Sprigge and Velona Pilcher are opening a new club theatre in a basement off the Strand. It's going to be called the Watergate, and they've asked me to come and direct. So you must get over and see it right away, as we're all going to work there.'

I passed on the news to Eva Sköld and we jumped on a bus without more ado. Following Ken's instructions, we found Buckingham Street, one of the streets that led down from the Strand to the Embankment, and next door to Villiers Street where the Players' Theatre, having been bombed out of their Covent Garden premises during the War, had found a new venue, the old Forum Cinema, 'underneath the arches' of the Southern Railway. At the bottom of Buckingham Street stood the eighteenth century 'water-gate' that gave the new theatre club its name. It was reached by a staircase, at the bottom of which, Ken told us, was to be the lobby and box office; to the right there would be a bar, which would also serve as an art gallery, and beyond there was to be a small restaurant; to the left would be the theatre, seating about a hundred and fifty people. There was not a great deal of evidence of this at the moment since the conversion had only recently begun from what was reputed to have been a Chinese bawdy house; but Eva and I made approving noises and then went off to have a cup of tea and speculate about the Watergate's future possibilities.

Peter Wildeblood had also been alerted by Ken. Having parted company with my mother and Brooke House Hotel, he was now beginning to make his mark as a journalist on the *Daily Mail* and had also had a topical comedy, *Prudence and the Pea-Nuts*, produced on a Saturday night at the Playhouse Theatre. He was collaborating on a dramatization of *Cold Comfort Farm* with Ken, who he was convinced was on the up and up.

'So I think one had better just cling onto those plum-coloured coat-tails, don't you,' he confided in me, 'and hope to get dragged to the top.'

I was not so sure. I had no doubt that Ken would make it, in any or all of the capacities in which he saw himself, but I was not at all certain that I wanted to pursue my career under his aegis or in his shadow. However I passed on the information about the Watergate to Celia and Angela, who had now established themselves in a room in Eaton Terrace, and suggested that, as Ken envisaged avant-garde drama alternating with revue, they should audition for the management. Eventually the Watergate had a grand opening to which none of us was invited; but I heard that Sybil Thorndike had been much in evidence, and the first thing to greet the guests as they descended the staircase was a sculpture entitled 'Laughing Buttocks'.

As yet no production was announced, and when I took Angela and

Celia to their audition, the only part of the club that was functioning was the restaurant, run by Bill Staughton, an Australian actor, where Miss Sprigge and Miss Pilcher were at present tucking into a dish of the newly fashionable delicacy, scampi. Eventually they emerged and sat appreciatively while Angela and Celia tore through their girl-guide routine in the icy theatre. They promised to let us know as soon as any revues were in the offing, and returned to their dinner. No revue did materialize, but Bill Staughton took the girls on as waitresses in the restaurant, where they worked for their tips and as much as they could eat; they had also been acting in the same capacity at Brooke House, where my mother had instituted what she called Business Lunches at two and ten a head, with coffee. Like me, Angela and Celia were clinging on to any toe-hold they could find in the business, in the firm belief that sooner or later that famous break would come.

Life became rather more precarious for me at that moment when the management of Northways informed my mother that unless she took up occupation of her flat in person, her lease would be terminated. She was of course in no position to do so, and Hugh, Sylvia and I had to find a new home very quickly. An agent sent us to a basement in the nearby Crossfield Road, which had two rooms, a kitchen in the hall-way and a bathroom, with an overgrown garden at the back. There was no heating, and it promised to be damp and cold in winter, but the rent was only thirty-five shillings a week and we needed somewhere in a hurry. There was one snag: a fee of two hundred pounds for the 'furniture and fittings', which consisted of two chairs and a table, a couple of thread-bare carpets and a broken gas oven. Luckily I had a life insurance for which my father had painstakingly kept up the premiums throughout the Twenties and Thirties; it was the only security I had, but I cashed it and we moved into the basement.

Hugh had a cousin, Elizabeth Schooling, one of the original ballerinas in Marie Rambert's company at the Mercury Theatre, who had married the choreographer, Frank Staff, and lived in a very pretty house off Kensington High Street where Hugh and I were often asked to dinner – an occasion for which we were always very grateful. Elizabeth was blonde and slightly daffy in a most charming way, while Frank, with his fierce black eyes and sardonic attitude, was an enigmatic character whom I found difficulty in getting to know. But he seemed to be genuinely interested in my work, and he kindly arranged for Hugh and me to go free, whenever we liked, to the Empire, Leicester Square, where he was choreographer to the ballet company, part of the live stage show with which the management was attempting to lure the public away from Television. He also introduced me to his agent, Leon

Cassel-Gerard, as he felt I should have somebody to represent me. Leon signed me up, and now all I needed was some work for him to represent.

Geoffrey and I had finished *The Rivals* and were now in the process of trying to get a management to take an interest in it. By way of giving the score an airing, two friends of Geoffrey's, Neil Crawford and David Smith-Dorrien, laid on a soirée at their house, to which we could invite anyone we chose and in the course of which the songs from *The Rivals* were to be performed by a group of singers, led by Diana Maddox. I naturally invited Ken, and the evening seemed to go quite well; but afterwards he came up to me and said,

'You know, Sandy, what this score needs is a really gutsy, show-stopping number like *Doing What Comes Naturally*.'

Considering we were presenting an adaptation of a Sheridan play, this seemed to me to be quite on the wrong tack. But on reflection I think he was right: the whole thing was a little too much on the dainty side – a besetting sin of many another English musical. But we went ahead and sent the script to H. M. Tennents, deciding that there was nothing like beginning at the top. It came back with a brusque note from John Perry: 'The script is so involved that I had to refer to the original play to discover what the story was. To compensate for this, the music would have to be sensationally good.' But he made no indication of wanting to hear it.

We were planning where to turn next, when Geoffrey announced that he had been asked by Jack Waller to compose the score for a musical version of a play called *The French for Love* by Marguerite Steen and Derek Patmore, which had achieved quite a success early on in the War when Alice Delysia starred in it at the Criterion.

Jack Waller was an impresario of the old school, whose greatest hit had been *No, No, Nanette* in 1925, and he had also, in partnership with Joseph Tunbridge, written songs for a number of English musicals, usually starring Bobby Howes and Binnie Hale. Geoffrey had already been involved with him over another project:

'Through Diana Morgan I was brought in on a curious show with a book by Fred Thomson, who was very old then but went right back to the small Jerome Kern musicals. It was called *He Saw Virginia* and was all about a man who fell asleep and dreamed about the Pilgrim Fathers, and why they wanted to do it here and not in America I've no idea. I came in and composed several settings and a point number which Diana wrote and which impressed Jack tremendously. Then Diana fell by the wayside and Eric Maschwitz wrote some more lyrics, and finally the whole thing collapsed. Later on Jack came to me with this adaptation of *The French for Love*; but they hadn't got a lyric-writer. So I suggested you.'

It seemed unlikely that Jack Waller would even have heard of me, but Geoffrey was asked to bring me along to meet him and the show's director, William Mollison, in the latter's flat. We were given a drink and then Mollison proceeded to read aloud the whole book. At the end Jack turned to us and said, in his marvellously rasping voice,

'Well, boys, wot'jer think?'

I forget what I replied, but it must have been right, because there and then I was given the job.

The story of *The French for Love* – or *Caprice* as we called the musical version – concerned a middle-aged Englishman, Victor, who is living in the South of France, with all his wants attended to by his mistress, Lucille, and Pierre, a womanising valet. This idyll is interrupted by the arrival of Victor's stuffy wife and their daughter, Joan, together with Joan's fiancé, a virgin Englishman called Robin, and his father, an apoplectic Admiral, who wishes to investigate Joan's family background. In order to preserve Victor's respectability Lucille pretends to be his housekeeper. The obvious complications ensue and, influenced by the conventional Riviera atmosphere of sunshine and 'oo-la-la', Joan embarks on a flirtation with Pierre and Robin receives his initiation into sex from Lucille, while the Admiral rushes off to Monte Carlo with Colette, the obligatory soubrette maid. But all ends happily: Victor and Lucille are reunited, the English contingent return home, and Pierre departs for the USA with a rich American widow.

It was not a bad basis for a musical comedy, and the book was considerably improved when Michael Pertwee was called in to make a new adaptation. Henry Kendall, a comedian of style, who had partnered Hermione in several revues, was cast as Victor, and for the part of his daughter, Joan, Jack announced that he had discovered Sally Ann Howes, the daughter of Bobby Howes. She had made several films as a child, but was now grown up into a staggeringly beautiful girl and, unknown to anyone else as yet, was possessed of an excellent singing voice: this was to be her musical début. Pierre was to be played by Jacques Jansen, a handsome baritone from the Opéra Comique, who had recently scored a success as Danilo; his English was almost non-existent, but Bill Mollison undertook to have him word-perfect in time for rehearsal. The main casting problem was Lucille, and for several weeks a stream of Continental ladies passed through Jack and Cecilia Waller's flat in Queen's Gate, all to be rejected for one reason or another. There was even talk at one point of approaching Marlene Dietrich, but nothing came of it. Finally one afternoon an English actress was announced by the name of Lisa Lee. Her appearance was striking: a handsome face with flashing eyes combined with the figure of what the Edwardians would have called 'a fine woman'. We were further impressed when she launched into a faultless rendering in French of *Un Jour Sans Toi*. Her only draw-back was that she was English and Jack had set his heart on presenting a Frenchwoman in the rôle.

'But I am *partly* French,' said Lisa, who had set *her* heart on getting the role. 'In fact I have worked under the name of Lisa d'Esterre.'

And so it was decided that Lisa would play Lucille in the guise of a French discovery. She turned out to be, as a real-life character, at least as colourful as any Continental star could have been.

In the meanwhile Geoffrey and I had produced what we felt was a very promising score which included some of the best melodies Geoffrey had ever written. Jack was full of enthusiasm and when Geoffrey came up with a tune that particularly appealed to him, he would rush to his violin-case, snatch up the instrument and join in on the repeat chorus. His musical knowledge was sound and based on long experience, but, to Geoffrey's horror, he had promised his partner, Joe Tunbridge, the conductorship of *Caprice* and also insisted that five of their own compositions be included in the score. Whatever Joe's standing may have been in the Twenties and Thirties, he was now a dithering little old man who was still suffering from the effects of a War-time nervous break-down; but nothing would induce Jack to go back on his promise, and, on top of that, he himself became ill and from dress rehearsal onwards the responsibility of the show rested on Bill Mollison, whose favourite solution to any problem was a good strong drink.

Despite these presages of disaster, I was still totally dazzled by my involvement in a bona-fide professional musical and looked forward excitedly to our opening at the Alhambra, Glasgow, as did Lisa, apart from the obvious reasons, since she had an ex-lover in the local gaol whom she was intending to visit, unknown to her present husband, a left-wing violinist. 'My marriages always last three years,' she confided to me, 'and the Red Fiddler and I have now been married for two. So . . .' We all installed ourselves at the Central Hotel and entered on the final period of band-calls, technical run-throughs and dress parades, the latter being complicated by the appearance of six gold lamé evening dresses, designed by Mrs Waller, which Jack insisted must appear in the show, in spite of the fact that most of it took place in the garden of a villa in broad day-light. I had the bright idea of introducing them into a number we had written for Henry Kendall and the male juvenile, Patrick Melany, an American protegé of Tessie O'Shea's who had been unaccountably cast as Sally Ann's ultra-English fiancé: the song was called *To Hell With Women* and I suggested that a vision of female devils be interpolated. Six of the girls were fitted out with sequinned horns, and the gold lamé dresses, lit to look red, duly made their appearance.

On the opening night Geoffrey, Michael and I sat together in a box with our note-books at the ready. The show got off to a good start: Harry Kendall played all his laughs beautifully and provided solid partnership for Lisa, who made a strong impression, in spite of an unbecoming wardrobe, designed, on her own insistence, by her friend, Honoria Plesch, who later had more success decorating the windows of Lyons Corner Houses. The audience also took to Jacques' good looks and beautiful singing voice but failed to understand anything he said, not surprisingly, since Bill Mollison had turned his English lessons into drinking sessions, in which Jacques had declined to participate.

Sally Ann entered, looking exquisite, to an appreciative round of applause, and shortly afterwards commenced a duologue with Patrick to introduce her first song, which also happened to be the first song she would sing on any stage, anywhere. Halfway through the scene there was a slight disturbance in the orchestra pit: we looked down to see that Joe Tunbridge had let the entire score slide off his stand and was now on his knees amidst a heap of music manuscript trying to find Sally Ann's number. It was called *Heart to Heart* and, unaware of what had occurred, she uttered the cue for song: 'Don't be silly, darling. What does it matter where we are?' Not a sound from the orchestra, and Joe was still scrabbling about on the floor. Sally Ann glanced in his direction, saw that he had apparently vanished, and, turning help-lessly to Patrick, launched into the verse, quite unaccompanied. After a few bars the lead violin took it upon himself to join her, but not of course in the same key. Gradually the other instruments followed suit and Sally Ann, by a series of agonising modulations, adjusted herself to what they were playing. Geoffrey meanwhile had collapsed with a groan at the back of the box and could barely be induced to watch the rest of the show.

At the end of the scene Sally Ann, now thoroughly demoralised, dashed offstage and into the arms of her mother, Pat Howes, who was waiting in her dressing-room. As I heard it later, she explained, between bouts of hysterical weeping, what had happened, and refused to go onstage again, whereupon Pat, a former actress, slapped her smartly on the face. 'This,' she added firmly, 'is Show Business', and ordered her daughter to repair her make-up for her next entrance.

On the whole the reception in Glasgow was favourable, but there was clearly a lot more work needed on the show, and we set about re-writing and interpolating new dialogue and numbers. But I could sense that Geoffrey's heart was no longer in it, and Bill Mollison seemed quite incapable of suggesting or implementing any improvements. Jack was still in hospital in London, and there was no-one to take control at a time when it was most needed. The show moved on to Manchester, where business was only fair, and then to Birmingham, its last date before London. Here a move was set on foot by some members of the cast to have Harry Kendall take over the direction, but he was reluctant to embarrass Bill Mollison, and it came to nothing. Jack informed us that we had a good chance of going into His Majesty's, but when the theatre management came to see the show they decided instead to take *Blue for a Boy*, a Fred Emney vehicle. There was now nothing to do but close *Caprice* in Birmingham.

Whereas for Geoffrey *Caprice* had proved frustrating and depressing, as far as I was concerned, in spite of its failure, it had merely whetted my appetite. As *The Rivals* seemed to be getting nowhere, I suggested to Geoffrey that we try an original subject set in the 1920s. Somehow a revival of that period seemed to be in the air. I had just read a new reprint of *The Great Gatsby*, and in a Cecil Landau revue Joan Heal had brought the house down dancing the Charleston. In the winter of 1950 my sister Christian returned to London for the first time since 1938, having lost her husband after a long battle with Parkinson's Disease. She asked me to come to Paris with her for the week-end, and while we were there Virginia arranged for us to attend a show at Pierre Balmain's: many of the models appeared in low-waisted chemise dresses and wore adaptations of the cloche hat. The fashion did not catch on, but it was a straw in the wind. Hugh and I decided to give a Nineteen Twenties party in the basement at Crossfield Road. I scoured Charing Cross Road for old sheet music and gramophone records, and everyone was asked to turn up in the costume of the period. The response was amazing: Diana discovered a beautiful jet-embroidered evening dress in the wardrobe of the Players' Theatre, where she was currently working; Peter Wildeblood arrived in full panoply as the Sheik, with his lady agent slung across his shoulder; and Angela and Celia, who already had their wardrobe, gave us a cabaret. They had now perfected their act with the addition of several genuine numbers of the period such as *The Song of the Gold-Diggers* and Irving Berlin's *Simple Melody*, and had tried it out on an Army audience in West Germany, where it was an instant success. From then on, as Lee and Helda of the Roaring Twenties, they performed in London night-clubs, touring Variety,

Middle East troop concerts and cabaret in India and South Africa. For them the 1920s were already paying off.

I suggested to Geoffrey that we do a new version of the Faust legend, with a female Faust called Kate, who is offered by the devil a return to her youth in exchange for her soul; but instead of becoming young in the present day, she relives her youth in the 1920s. The scene after her transformation took place in a villa in the South of France and opened with the influx of a crowd of girls carrying hat-boxes. Somehow we never got further than that, and I sensed that Geoffrey did not find the subject inspiring. What is more, much as I enjoyed working with him, I was feeling a growing urge to write my own music again. So we parted company professionally, but remained firm friends.

1951 was the year of the Festival of Britain, when a wonderland of pavilions dedicated to the Arts and Sciences arose from the desolation of the South Bank, at its centre a sparkling new Concert Hall. There were complaints about the folly of such extravagance at a time of domestic and international crisis; but I considered the whole thing a splendid gesture on the part of the Labour Government, although it turned out to be its swan song as well. Simultaneously part of Battersea Park was transformed into a Pleasure Garden of a delicacy and charm which it is hard to imagine when faced with its tawdry remnants today. It contained, among many other attractions, an open air theatre in which Madame Rambert presented a ballet of Orlando the Cat and where later on Angela and Celia appeared in a revue performing my tea-shop sketch from Oxford.

In the spring I was called up from Paris by a friend of Geoffrey Wright's, the lyric-writer Geoffrey Parsons, who was over there working on the script for a dubbed version of a French film, *Nous Irons à Paris*, a lightweight comedy with music, featuring Paul Misraki and his Band and a trio of enormous black women called the Peters Sisters. There was a song sequence in the middle of it which Geoffrey felt he had no time to cope with, and he had suggested that I be brought over to do it. The fee was fifty pounds, plus all expenses and an allowance while I was in Paris. Naturally I jumped at it. The work was extremely difficult since the sequence in question was a collection of parodies on Paul Misraki's hits, so that it not only had to match the singers' lip movements and fit the music, but be funny as well. I spent morning after morning in a projection room at Joinville shouting lyrics into a microphone while the sequence was run over and over again. But, largely thanks to Virginia's presence in Paris, the evenings made up for it. Eventually the dubbing was completed and I awaited news of the film's London première. Months later it turned up as a second feature at the local, and I rushed to see it. Breathlessly I sat through the opening reels, only to find, when 'my' sequence was about to start, that the whole thing had been cut.

One morning while I was in Paris Hugh rang me from London: Christopher Hewett, Hermione's friend and her victim in the Masseuse number, was trying to get hold of me. The Watergate had finally established itself as a club theatre and had instituted a highly successful series of late-night revues, written by Peter Myers; but Peter had had a difference of opinion with the management and had taken himself off to a rival club theatre, the Irving. Chris was directing a special Festival Revue, called *Mid-Century Madness*, for the Watergate and urgently needed some more material. Could I supply it? I told Hugh to ring at once and say that I would. As soon as I returned to London I went down to the Watergate to see Chris and find out what was required. I was enormously excited because I had a feeling that this was the opening I needed.

In the next day or so I produced four numbers, all of which went into the show, and one of which, a send-up of the Dale family in a long-running radio serial, received special mention from the critics. The revue as a whole was only moderately successful, but John Jones and his wife, Mary Harris, who were managing the Watergate for Miss Sprigge and Miss Pilcher, asked me to write a complete show for the autumn. It was the chance of a life-time and I agreed on the spot.

I went to announce the good news to Leon Cassel-Gerard, but his reaction was hardly what I expected.

'You don't want to waste your time in a hole like the Watergate,' he said.

'Oh, but I do,' I replied, 'and I don't think it will be a waste of time.' I then went on to suggest that he might like to terminate our contract, since he did not approve of my decision. He had in fact taken very little interest in my work and had not even bothered to come and see *Caprice* until it was closing in Birmingham, and now he appeared to have no objection to our parting company. There seemed no point in going to another agent and I made the agreement with John Jones and Mary Harris myself.

The Fringe Theatre is now an accepted phenomenon and probably makes a more original and constructive contribution then did London's club theatres of the 1950s; but the Watergate, whose name will unfortunately go down in history in quite another context, was something special. To begin with, it was slap in the middle of the West End, and while it had a reputation for experiment and the avant-garde, it was also rather chic: in the words of the *Sunday Express* critic, it was the place 'where mink meets corduroy'. Whereas the Fringe Theatre of today is largely Youth- and Left Wing-orientated, the Watergate seemed to have something for all ages, classes and political persuasions. From the moment one passed beneath 'Laughing Buttocks' and entered the lobby, there was an atmosphere of activity, of life and bustle, of old and new conflicting and merging, of intellectual intensity and of light-heartedness: it was, in short, a microcosm of what, to my mind, Theatre should be, and I adored it.

In spite of Ken's prognostications, I had not been asked to work there until Chris Hewett approached me over *Mid-Century Madness*, but, owing to Angela and Celia, I had been a frequent visitor. They had graduated from the restaurant to the stage, and had featured particularly in a series of plays initiated by Ken Tynan. The first of these was *Desire Caught by the Tail*, Picasso's only play, written to entertain his friends during the Occupation. After the first reading Ken had apparently lost confidence in the project and the season was taken over by Billy Jay, a former stage manager at the Oxford Playhouse, who had, in Angela's words, 'the nerve of the Devil'. She and Celia appeared in several rôles, including Fat and Thin Anxiety, and the play, which would never have seen the light of day without Picasso's name attached to it, had quite a succès de scandale. I was rather more interested in Billy's next effort, a production of another only play, this time by Ronald Firbank. Someone had told me that if I was interested in the Twenties, I should read Firbank's novels. He was quite wrong of course, but it so happened that all Firbank's works had just been published in a two-volume collected edition, and I bought them, was baffled at first, and then, by dint of reading them aloud with Hugh, fell under the spell. Billy announced that he was going to produce Firbank's play, *The Princess Zoubaroff* – for the first time ever, I believe – and Celia was cast as one of the abandoned wives, Nadine Sheil-Meyer, and Angela as the novelist, Blanche Negress.

The play is insubstantial to the point of flimsiness, but it is full of delicious dialogue and possesses the elegant outrageousness that was later to delight a whole new generation of Firbank-admirers. Within the limitations attendant on any club theatre production, Billy did a commendable job, and it was just the kind of event for which the Watergate had been intended. The production was later revived at the Irving with the additional attraction of Brenda Dean Paul, the celebrated drug-addict, as the Princess, but that is another story.

Having established itself as a straight theatre, the Watergate now entered on a policy of late-night revue, at a curtain time of ten-thirty. Since most West End theatres in those days went up at seven-thirty, this meant that an artist could come after his performance and appear in the revue, which not only facilitated casting but also enabled actors and actresses to manage financially. No salaries were paid at the Watergate, only a percentage of the take; in a good week this could amount to several pounds, but I remember the cast of one unsuccessful play being doled out seven-and-six each. This policy of two performances a night put a considerable strain on the stage staff, since one lot of sets and costumes had to be rapidly removed to make way for another, and so restricted was the space backstage that one frequently came upon flats and dress-racks standing in the lobby or the bar. But somehow everyone managed and the show went on.

We decided to call the new revue *See You Later* and this time Chris was to be in it, and John Jones and Mary Harris called in a friend of theirs, the actor John Byron, to direct. The revues always had a cast of six, three girls and three boys, and the other two boys were Charles Ross, who had been in *Mid-Century Madness*, and Dennis Wood, recruited from the Players' Theatre. I suggested Diana as one of the girls, which was readily agreed on, and another was a very pretty protégée of Aïda Foster's School, Yvonne Marsh. For our leading lady Chris came up with a surprising proposition: Dulcie Gray. Dulcie had made a colossal reputation in British films playing long-suffering wives and put-upon heroines, and was married to Michael Denison. Together they seemed to represent the rather drearier British virtues and the last place one would expect to find Dulcie was in a theatre club doing a late-night revue. But she had made up her mind that it was time to destroy her current image:

'I wanted to get away from the sort of stiff upper-lip British gentle-woman I had played so often, because I felt I was getting in a beastly rut, and this seemed like a god-send. I'd never worked in that sort of theatre before, and I just wanted to do the whole thing – to break out.'

Chris brought Dulcie up to Crossfield Road one evening to meet me, and I was astonished to find that she was the antithesis of her screen persona: jolly and voluble, with a wicked sense of humour and an enviable gift of self-mockery. She had a notion for her first solo number: she would appear in Kate Greenaway costume, wearing a straw hat and carrying a watering can, and looking thoroughly demure and olde-worlde; and then she would reveal that her garden was crammed with hashish, opium poppies, toadstools, deadly nightshade and every kind of noxious plant imaginable. I wrote the number and called it *Garden Girl* and Dulcie agreed to do the revue. She worked tremendously hard, particularly on the musical side, since she had never sung a note or danced a step onstage in her life, and here we were fortunate in having Donald Swann as our accompanist. He was endlessly patient and good-humoured and, as an additional asset, through the entire run of the show he would sit at his piano during non-musical items laughing his head off at every funny line, which encouraged both audience and actors no end.

Dulcie managed to integrate herself into the Watergate atmosphere remarkably well, although it took us a little while to get used to her habit of throwing her mink coat on the floor before she went onstage and her tendency to ask for 'a teeny-weeny double brandy' in the lunch break, when the rest of us were drinking light ales. The only person Dulcie failed to win over was Diana:

'I don't think she really approved of me. There's something about being an English film star that drives people mad, critics and everybody. After all, right the way through my time in films I was also acting on the stage, but in some curious way British films of that era make people more apoplectic than almost anything else that's ever happened in British history.'

However, despite one or two flare-ups, rehearsals were reasonably smooth, and Chris's gifts of mediation were invaluable. As a director, John Byron was intelligent and imaginative, but lacking in authority, with the result that Diana ended up by directing herself in her solo numbers, unethically but effectively. The sets were designed by Desmond Healey, according to a scheme devised by John, which, it was discovered in the dress rehearsal stages, simply would not function. So we all had to set to work sewing together black tabs – the conventional stand-by in any revue. Even Hugh was hauled in to help, and when a similar crisis occurred in the wardrobe, Dulcie could be found lending a hand at the sewing machine. In the final stages we were beset by another, totally unexpected, hazard. As Dulcie puts it:

'Our darling director had a call from God – on the Thursday before opening night, just as I was learning my bumps and grinds. He told me that God did not approve of the Theatre, and I told him that perhaps He could wait at least until after the First Night.'

The First Night itself nearly failed to happen. The audience, including the critics, were kept waiting for an hour because the front curtains – or 'house tabs' – refused to open and close. Frantic attempts were made to repair them, to no avail, and eventually Michael Denison offered to stand behind them onstage during the entire show and pull them by hand when required. If anyone ever laughs at the Denisons in my hearing, I challenge them to match this example of husbandly loyalty – which, incidentally, was performed in complete anonymity.

In spite of having been kept waiting so long, the critics were unanimous in their praise. They naturally devoted a good deal of their space to Dulcie's theatrical volte-face. The *Evening News* headed its notice: 'Dulcie Non Decorum', and went on to say, 'From the moment she appeared as a sweet girl who was dying to feed the Vicar to her man-eating orchid we knew it was going to be all right.' John Barber singled out her aged French diseuse – 'all bosom and goitre' – in a send-up of a Follies show, and Peter Wildeblood, now a critic on the *Daily Mail*, considered that she had hitherto been outrageously miscast and was 'plainly more at home on a broomstick'.

I was pleased to find that Diana also came in for a large share of the credit. At her suggestion I had written a song about a Gaiety Girl who is fed up with having champagne drunk from her slipper. It was called *Damp Shoes* and she did it exquisitely. We also included a fairly cruel imitation of Joyce Grenfell, during which she sang a little waltz song entitled *I'm Rather Keen on Life*. Of this the *Guardian* said that 'Miss Maddox looks nothing like her victim but by projecting an optical illusion across the footlights appears to be her twin.' Everyone else received mentions and Chris had particular success with the Watchman number from *Slings and Arrows* which he had always had his eye on.

I was more than satisfied with my own reviews and delighted with John Barber's remark that I wrote 'words worth hearing to tunes worth cheering'. In a small way, I appeared to have arrived, and for the first time I could believe that my future in the Theatre might be assured. On the first night my mother, as if to award me a kind of accolade of her confidence, produced an orchid on her arrival at the Watergate and pinned it to my lapel. It would hardly be true to say that her faith in me had never faltered; she had on the contrary tended to sit back and let me show what I could do. But now, with a kind of second sight, she seemed to know that I had made it. I would never be a bishop, but what I had chosen to do instead I could, it seemed, do well.

One of the most successful items in *See You Later* was a sketch called *Desert Song*, which had originally been in two parts, contrasting the Rudolf Valentino image of the Middle East with its present-day turmoils. It was found during dress rehearsals that it was almost impossible to make the costume changes between the two halves, and we decided to present the first half as a complete sketch in itself. Dennis, who had the necessary smouldering good looks, played the Sheik and Diana played the pure English girl whom he seduces. She designed and made her own costume and looked like a perfect recreation of Agnes Ayres or Vilma Banky. It was obvious that she had the same feeling for the period as I had, and one day after the opening night brou-ha-ha had died down we had a chat about it.

'Why don't you write a complete show in the style of the Nineteen Twenties?' she asked me.

This time I greeted her suggestion not just coolly but with incredulity.

'People would never sit through it,' I protested. 'A sketch or a number in a revue is all right, but a whole show –!'

'I think you're wrong,' she said calmly. 'I'm going to suggest it to the Players.'

I knew there was no point in arguing with her, but I had little confidence that the Players would take any interest. I had worked for them briefly a year or so before, when Ronnie Hill, who was putting on a revue there, asked me to write a number for one of their best-known artists, Joan Sterndale Bennett. I had met the three directors, Don Gemmell, Reginald Woolley, who was also resident designer, and Gervase Farjeon, son of Herbert Farjeon, whose Little Theatre Revues first inspired me to write lyrics. I also knew that Gervase had been to *See You Later* because he was good enough to tell me that my work reminded him of his father's, which was the highest praise I could imagine. But the possibility of the Players putting on a show of mine, let alone the kind of thing Diana had in mind, seemed very remote, and when John and Mary asked me to think about another revue to follow the Watergate pantomime at the beginning of 1952, I forgot about it.

The first thing we were concerned with was to find a new director. John Byron's attack of religious mania had led him into a monastery, so that, if for no other reason, he was out of the running. Chris had been offered the lead in the tour of *Kiss Me, Kate*, so he was unavailable. I had no suggestions to make until one evening Geoffrey Wright asked me to go with him to a new revue at the Unity which had been mostly written by Geoffrey Parsons and his composer partner, Berkeley Fase. It was fast and witty and done with style. I looked at the programme for the name of the Director: it was a woman, the actress whom I had first seen in Herbert Farjeon's Little Revue, Vida Hope.

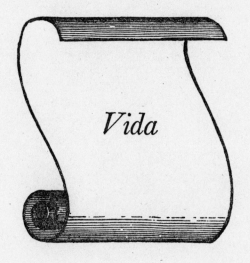

Vida

ON the night of her death, Vida's husband, Derek Twist, asked me if I knew the meaning of her Christian name.
'No. What is it?'
'It's the Spanish for "Life".'
Life. And Hope. That was Vida.

I first met her in the spring of 1951. For some time previously Douglas Cleverdon, the BBC producer, had been trying to launch a revue on the Third Programme (now called Radio 3), which would combine entertainment and culture, rather along the lines of Laurier's original conception of *Tuppence Coloured*. He had roped in various writers and assembled a cast, one of whom was Diana, and she had, as usual, asked me for a number to perform. I gave her a song based on the medieval round, 'Sumer is I-cumen In', which was accepted, and she recorded it. The whole project had various false starts but was finally completed, and everyone concerned in it was invited to Broadcasting House one evening in April to hear the result. Donald Swann was also there, as was his collaborator, Michael Flanders, but apart from them the only person I knew was Diana. We were all seated round what appeared to be a board-room table and, after an introductory speech from Douglas Cleverdon, the recording was played.

After the first few moments it was fairly obvious that the experiment had not succeeded, and for the rest of the programme we just sat in embarrassed silence, forcing ourselves to laugh when we felt it was required, and trying not to catch each other's eyes. When the recording finally came to an end, we all congratulated poor Douglas Cleverdon in as sincere a manner as we could muster and then made an unseemly bee-line for the exit. In the lobby of Broadcasting House Diana caught up with a rather plump woman, with unruly dark hair round a wide, open face, who had smoked incessantly through the proceedings.

'Vida! Vida!' she called. 'I want you to meet Sandy Wilson.'

F

Vida barely looked at me.

'Christ!' she said – or rather 'Chritht!', as she had a pronounced lisp which seemed to issue from the corner of her mouth. 'Let's go and have a drink!'

We went to a pub nearby, and after a port and lemon she cheered up and began to chatter to Diana. Every now and then she would throw back her large head, shake the untidy hair, and utter a raucous giggle. She didn't say very much to me, but I was quite happy to watch and listen as these two lively creatures made fun of the whole programme we had just heard. And always afterwards, even in our direst moments, I knew that when Vida was around sooner or later that laugh would break out and we would be making fun of everything.

Derek Twist was a film director and he first met Vida when she came to see him about a part in his film, *Green Grow the Rushes*, for which he had hoped to get Megs Jenkins:

'She came into the room where I was interviewing lots of artists and we both nearly fell off our chairs. It was one of those things, from the word go.'

Derek was married, but had been separated from his wife for some time. When she finally agreed to divorce him and he asked Vida to marry him, it gave her for the first time in her life the hope of domestic security:

'Vida's father was an old "actor-laddie" and he was in the First World War. I'm not sure if he was gassed or shell-shocked, but anyway, when he came back, he still went on living in the tradition of the old actors: he didn't believe in directors or all this "naturalistic nonsense" that was going on. His idea was to get his lines, walk straight to centre stage, and spout. Consequently he got no work, and had no money at all. If it hadn't been for some charity organisation for the children of officers, Vida wouldn't have had any education at all. They used to live in Clapham and Vida's bedroom was the landing, screened off by the flags of all nations, which they happened to have. On one occasion she was sent back from school with a note saying she was under-nourished. Her silly old father would go out on to Clapham Common with his war-time revolver, after announcing he was going to shoot himself; but he did it so often that in the end no-one believed him. Her mother worked in a corset factory, and if it hadn't been for her they wouldn't have eaten.'

From her childhood Vida had wanted to go into the Theatre, but her parents would not allow her to, and in her early teens she went to work in an office. From there she graduated to copywriting for an advertising

firm and was doing very well at it But she began acting with an
amateur company, and this led to a part in a revue at the Unity Theatre.

'That's where she was spotted by Herbert Farjeon. He said "Stop
all this nonsense of copy-writing. You're an actress, and I'm going to
put you in the Little Revue."'

She continued to work in Revue and Cabaret after the War broke
out, and it was in another Farjeon opus, at the Criterion Theatre, that
Joan Sterndale Bennett first met her:

'I'd been on tour with this revue, *The Best of Farjeon*, and we were
out of Town when the raids started. Then we came back to London, to
the Criterion, and that's where Vida joined us; but we only lasted a
week, because a time bomb fell in Piccadilly. I think it was probably
through me that she first went to the Players in 1941. She was so
different from anybody else – this rather large lady as a little girl, a
nice, funny little girl, singing *Daddy Wouldn't Buy Me a Bow-Wow*.
Then she did a dramatic piece called *Bristol Bett* which was really very
good. I've been asked if I would do it, but I couldn't, because I could
always see Vida doing it. That was when the Players was in Albemarle
Street, and we shared a dressing-room and really got to know each
other very well. We used to have cod rows and shouting matches, and
the members were so close that one could see their startled faces
through the door. In later times we hardly saw each other, but when
we did it was as if we had never been apart, and when she went it was
something I never got over – it left a hole.'

In 1942 they were both in another Farjeon revue, *Light and Shade*,
at the Ambassadors, which lasted for about six weeks, and it was during
rehearsals for this that Geoffrey Wright met Vida for the first time:

'She did a rather elaborate number in the show called *Beasts of Prey*
which Bertie Farjeon had written and which I had set. As Vida sang it,
it came out "Beathts of Prey" and I think people found it rather hard
to take the song seriously.'

I went to the revue with my mother and remember Vida chiefly as a
Rubens nude in a picture frame, with her back to the audience, during
a sketch about an art gallery. But she was also making a reputation as
a straight actress and could be glimpsed from time to time on the
screen, usually in the part of a slut or a factory worker. Towards the
end of the War she was asked to join the Old Vic Company, under the
direction of Laurence Olivier and Ralph Richardson, and it was then
that she struck up her friendship with Diana.

When I approached Vida about directing my second revue at the
Watergate, she was appearing at the Vaudeville in a play about a home
for unmarried mothers called *Women of Twilight*. It was considered

rather sensational for its time, since it mentioned such things as abortion, and she was, as usual, cast as a slut, the sleazy maid-of-all-work in the establishment whose villainous proprietress was played by Barbara Couper:

'I first met Vida at the Embassy Theatre, where we started. She had this incredible ease in obtaining an effect – which of course, as we know, is not at all easy. It means an enormous amount of creative work and study by yourself; but when she did it, it gave this appearance of great ease. I used to think "My God, this woman – how she can act!" And her humour of course was so gorgeous. That terrific laugh she had, a bawdy laugh – marvellous!

'We liked each other from the start, and one day she said to me, "I want to produce plays." And I said, "Oh, you do, do you?", because I always thought it was a terribly difficult and wonderful thing to do. And she said, "Yes, that's what I want to do. And I'd love to produce *you* in something." '

A few years later Vida's wish was fulfilled when Barbara Couper played Mrs Hurstpierpoint for her in my musical version of Ronald Firbank's *Valmouth*.

'As a director she never forced anything on you unless you were absolutely and utterly wrong. She would have thought very deeply about it, but she would never be fussy or despotic, and when you wanted advice, she would just say, "Well, darling, as I see it . . .", and I very rarely knew her to be wrong. She was so generous-minded, but she could be very firm when necessary, and rightly so, because if you have a director who's wiffly-waffly, where are you?'

Being an actress, Vida could readily assume any part in the show, and often did, not always to the liking of whoever was playing it. But for 'Barney' Couper it was enlightening:

'I adored it, because her incredible ease came out. Suddenly you saw it like a beautiful Persian carpet unrolling, with all the patterns in the right place. But she would always end up by saying, "Of course I can't tell you how to do it, darling, but that's the sort of idea", and this was so helpful, because there was kindness and sweetness there – and *humour*. And Vida had beautiful manners – and you don't get much of that nowadays. She would be grateful and thank you, and she would make sure that people were happy.'

Also in the cast of *Women of Twilight* was a waif-like actress with huge eyes and the air of an abandoned sparrow. Her name was Maria Charles, and she was later to play the part of Dulcie in *The Boy Friend*:

'I felt very strongly about Vida, because she had always been absolutely super to me. When we started in *Women of Twilight*, I had a couple of scenes with her, and I realised at once that this was a woman who knew everything about the Theatre, and who *gave* it to you. That was why she was so marvellous as a director. All I wanted to do was to be good for Vida's sake, because nobody could teach me any better. She could make you do things that you didn't know you could do – suddenly, and as long as she was there, you knew it was all right!'

In the New York production of *The Boy Friend* Dulcie was played by Dilys Laye, who responded in the same way to Vida's personality as a director:

'She was wonderful, because she *loved*. It's difficult for a woman to direct, or in fact be an actress, because there's such a fine line between the professional and the woman, and there's still that sex thing. Vida could love you with an all-enveloping warmth, and yet you'd never go over the line with her, you'd never take advantage, because you had such great respect for her.'

Because Vida, despite her great strength, was so essentially feminine, her cast tended to look upon her as a mother, and she invariably referred to them as 'my children' – children who had at times to be scolded as well as cajoled. Harry Naughton worked as choreographer with her on *Valmouth*:

'She was a little confusing at first, because she would scream like a fishwife if she was a bit frustrated. Then she would hug and kiss everyone because they'd done something frightfully well, and of course they were totally bewildered. But somehow, through her screaming and then her individual attention, she got the best out of people, because she kept them on their toes all the time. She used to say, "Doing a show is like giving birth to thirty babies, because each one of the cast has to be mothered and coddled and taken care of. They also have to be beaten, but they especially have to be loved and encouraged." '

She was also, in some ways, a child herself, and when success came to her, she never lost her child-like delight in the pleasures and advantages that it brought with it. One evening I took her to dinner at the Caprice, then the fashionable rendezvous for Theatre people. After looking at the menu for a few moments, she announced with an excited gurgle, 'I'm going to have melon frappé. I *adore* melon frappé, don't you?' Coming from anyone else that would have sounded affected: 'melon frappé' is after all only cold melon. But Vida really meant it.

'One would have walked through fire and water for her.' It is Jimmy Thompson talking: now a successful comedian, early on in his career he played one of the 'boys' in *The Boy Friend*. 'You'd be sitting in the

Players, and long before the door opened the pong of Miss Dior wafted into the theatre, and you knew that Vida was on her way. She was just a scalding hot smashing lady.'

The remarkable thing to me about my association with Vida Hope was how little we needed to discuss the matter in hand. I would write the material, play her the songs, and she would just say, 'Yes, I see,' and get on with the job. It was, in a way, an extension of the relationship I had with Diana, and, like Diana, Vida, in the more responsible capacity of director, seemed to know instinctively, without my needing to explain to her, just what I had in mind when I was writing something. And then, as often as not, she would discover an extra dimension in it which I myself had hardly been aware of. As a result there existed between us a feeling of absolute trust, which is the most valuable quality there can be in any author-director relationship.

She was so obviously gifted that it amazed me when, after the success of *The Boy Friend*, she was not inundated with work, and Derek Twist considered that any man who had had the same success would have been offered far more things than she was.

'But her home life meant a hell of a lot to her. For some years after we had been living together I don't think it ever crossed her mind that I would marry her and we would settle down. But when it did happen, it became tremendously important to her. You see, until Vida and I married she had never had her own bedroom in her life, and the idea of having a bedroom *and* a sitting-room was something so enormous. And that was why she never wanted to go away. When we went abroad, she was restless the whole time because of this terrible feeling that when we got back she might find it was all a dream. Her home and her marriage gave her a new viewpoint on everything. She loved working in the Theatre, but there was a stage beyond which she was not prepared to sacrifice her personal life. It had suddenly all come right.'

The last time Joan Sterndale Bennett saw her, Vida had acquired a new toy, another 'perk' of success:

'I was going into the Players, as she was leaving, and she was terribly excited because she had just bought her little red car. She said, "You've got your car, and I've got mine! Bye-bye, darling – I'm dashing off to meet Derek at London Airport." That was the last I saw of her – driving up Villiers Street.'

The Watergate management agreed to my choice of Vida as director, and we decided to call the new revue *See You Again*. To replace Chris Hewett we had Eric Berry, an accomplished straight actor who had made a hit as the Dame in Julian More's *Puss in Red Riding Breeches*, the Watergate's Christmas panto. The Principal Boy had been Gabrielle Brune, an artist of great elegance and beauty, who had sung Geoffrey Wright's *Transatlantic Lullaby* in the Gate Revue, and she was our new leading lady. The other boys, Charles Ross and Dennis Wood, stayed with us, but instead of Diana we had Joan Sterndale Bennett whom Vida had winkled out of the Players and induced to come over to the Watergate. Towards the end of the run of *See You Later* Yvonne Marsh had been obliged to leave to fulfil a pantomime contract and we had replaced her very successfully with June Whitfield. June was asked to be in *See You Again*, but at the last moment received an offer to go to New York and play Maria Charles' part in *Women of Twilight*. So we called auditions at the rehearsal room in the old Stoll Theatre to find a replacement. Vida decided to ask Maria to attend.

'She said to me one evening after the show, "Do you sing and dance?" and, liar that I am, I said yes. So she said would I come along and audition for her. Auditioning for me meant going along to a theatre and being given a script and reading it, but she muttered something about having to learn a song. Well, *South Pacific* was on at Drury Lane and everybody was Mary Martin – including me – and *Honey Bun* was all the rage. So I learned that.'

At the moment when Maria arrived for her audition we were listening to a girl from the *South Pacific* company, Joyce Blair, giving a Merman-sized rendering of *I've Got the Sun in the Morning*.

'I was standing outside, and I heard this marvellous voice blaring out and I thought, "Well, you'll have to be louder than that!" Then I went in and everyone was there, including you, whom I'd never met. And Vida of course. And someone said, "Have you got any music?" and I said, "No. But I can sing *Honey Bun*, if anybody knows it."'

It happened that I did, and I offered to play for her. But the piano was placed in such a way that I had my back to her and was unable to watch the audition. However what I heard was so extraordinary that I decided there and then that, no matter what anybody else thought, we must have Maria in the show. After the auditions were finished, Vida came over to me.

'Well, I suppose it'll have to be Joyce Blair. John Jones obviously thinks she's very sexy.'

'I don't care,' I said. 'I want Maria.'

We returned to John and Mary, prepared to do battle for our choice, but, to our amazement, John, beaming all over his face, told us that he thought Maria was marvellous and we should take her. We must have both looked rather incredulous because he added anxiously,

'Don't *you* think she's marvellous?'
We assured him immediately that we did, and Maria was cast.

From the first time we worked together onwards Vida and I seemed to have a tacit understanding that, after the first day of rehearsals, I would not reappear unless I was required, either to do some re-writing or to give an opinion on something she was undecided about – which was a rare occurrence. I think that in any case the presence of the author or, even worse, of the composer (and I happened to be both) can be unnerving for the company in the early stages, before they are sure of their words and music, and as we once again had Donald Swann at the piano I had nothing to worry about in that respect. He also, at Vida's suggestion, contributed his very pretty setting of John Betjeman's *Subaltern's Love Song* for Dennis Wood to sing, resplendent in guards officer's uniform, and altogether the show promised to be even better than its predecessor. After puzzling some time over Eric Berry's material, because he was an unfamiliar personality, I suddenly had two ideas in quick succession, which suited him perfectly: the first was a send-up of Godfrey Winn, then at the height of his career as a women's magazine columnist, entitled *Thank God for Me*, and the second was a music-hall number for Hengist, with the opening line, 'Has anybody here seen Horsa? H-O-R-S-A.' Everyone else seemed to be well suited with material, and rehearsals proceeded smoothly.

The only discordant note was struck during the first week by Gabrielle Brune who developed an un-nerving habit of visiting our rival, the Irving Theatre, and returning to the Watergate with rapturous descriptions of the brilliant material Peter Myers had written for their new revue. This unsettled the cast and irritated Vida and me, and the situation was further aggravated when Gaby began comparing her own material unfavourably with what she had heard at the Irving. One day Vida asked me to come down and see her in the lunch break.

'Darling,' she said, 'I simply can't cope with her any longer. I think she'll have to go.'

It was the first time in both our lives that we had been faced with the prospect of sacking somebody, and it made us very unhappy, on top of which we knew quite well that John and Mary adored Gaby after her huge success in the pantomime; but there was nothing for it but to get rid of her. John agreed with us, very reluctantly, and then we were faced with the problem of replacing her. Fortunately Joan Sterndale Bennett was able to take over quite a lot of her comedy material, including a spinster's impassioned declaration of love for Gilbert Harding, a bombastic radio and television personality of the time. Finally one morning John told us that he had come up with a master-stroke: we were going to have another film star! And he led in a peerlessly beautiful blonde who reminded me more than a little of my adored Madeleine Carroll. She turned out to be Patricia Wayne, who had been discovered in a blaze of publicity by Robert Montgomery to be his leading lady in a film called *Your Witness* and had then, along with the film, sunk without trace, after a very damaging interview in the *Sunday Express*. It turned out that so far from wishing to appear as a 'film star' Patricia wanted to resume her own surname of Cutts, put her brief film career very firmly behind her and commence a new one at the Watergate. We were impressed by her bravery more than anything else and Vida agreed to play her. As Pat would be the first to admit, she was no Gabrielle Brune, but she was delightful and decorative and just right for such items as a sketch mocking Jane Russell's adoption of an English orphan and a duet with Dennis Wood celebrating the romance of the moment, Cecil Beaton's passion for Greta Garbo.

This time there were no first night mishaps, and the notices were, as I had hoped, even better than before, and all of them made mention of Vida's direction. Everyone in the cast received complimentary reviews, and Maria was described variously as 'a jolie-laide with wit' (*The Times*), 'a wicked imp of twenty-two' (the *Express*) and a 'bright-eyed chirpy sparrow of a girl' (the *Mail*). Joanie and Eric were considered excellent in everything they did and the *New Statesman* quoted a line from the former's monologue as an Edith Evans-like adjudicator of an amateur production of *Ghosts*: 'Steady with the eye-shadow, Oswald!' The Watergate did capacity business, we were asked to do an excerpt from the show on television, there was even talk of a transfer to a public theatre. Everyone was happy, but the one person who was unable to enjoy it was Vida.

'There was that awful performance of *Women of Twilight*,' as Barney Couper describes it. 'It was a matinée and there were Vida and I acting away quite normally, when suddenly Vida was all over the place. She was crying, she was trembling, she was swaying on her feet. I thought, "My God, what's happened to her?", and probably some unkind people supposed she was tight. She just managed to get through, and then she collapsed on the floor and had to be carried to her dressing-room. It was the start of a terrible go of rheumatic fever.'

By the time Vida had fully recovered, *See You Again* had finished its run, and I was wondering what to do next. John and Mary were uncertain of their future at the Watergate, and there was talk of another management taking over. I was asked by H. M. Tennents to contribute Diana's Gaiety Girl number to the Globe Revue, which had already opened and was enjoying a moderate success. When I went to see it, the song had been cut in half and ruined by inept direction. A few days later I was informed that it had been removed. As it was my sole source of income at the moment, the outlook was depressing. I looked up the number of Gabbitas Thring in the directory once again. Before I could dial it, the 'phone rang:

'Is that Sandy Wilson? This is Gervase Farjeon speaking. Can you come down to the Players tomorrow at lunch-time? We want to discuss something with you.'

Back
to the
Nineteen
Twenties

THE Players' Theatre, as I mentioned earlier, was now situated in the old Forum Cinema, a long tunnel-like auditorium built into one of the arches of Hungerford Bridge which carried the Southern Railway across the River. It was still the home of the Late Joys, the Victorian music-hall entertainment which I had seen with Frank and Virginia Vernon in the summer before the War, but it now had a membership running into several thousands and a world-wide reputation. Attached to the theatre is a restaurant, usually referred to as the Supper Room, and it was here that I met Gervase Farjeon and Reggie Woolley, who designs all the Players' shows. Gervase has a charmingly shy manner which borders at times on incoherence, while Reggie combines a faintly mandarin appearance with a misleadingly destructive sense of humour. Between them they made it a little difficult to understand what we were meeting to discuss, but one thing seemed clear: unlikely as it had sounded at the time, Diana's suggestion had been taken up and I was being asked to write something for the Players. Later I learned that Lisa, now thankfully re-anglicised as Lisa Lee, had also put in a word for me. 'You know Sandy Wilson's work,' she had said to Reggie one evening after the Joys. 'Well, he's terribly down on his uppers. Couldn't you do something of his here?'

The Joys are presented in three acts, or what are facetiously referred to by the Chairman as 'halves', and I was being asked to write an entertainment to fill the second and third half, which would be preceded by a first half of Joys. The type of entertainment seemed to be left to my choice, and, remembering Diana's promptings, I very hesitantly suggested doing something in the period of the Nineteen Twenties.

Reggie and Gervase looked at each other and then back at me.

'That would be fine,' said Gervase.

And so it was agreed. They suggested that the whole show should run about an hour, and it would be put on, probably in the autumn, for a season of three weeks. I was to be paid twenty-five pounds now and

I COULD BE HAPPY

twenty-five more on completion. I left the Players feeling elated, but at the same time rather bewildered. Now that I had actually been asked to write a whole show in my favourite period, what form should it take? Should it have a story? And if so, what should the story be about? The restricted length was a handicap, as was the fact that it had to be in two acts instead of three, which was the custom in the Twenties. I also realised that I would be expected to write parts for some of the Players' regular performers who would be appearing in the first act of Joys. Hattie Jacques was one of the most popular at the time: I would have to provide a large rôle for her. Also it would be politic to write a part for Gervase Farjeon's wife, Violetta, who specialised in roguish French chansons.

All these considerations passed through my mind as I travelled back to Crossfield Road. But in the next few days only two things emerged. First, the title: as a mark of respect to Rodgers and Hart, whose songs had meant so much to me and whose musical, *The Girl Friend*, had one of the best scores of the period, I would call my show *The Boy Friend*. I had no idea who the Boy Friend was going to be or what story I was going to build round him, but at the moment that didn't seem to matter. I also decided that the heroine would be called Polly. There was no significance or reason behind the choice of name; it just seemed to sound right.

When I began to think about a plot, I found myself returning irresistibly to that moment in the Faust musical which Geoffrey and I had never written: a villa in the South of France, French windows with a view of the sea, and in rush a crowd of girls carrying hat boxes. But under the circumstances a *crowd* of girls would be too extravagant; I had better make it just three. What should *their* names be? Dulcie, Fay and Letty. No, Letty didn't sound right. I remembered a line from the Valentino sketch at the Watergate, about 'Madcap Maisie'. I changed Letty to Maisie.

But what were the girls doing in that villa – I decided to call it the Villa Caprice, perhaps as a gesture towards Jack Waller's ill-fated musical – and why were they carrying hat-boxes? Well, if the villa were in Nice, it could be Carnival time and they could be bringing their costumes back from the costumier's, and that would provide a Finale: the Carnival Ball. But why were they in Nice in the first place? The presence of Hattie Jacques loomed up again: Hattie as a head mistress in charge of a finishing school where Dulcie, Fay and Maisie – and of course Polly – were pupils. Now where would Violetta fit in? I remembered a production of *No, No, Nanette* which Diana and I had seen some months previously at the People's Palace in Mile End Road:

Nanette, so Jack Waller had told me, was always on somewhere, and this was a touring version, done of course in modern dress, but in every other respect unchanged from its first appearance in 1925. That too began with an influx of girls, which interrupts a 'phone conversation by Pauline, the cook. Instead of a cook I would have a maid, a chic French maid, and her name would naturally be Hortense. The girls would come rushing on, chattering and giggling, and Hortense would call them to order and remind them that they were supposed to be Perfect Young Ladies.

I now had a setting and the title of an opening number. The next thing to do was to bring on my heroine, Polly. Through the French windows of course, and, because tennis always seemed to figure somewhere in the shows of the 1920s, one of the girls could announce her arrival by saying, 'Oh, look! Here comes Polly across the tennis court!' Polly who? Something simple, but at the same time genteel. Polly Browne. Browne with an e. 'Here comes Polly Browne across the tennis court!'

Now that my heroine was on, what was to be done with her? I remembered the title of one of Noël Coward's songs, *Poor Little Rich Girl*. Polly would be rich, and of course very pretty, but she would also be unhappy. Why? Because, unlike all the other girls, she had no boy friend. Her father – her widowed father – was so afraid of fortune-hunters that he would not let a man near her. So poor Polly, in order to keep her end up, has to invent a Boy Friend. And of course she sings about him. There was my title number.

Under the heading *The Boy Friend* I began to write a list of characters: Hortense, a French maid, Maisie, Dulcie, Fay and Polly Browne, pupils at the Villa Caprice, a Finishing School. Whose Finishing School? I imagined Hattie, severe but stylish, probably in black and white. What should I call her? One of the first things I saw when I met my sister Helen in Paris in 1937 was an advertisement: DUBO, DUBON, DUBONNET. Madame Dubonnet. She would be strict but warm-hearted, and she would guess at Polly's deception – how? A letter from the imaginary Boy Friend with a Nice post-mark when it is supposed to have come from Paris. Polly admits all, and Mme Dubonnet promises to have a word with her father, who happens to be visiting the school that day. I knew that luck and coincidence featured strongly in the plots of the 1920s, and I intended to make full use of them.

At this point I felt it was high time to introduce some dancing, and of course the dance would have to be the Charleston. Who was to perform it? Not Polly: it would be too undignified. Why not Madcap Maisie, who, in contrast to Polly, has plenty of boy friends. One of them could just happen to look in at the Villa Caprice – again through the French windows – to remind Maisie of her promise to dance with him at the Ball. As he was a dancer, perhaps he'd better be an American, the sort of American who might have appealed to Lorelei Lee – 'that terribly rich and handsome American who's staying at the Negresco' – and because so many Americans seemed to have Dutch surnames, I called him Van Husen – Bobby Van Husen. Talk about the Ball could lead quite naturally into a dance: 'Won't you Charleston with me?'

Now what else was to be done with Madame Dubonnet? If Hattie were to play her, she couldn't just be a school mistress. Why not make her an old flame of Polly's father, Percival Browne? They could have met in Paris during the Great War – on Armistice Night, in Maxim's. Memories of Irving Berlin waltzes came back to me – *Always, Remember, All Alone.* When Mr Browne comes to visit Polly, Mme Dubonnet recognises him, but he, being a rather pompous, puritanical character, pretends not to know her. So naturally she reminds him of the waltz the band was playing that night they met, and it happens to refer to the present situation: *Fancy Forgetting.*

I already had almost enough material for the first half of the show, and I still had not introduced the title character. The Boy Friend. I recalled that heroes and heroines of old musical comedies often displayed an urge to disguise themselves as servants – maids, butlers, page-boys. A picture of Bobby Howes as Buttons flitted across my mind: the Boy Friend could be a messenger boy who arrives at the Villa Caprice with Polly's costume for the Carnival Ball. They fall in love at first sight and Polly, greatly daring, asks him to come to the Ball with her. And they sing a love song of course – what about I had at the moment no notion. But now that I had brought on the Boy Friend, what should I call him? There seemed to be only one possible name, a name that to me was somehow both heroic and endearing: Tony.

But of course Tony was not really a messenger boy at all, and now I had to think about the next act. I had already decided that, in spite of the specifications I had been given, I would make it a three-act show, but compress the second and third acts into one 'half'. Recalling *Nanette* again, I felt it was only common sense, since we were in Nice, for the second act to take place on the beach or 'Sur le Plage' (I mistook the gender then and never corrected it), thus enabling the girls to appear in the bathing costumes of the period. After an opening chorus, Polly and Tony could have a rendezvous and sing another song, probably about their future together. Romantic couples in the 1920s always seemed to be yearning for the simple life, *A Room with a View,*

Tea for Two. I pencilled in the title *We Want to Live in a Mews*, decided that it sounded too grand for nowadays, and eventually changed it to *A Room in* – where? – 'room' and 'bloom' would make an internal rhyme, which was characteristic of 1920s lyrics – *A Room in Bloomsbury*.

Most of the remainder of Act Two could be taken up with beach-side frolics: Mme Dubonnet in a bathing costume (how killing Hattie would look!) trying to induce Percy Browne to come for a swim and singing the Blues, and Maisie doing a number with the Boys, because I had recently seen a touring revival of Jerome Kern's *Sally*, and the high-spot of the second act was her solo with a male chorus. All that remained was to devise a tragic climax, in which Polly and Tony would be parted. Why? If he was not really a messenger boy, who was he? Well, the son of a Lord of course. And the Lord – with his Lady – could just happen to be in Nice, on holiday. All they know is that Tony has disappeared – from Oxford – and when they spy him on the Plage, they call a gendarme to follow him. Polly thinks Tony is a thief – just another fortune-hunter. Curtain.

I could now complete my cast list: Madame Dubonnet, Bobby Van Husen, Percival Browne, Tony and Lord and Lady – what? There was a road, somewhere near where we had lived in my childhood, which seemed to be full of grand and forbidding mansions: Brockhurst Road. Lord and Lady Brockhurst.

Now for Act Three, the Carnival Ball. All that was required to be done was to reunite Polly and Tony and bring about a happy ending. But there had better be a couple more songs in the process. In *Sally* the elderly comedian had had a number with a young girl. If I made Lord Brockhurst (whom I had decided to call Hubert) an incorrigible flirt, with a battle-axe wife (called Hilda), he could have a number with – let's see – Dulcie? Something about not being too old to have a fling. And Dulcie could respond with the essential 1920s refrain, 'Boop-a-doop!' After that Polly could appear at the Ball, looking delightful, but absolutely miserable, in her fancy-dress costume – as Columbine? Mme Dubonnet could take the opportunity of singing to her, to buoy up her spirits: *Lonely Little Columbine*. No, that didn't sound very mellifluous. One of Noël Coward's early successes was *Parisian Pierrot*. If Tony were Pierrot, then Polly could be Pierrette, and Mme Dubonnet could sing *Poor Little Pierrette*. The song has barely finished when Pierrot appears, masked. After a suitable preamble Polly recognises him, as do Lord and Lady Brockhurst. Explanations, reconciliations, proposals – including Bobby's to Maisie: 'Now how about that Charleston?' Grand Finale, with balloons and streamers.

*   *   *

The Players had asked me to submit a synopsis, and, now that I had completed the plot, I duly wrote one out and arranged to meet all three directors in the Supper Room the following evening. We sat down together, with a glass of wine, and I proceeded to read them the story of *The Boy Friend*. As it progressed, it seemed to sound sillier and sillier. How could anyone in his right mind wish to put on a show with so trivial a plot about such thin, unconvincing characters? What had appeared amusing to me at home when I was imagining it now sounded ridiculous and artificial. I faltered on towards the dénouement, quite convinced that they would either tell me to go away and try again or, more probably, turn the whole thing down flat.

'. . . All ends happily with a Charleston.'

I closed my note-book and took a gulp of wine. Don, Gervase and Reggie exchanged glances. It was always a puzzle wondering which of them would be the first to speak. In this case it was Reggie.

'Yes . . .' he said slowly, 'we think it sounds fine.'

There was a certain slight lack of conviction in his voice, but they all seemed to be smiling. Sheer kindness probably, I thought to myself, but now it was up to me to go away and write the thing. The first twenty-five pounds changed hands and I returned to my note-book:

'Act One. The Drawing-Room of the Villa Caprice, Mme Dubonnet's Finishing School on the outskirts of Nice. At the back, French Windows . . .'

It would probably sound more convincing, and certainly more traditional, if I described the creation of *The Boy Friend* as a tortured struggle, with numerous false starts, constant re-writes, agonised re-appraisals and all the other problems attendant on a primum opus. The truth is that it was by far the easiest thing I have ever done. From the moment I began it the whole show seemed to come tumbling out of me as if it had been waiting for years to be born – which, I suppose, it had. I wrote the script through from beginning to end in a matter of days, and, with the alteration of the odd word here and there, that is how it finally appeared. There was only one major interpolation in the course of writing and this came about, naturally enough, from a suggestion by Diana. It goes without saying that both the Players and I had assumed that she would take the lead, and I asked her up to Crossfield Road one morning to hear what I had written so far. She was delighted with it, but felt the plot needed just one further complication.

'As Polly is so afraid of fortune-hunters, shouldn't she also pretend to be just a working girl – a secretary? Yes, that's it – Madame Dubonnet's secretary!'

I agreed. Tony could imagine that she is one of the wealthy pupils, with expensive tastes, but Polly would hastily deny it.

'She could say, "Oh no, I'm quite content with simple things",' suggested Diana.

'And then Tony could say, "How ripping! So am I." '

We clutched each other and giggled helplessly.

'Do you know, Sandy,' said Diana, after we had recovered, 'I have a feeling about this show. I think it's going to be the most colossal hit – all over the world.'

It was the first time that it had ever occurred to me that *The Boy Friend* would be seen anywhere after its three weeks' run at the Players. I decided this was another of Diana's unlikely fancies, and went back to work.

The lyrics and music followed the script with almost equal ease: all the songs which had been running round my memory ever since I heard them on the gramophone in my infancy seemed to coalesce into the essentials of a new score, which echoed them but never, I tried to ensure, imitated them. Within a few weeks I had completed every line and note of the show. The only thing that caused me any trouble was Polly and Tony's first number. Unlike most of the others, it had to be sentimental and convincingly so, and yet at the same time in a dated idiom. *I Want to be Happy* was the big hit in *Nanette* and I felt the word 'happy' should appear in the title. The fact that the two of them had only just met did not really signify, because this was a musical comedy; but I felt that, all the same, there should be something tentative about their first song together. 'I *Could* be Happy' perhaps, instead of 'I Want to be Happy'. *I Could be Happy with you* – but only, of course, – 'if you could be happy with me.' Trite enough, but at the same time true. I sat down at the piano and began to set the complete line. All too easily it lent itself to what I felt then and continue to feel is a musical phrase of pure saccharine. I overcame my distaste and completed the song. It still makes me wince a little, but perhaps that too is correct and in keeping.

Now that the score was finished, I rang the Players and asked them if they would like to hear it. As Reggie Woolley described it to me much later:

'Gervase and I came out to your basement flat, and you played the songs over to us, and we said "Yes." But at that moment we didn't realise what we were listening to. So, quite frankly, Gervase and I said to each other, "Well, we've commissioned it; we'd better do it." It was as absurd as that.'

But they told me that it would be impossible to put it on that year;

it would have to wait until after the pantomime, which meant the spring of 1953. This was a blow, as I had no other work lined up in the meanwhile; but I received my second payment of twenty-five pounds and decided I would just have to be patient.

When I look back at that time, I am really not quite sure how I managed to live. During the summer Hugh had got me a part-time job in the antique shop in Notting Hill Gate where he was working, which consisted of sitting in a cellar and attaching coded price labels to the merchandise. It was meant as a helpful gesture, but I detested both the work and the atmosphere of dusty chicanery in which the antique business is transacted, and that experience, coupled with the fact that our flat seemed to be furnished entirely with crockery that was too cracked or worthless to sell in the shop, gave me a life-long antipathy towards junk of any description. In any case Hugh had been offered a job by another dealer which would take him to New York for six months of the year and I could no longer rely on his help.

Of course I continued writing numbers for revue and cabaret, and one of these brought about an unexpected windfall. A few months previously, at a party given in a mews off Baker Street by someone with the unlikely, but appropriate, name of Montagu Joyston-Bechel, I had been introduced to a girl with black hair, in a strapless evening dress, called Fenella Feldman. She was immediately attractive, but her most compelling feature was her mouth, which she seemed able to manoeuvre from moment to moment into the most unlikely shapes and expressions, and from which emerged a voice with the texture of crumpled damask. She told me that she was an amateur actress but was intending to turn professional shortly, and also that she was interested in doing revue. I promised to keep in touch and let her know if I heard of a suitable opening.

One of the people who approached me about cabaret material was Estelle Brody, a star of silent films, who had made a come-back in the theatre playing the fairy in the Watergate pantomime, *Puss in Red Riding Breeches*. I wrote her what I thought was rather a good woman's number called *You Know the Man*, but she turned it down and shortly afterwards retired again. I forgot about the song until a few weeks later when Fenella rang me. She had got her first professional cabaret engagement and needed some material immediately. Did I have anything? I asked her to come round and I played her *You Know the Man*. As soon as I had finished, she said, without hesitation:

'I want to buy that. How much is it?'

I was completely taken by surprise and had not the least idea what to ask. I couldn't refer her to my agent, because I still hadn't got one.

I took a deep breath and said, 'Twenty-five pounds.'

'All right,' she said, without flinching. 'But I can't pay it to you all at once, because I don't have the money. But I'll give you five pounds whenever I can, until I've paid it off. Will that do?'

And she did precisely that. During the next few months, usually at a moment when I was wondering how to pay the telephone bill or next week's rent, Fenella would appear with five pounds. It is probably years since she last sang *You Know the Man*, but, as far as I am concerned, it is hers for life.

When Hugh left for New York in the autumn, I decided that I would have to find someone to share the flat with me, partly because I needed help with the expenses, but mostly because I hated living alone. I began by advertising locally, but the results were either uncongenial or faintly alarming, and in the end I asked a friend of mine, Jon Rose, who was living in a minute bed-sitter in Bayswater, to move in. Jon was Australian and a singer, one of a growing colony of Australian immigrants in London who had come to Europe seeking the culture and fulfilment which their own country seemed to deny them. He was volatile and articulate – at times excessively so – and possessed of a personality with either charmed people into the ground or sent them screaming out of the room. We had a close and stormy friendship which lasted for several years, and no account of the following events would be complete or honest if Jon's part in them were omitted.

At the time of his moving in Jon's singing career seemed to have come temporarily to a halt and he was making a precarious living at other occupations such as modelling for art students and working on the night shift in Walls' Ice Cream factory, a useful, if unpleasant, job for out-of-work actors at that time. Christmas usually produced a wider selection of employment, and that year Jon worked in a children's book factory at what was called 'popping-up', a process whereby certain pages of the book when opened would become a standing model of a scene from a fairy tale. His opposite number on the popping-up section was a belligerent and discontented actor called Kenneth Haigh.

On Saturdays we always went to Portobello Road with a large shopping bag and bought cut-price tinned food from the market stalls, which supplied our dinners for the week. Angela and Celia were in the same financial state, but we somehow managed to entertain each other, our meals consisting usually of soup made from Heinz Baby food and tinned steak pudding, and theirs of spaghetti and corn flakes. One day, when the spring seemed particularly far off and I had nothing at all to occupy me, Jon suggested that he and I should get together a cabaret act: I would play the piano and do the 'point' numbers, he would take care of the vocal numbers, and we would occasionally combine for duets. I had a good deal of unused material, including one ballad which Jon was very keen to sing and which I had written some time before, when Jack Hylton, the impresario, had sent out an SOS to song-writers to supply an extra number for Irving Berlin's musical, *Call Me Madam*, because Anton Walbrook, who was playing the male lead, considered that his share of the score failed to match the leading lady's. I wrote a song called *Learning to Speak your Language* and was asked to bring it along to the Adelphi Theatre, where *Call Me Madam* was rehearsing, and play it to Mr Walbrook. He seemed quite taken with it, but began to tell me about a number he had sung in a film called *La Ronde*.

'Perhaps you know it,' he said. 'It goes something like this –' and he hummed a tune which we all of us at the time knew only too well. My song was in quite a different tempo and bore no resemblance at all, but Jack Hylton leant close to my other ear and in his well-known Yorkshire accent whispered:

'Play it as a waltz, lad, play it as a waltz!'

I obediently did so, and Mr Walbrook's face lit up. But he eventually decided that the inclusion of another composer's song in an Irving Berlin show might put him in wrong with the critics, and *Learning to Speak your Language* was returned to me.

When we had assembled an act and rehearsed it sufficiently, we contacted every agent we could think of and informed them that we were available. The response was unenthusiastic, to say the least. One gentleman offered us, by way of an audition, an unpaid engagement at a Rotarian dinner at the Hyde Park Hotel. We arrived at the appointed hour, wearing the cut-price dinner jackets which we had bought in Shaftesbury Avenue, and sat in an ante-room while the diners indulged in a series of toasts, speeches and ceremonials which dragged on long after the time we were supposed to go on. When at last we were summoned to appear, our audience was so befuddled with alcohol that none of them knew or cared what we were singing about. We received no further bookings. We were also taken up briefly by Hermione's friend, Elma Warren, and her husband and partner, Lord Ulick Brown, who procured us an afternoon engagement at the Café de Paris, providing part of the cabaret for a group of débutantes and their escorts called the Monkey Club, a depressing occasion made even more so by the fact that neither Elma nor Ulick felt it was worth their while to be present.

One day I had a letter from a Cambridge undergraduate asking me if I could suggest someone for the cabaret at his college ball. After a quick consultation with Jon, I wrote back by return and suggested ourselves. The reply was fairly enthusiastic but said that the committee felt a girl should be included in the act. I rang Fenella, who had now changed her surname to Fielding, and asked her round to meet the gentleman from Cambridge. We were offered the job, but he told us there would be no fee, only our fare to Cambridge and our accommodation at the University Arms. This was a blow, but at least it was work, and we accepted.

Fenella rather craftily arrived in Cambridge by car, driven by her then fiancé, Tony Shaffer, who at the time was nothing to do with the Theatre but who later wrote the vastly successful *Sleuth*. This meant that she would at least make the rail fare out of it, although she nearly gummed up the entire works by claiming for Tony's accommodation as well as her own; but I think we were all feeling a bit ratty, since our audience had shown a marked preference for the undergraduate entertainers who had preceded us. Our way out of the college lay through the kitchens, where all the supplies for the buffet were in evidence, and Jon slipped a bottle of gin under his overcoat, muttering 'That's the least they can give us.' We made it last for two months.

The only person of note to hear our original cabaret act was Hermione whom I asked for criticism and advice. She invited us round to Kinnerton Street for tea and, on our arrival, said that she hoped we wouldn't mind if a friend of hers called Nancy Spain listened to the act with her, as she was there to work with Hermione on a magazine article. We were introduced to a lady in corduroy trousers who said very little and remained very much in the background while Hermione gave her opinion of our performance.

'And now, my dears,' she announced, 'I've got to go out to some beastly theatre. But you two stay here with Nancy and help yourself to drinks.'

We did as we were told, and after the first drink Miss Spain became more communicative and began to reveal the mischievous vitality which I am sure everyone who knew her still misses.

'Are you working on anything else?' she asked me.

'Yes, I am actually,' I said.

'Go on. Play some of it,' Jon prompted me. I was not particularly keen to since I had already had a disconcerting experience a little while before when we invited a group of friends, including Heather and Michael, to the flat one evening to listen to the score of *The Boy Friend*. They sat through the entire thing in baffled silence and responded at the end with a little polite applause. However Nancy seemed so genuinely interested that it would appear churlish to refuse. So, after a brief explanation of what the show was about, I launched into the chorus of the title number.

Nancy reacted as if the clouds had opened above her to reveal a vision of Paradise.

'My God!' she cried, collapsing across the piano lid. 'That is the most brilliant parody I have ever heard in my life. More! More!'

I went on to play as much as I could manage from memory, and her enthusiasm continued to mount.

'When's it coming on? I want to see it! I want to see it at once!'

I told her that the Players hoped to do it some time in the spring.

'In the spring? But they should be doing it now! It's bloody marvellous!'

Dear Nancy – she was, as it were, the first member of the Public to hear *The Boy Friend*, and her encouragement, as always, cheered me up no end. I left Hermione's that evening with renewed faith in the show, and a few days later I rang Diana to have another chat to her about it.

When she answered the 'phone, there was obviously something wrong. She sounded as if she had been crying.

'What's the matter, Diana?'

'Andy's ill. I think –' her voice faltered, 'I think he's – dying.'

She could obviously say nothing more, and I mumbled something about hoping he would get better and rang off. Diana had married Andy soon after he came down from Oxford and they were now living in a flat in, of all places, Bloomsbury. A day or two later I heard what had happened. Diana had gone away for the week-end to her family in Wales and, on returning home, discovered Andy lying unconscious in the gas-filled kitchen. He had been rushed to hospital, but it was too late. He left a note completely exonerating Diana of any blame for his suicide; he wanted desperately to do something creative, but the only work he could get was translation from the Polish. The feeling of failure and frustration became too much for him and he decided to take his life. Diana asked me to come to the cremation at Putney Vale Cemetery.

By Christmas she had more or less recovered, and the Players asked her to appear in the pantomime, *Babes in the Wood*. Jon and I went to see it, and she seemed to be her old self again, looking delightful and singing beautifully as the principal Good Little Fairy-Bird, with Violetta as her recalcitrant French side-kick. One of her greatest successes at the Players had been with the song, *The Boy I Love is up in the Gallery*. We knew she would never sing it again.

After the pantomime closed, the Players told me they would definitely put on *The Boy Friend* in mid-April, and Don Gemmell, who normally produced the Joys, asked me if I had any ideas about a director. Without hesitation I suggested Vida. He did not appear immediately enthusiastic.

'You don't think,' he said, 'she's a bit modern?'

I was rather puzzled by his objection, but I discovered later that he had already made up his mind that *The Boy Friend* must be produced with total authenticity in keeping with the tradition of the Players, where fidelity to period had always been considered of paramount importance. However I explained to him the strength of the rapport between Vida and myself, and he agreed to ask her if she was interested. After reading the script, Vida arranged to come and hear the score, and she described the occasion herself in a preface to the published edition of *The Boy Friend*:

'I went round to Sandy's flat one bleak February morning to . . . hear the music. He looked pale, seemed over-anxious that I should like it, and, as always when he is nervous, played his own composition shockingly. But never mind; I saw, I heard, and I was conquered. Over coffee I declared my love for *The Boy Friend*, told Sandy I wanted to do it as a serious reproduction of a period and not as a burlesque, and from that moment on his whole demeanour brightened . . .'

Our designer would of course be Reggie Woolley, and I knew that the show would be in safe hands there, because he was a wizard at making the most of the tiny stage at the Players and his period sense was faultless. As choreographer Vida chose an old friend of hers, John Heawood, the dancer whom I had first seen in Laurier's *Tuppence Coloured* at Bournemouth:

'I was in a Jack Hylton show at the Adelphi, when Vida approached me about it. She said "Darling, I have this lovely piece which Sandy has written for Diana Maddox. I'll get you a copy of the script and you see what you think about it." So in the interval at the Adelphi I read it – it was very brief – and I called her the next day and said, "I think it probably is absolutely delicious, dear. The thing I'm slightly worried about is that there don't appear to be any *jokes*." And she said to me, very firmly, "Darling, you get on with the lovely dancing and leave the jokes to me." '

I had no notion of Johnnie's ability as a choreographer, but it turned out that his childhood background in Canada made him ideal for the job:

'I was old enough to have been trained by my father in all the new dance steps, from 1924 to about 1934. I literally learned to Charleston in 1926, and I became a professional dancer when I was nine, in 1929. My first song on the living stage was *Singing in the Rain*. So I really was prepared. All those years I had been getting ready for *The Boy Friend.*'

In addition he had the same kind of rapport as I had with Vida:

'Vida had the gift of words, and she appreciated it in other people. She was wooed by the text of *The Boy Friend* and that is why she was right as a director. She admired me as a stylist and that is why she felt I would be right to work with her. We did a great deal of chatting, but only about the mise-en-scène, never about the script. We had such understanding of each other that she seemed to have either thought of something just before me or to agree with me the instant after. I don't know that I've ever had the same sort of relationship with anyone since.'

At the same time Vida was proceeding with the vital business of casting, and now I had my first experience of her uncanny instinct for choosing the right person for a part, even if at first sight the choice might seem unwise or unsuitable. Because of her varied experience as an actress she knew the work of all sorts of people whom I had scarcely seen or heard of, and this was invaluable. As I have mentioned, I had mentally cast Hattie Jacques in the part of Madame Dubonnet, but as the show developed and it became clearer that it was going to be treated with a greater degree of seriousness and sincerity than I had ever imagined, I began to wonder if Hattie might not seem out of place. But when Vida told me her own choice, it seemed equally strange: Joan Sterndale Bennett. I had always thought of Joan as a character comedienne who could illuminate the humdrum and the ordinary with a satirical glitter, but never as a purveyor of glamour or chic. However Vida was adamant that she would be sensational in the part, and Joan herself, after some hesitation, said that she would like to do it:

'I had already heard something about it, because Maddox (Diana) was always fooling around in the dressing-room at the Players, and after the show one night she put a bit of ribbon round her head and did her hair in ear-phones, and said, "Wouldn't it be fun to do a Twenties show? I know Sandy Wilson. I'll ask him to write us something." Then somebody gave me a script to read – a few pieces of rice paper! – and I rushed through it and said, "Oh, yes . . .". I was surprised to be asked, and then when I knew you wanted Hattie, I had a terrible inferiority complex about it. But Vida said she wanted me.'

Hortense, the maid, would of course be Violetta and, because the part only appeared in the first act, it was decided that she would also, despite her essential French-ness, play Lady Brockhurst:

'I think it was a question of money – the Players wanted to save a salary! Also I thought what great fun it would be, and I persuaded

Vida that I could say "Hubert!" correctly, because I could always put on English character voices. Then Vida told me that I looked like an actress called Edna Best and I would have a wig done in her hair-style.'

Lord Brockhurst was to be Geoffrey Hibbert, an actor whose work I knew, having seen him in revue at the Irving Theatre as well as in films where he had first appeared as a boy. As Percival Browne, Polly's father, Vida cast Dennis Wood, who was familiar to me from the Watergate, but for the part of the American, Bobby Van Husen, her choice again seemed strange: Larry Drew, whom I remembered as a dancer in Hermione's revues at the Ambassadors. It happened because he knew Ann Wakefield, a regular performer at the Players, who had been cast as Maisie:

'I'd been at the Players, but I had left and gone to the Windmill (a theatre that presented a non-stop variety show, featuring nude, but static, chorus girls). Annie rang me up and said, "They're doing this 1920s show. Why don't you get in touch with them?" So I rang Reggie and he said, "Yes. Come along and meet Vida Hope." I went about three days later and met her in the Supper Room, and she said, "You're very pretty, darling. I think I like you. Can you Charleston?" I said "Yes." "Can you do an American accent? Right, you're in." '

But in fact Larry had not been Vida's first choice for the part. A few years previously she had been in a revue at the Duke of York's Theatre called *Four, Five, Six*, starring Bobby Howes and Binnie Hale. Also in the cast was a dancer by the name of Anthony Hayes:

'I was what was known in those days as "the juvenile lead" and Vida and I became great friends during the run, but I didn't see much of her after it closed. Then I came home one night at about eleven o'clock and the 'phone was ringing. It was Vida: "Oh, thank God I've got you. I've been trying to get you all day" – it was a Sunday, and I'd been away for the week-end – "I'm producing a show at the Players called *The Boy Friend*, and I think you would be ideal in it, because of your sense of period. There's a very good part for the boy who does the Charleston." I read the script and thought what a delightful piece it was, but I said to Vida, "I could never play Bobby, because my American accent is atrocious, it would never pass muster." She said, "Are you certain about that?", and I said, "Absolutely, Vida." So she was rather upset and said, "I must have you in the show, because your dancing is so ideal. I can only think that you could play the juvenile lead, but that's not a dancing part and the girl playing opposite you, Diana Maddox, isn't a dancer. But come and meet Reggie Woolley anyway." So I did, and Reggie thought I would be fine, and I said, "All right, let's take it from there, and let's see if we can fit in some dancing." '

And so Tony Hayes was cast as Tony Brockhurst. We needed two other boys to play the parts of Alphonse and Marcel, who had to do little more than partner the girls in the dance numbers. John Rutland, whom Vida knew from his appearances at the Players, was cast as Alphonse, and Malcolm Goddard, a dancer who had worked with Johnnie Heawood in the film version of *Where's Charley?*, was asked to audition for Marcel:

'It came to my turn to dance, and Johnnie asked me to do the Charleston. I'd never learnt it; I'd only seen Joan Crawford do it on the movies. But I threw myself into it, and it was only years later that I realised why Johnnie laughed so much: I did all the lady's actions and none of the men's. But I did end up with the job.'

Vida asked Maria to play the part of Dulcie, and it was decided to hold auditions for the part of Fay, because we needed a good all-round singer and dancer to add weight to the numbers. I happened to be there and of the several girls we saw the most gifted seemed to be a very pretty brunette called Anne Rogers. I asked her if she remembered how she first heard about *The Boy Friend*:

'Yes, I do actually. I saw in the *Stage* that James Shirvell was putting out yet another tour of *No, No, Nanette* and I thought I would like to play Nanette. But I got a letter back saying it was already cast, would I like to audition for an understudy? I was feeling very down, and I thought I might as well go along; but that morning, when I got up, I had the most ghastly laryngitis and couldn't utter a word. But I got all done up in me best hat and me best coat, and went off looking like something out of the Salvation Army – I'd only just come down from the North, you see. When I got there, they were lined up four deep on the stairs, but I thought, "I've got a special letter from James Shirvell." So I pushed my way up the stairs saying, "Excuse me! Excuse me!" and knocked on the door and went in. There were four people sitting there and I didn't know any of them, but one of them was Daphne Scorer. They asked me, "What are you going to sing?" and I whispered, "I've come to tell you I *can't* sing." So then they couldn't wait to get rid of me. But three days later Daphne rang and said, "They're putting on a little show at the Players, and we thought you might be right for it."'

For her audition Anne sang *Rag-time Cowboy Joe* and tap-danced, and then, when Vida asked for another song, she stunned us with a virtuoso rendering of the operatic aria, *Oh, My Beloved Father*.

'Thank you very much, Miss Rogers,' said Vida at the end of it. 'That was beautiful.'

'I could do much better,' replied Anne, 'but I've just had laryngitis.'

She was offered the part of Fay, but her agent insisted that she must have a number in the show. So, rather reluctantly, Vida took Dulcie's number with Lord Brockhurst, *It's Never too Late to Fall in Love*, away from Maria and assigned it to Fay. As Ann Wakefield was dark and Maria was a red-head Vida wanted Fay to be a blonde; so Anne Rogers agreed to wear a wig. The cast was now complete except for one small non-speaking role, the gendarme summoned by Lord and Lady Brockhurst to pursue Tony at the end of the second act. As we were obliged to play Act Two and Act Three together in the third 'half', it was decided to cover the scene-change by a brief Mark Sennett-style ballet of the Chase. For some reason which I never discovered we cast a girl, Claudine Goodfellow, who assumed a moustache for the part and who, in Johnnie Heawood's words, 'was known as the Colonel, because she was such a good chap. She later married a splendid rich gentleman and had many, many children.'

On a Monday morning towards the end of March the company assembled at the Players for the read-through and to hear the songs. At the end of it Vida made a short speech. She told them very firmly that there was no intention of doing a burlesque or a send-up of the Nineteen Twenties, and any tendency in that direction would be fiercely discouraged: she instructed them to think of *The Boy Friend* not as a re-hash of something old but as a beautiful, new show which they were rehearsing for the first time in 1926. It was to be 'witty, elegant, charming and tender' and if she caught anyone overplaying or making fun of it, she would 'smack their bottoms'. 'They listened politely,' as she puts it, 'then went away and had their lunch, when no doubt they expounded on the lunacy of their producer and their crack-brained author.' But in fact what she said had made a deep impression on everybody. 'After that morning,' Tony Hayes remembers, 'I think we all felt a bit inspired. We'd all seen the Twenties guyed before, but this had to be sincere. The moment there was any sign of overdoing it, Vida clamped down immediately. She really loved the show, and she made all of us love it.'

As at the Watergate, I stayed away from rehearsals unless Vida specifically asked for me, but whenever I looked in I was struck by the atmosphere of dedicated enthusiasm that pervaded the Players. Everyone appeared to be utterly absorbed in the show and intent on helping it and contributing to it wherever possible. Joan Sterndale Bennett discovered some bound volumes of Play Pictorials from the Twenties, and these gave Vida ideas for groupings and postures and were eagerly pored over by the whole cast. Tony Hayes had been dancing in musicals ever since the age of eighteen, when he had learned routines from Lulu's teacher, Buddy Bradley, and he suggested ideas and steps for Johnnie Heawood, and in the case of *I Could be Happy with You* devised an intricate tap dance for himself, during which Diana was to stand on a pouffe centre stage, whistling the tune, thus overcoming the problem of her shortcomings as a dancer. Violetta produced a beautiful white dress, given to her by a friend of her mother's, for Mme Dubonnet to wear in the first act, and Mary Bennett, Joan's step-mother, who was in charge of the Players' wardrobe, unearthed a cache of 1920s shoes among a collection of old clothes donated by a member. Diana discovered the whereabouts of Santos Casani, who had been responsible for introducing the Charleston to London, and she and I went along to his flat one evening and were instructed in the correct steps. 'We all contributed something,' Larry Drew recalls, 'with no qualms at all. We'd say, "Wouldn't it be fun if –", because there was such exuberance about the show at that time.' Within the first few days of rehearsal everyone connected with *The Boy Friend* seemed to have fallen in love with it, just as Vida had done, and to have become every bit as concerned that it should be a true and sincere evocation of the period. The fact that it was being produced at the Players, where authenticity was the order of the day, contributed immeasurably and I doubt whether the same dedication could have existed anywhere else.

Artistically then, everything was going even better than I had hoped, but from the start of rehearsals we were bedevilled by illness, beginning with an outbreak of German measles which progressed steadily through the company, but, as Vida put it, 'we manfully worked on – as we all had it, there was no question of infecting others.' Then in the first week Geoffrey Hibbert told her that he had been offered a part in a television play. 'Of course you must do it, darling,' Vida replied. 'This is only going on for three weeks.' The salary at the Players at that time was eight pounds a week, and it was understood that if anyone received a better offer they were at liberty to leave. What was more, the play was going to be repeated, which, in the days before tele-recording, meant two live performances and a double fee. So Geoffrey departed.

John Rutland was away from rehearsals, in bed with a septic throat: 'My doctor was seeing me one morning, when the 'phone rang, and it was Vida. She said, "Would you be interested in playing Lord Brockhurst?" I said, "Yes, very, very much!" and I rang off and said to my doctor, "I've got a bigger part!" He was so concerned that he sat down and read it through with me. I'd never played an old man before, but he said, "I think you can do it." '

With John moving up into the part of Lord Brockhurst, it became necessary to find another boy to play the part of Alphonse. Johnnie Heawood remembered Jimmy Thompson, who had shared his dressing-room during the run of *Oranges and Lemons*:

'I was doing an unbelievably tatty revue down at Deptford in a theatre that had been a cinema and was falling to bits. I had a call from Vida, whom I actually didn't know, and she said, "Oh, Jimmy darling, we're doing this thing at the Players, and we want you to be in it." And I said, "Is it *The Boy Friend*? Because if so, I can't possibly be in it. I've booked for the first night and I'm looking forward to seeing it so much." In any case Johnnie had told me that there was all this fantastic 1920s dancing in it, and I'm not exactly dainty nipper-feet.'

But Vida replied that she was trying out another boy the next day, and if he was no good, she wanted Jimmy. The following evening she rang again: 'You've got to come tomorrow, darling. You're in it.'

'I turned up the next morning, and she sat me down in one of those canvas chairs at the Players, and she said, "All right, boys and girls. Off you go!" And they went right through the show without my part. Then she said, "There you are, dear. Now you've seen it, you can do it." '

John and Jimmy had barely settled in when Dennis Wood asked to be released as he had been offered a part in a revue with Cicely Court-neidge. There was barely a week till the opening night, but Vida felt obliged to let him go. As a replacement she chose Fred Stone who had often appeared in the Joys:

'I knew Vida very well, and Joanie Sterndale Bennett too of course, as I had done numbers there with her. Vida came to me and said, "Could you do this, Freddy?" and I said "Yes" and took the script home with me and learned the part that night. I came in the next day and she said, "How would you have done it in the Twenties?" So I played it exactly as Cyril Ritchard did with Madge Elliott in *Love Lies* and *This is Love*.'

Freddy's presence in the show turned out to be another invaluable asset, since his experience went back to the Twenties themselves and he had actually been in the chorus of the kind of show we were trying to recreate.

'Vida was tremendously sensible. She realised that I had worked at that time and she made no bones about using everything I suggested. My first entrance was my own, and so was my exit. And that business of saying, "Good heavens! This is impossible –" then sitting on the pouffe – "most awkward", that was all mine. But, being an actor, I did far too much. So Vida would cut it down. She would let me do it all for about twenty-four hours, and then she said, "Now, darling, we'll tidy this up." '

One day towards the end of the rehearsal period Vida rang me:

'Darling, I'd like you to come down this afternoon. There's something I want you to see.'

When I arrived at the Players they were running through Act Two. At the climax, when Polly is convinced that Tony is really a thief, she goes into a short soliloquy followed by a reprise of *I Could be Happy with You*, sung on the verge of tears. As Diana did so, the whole company slowly turned round and faced upstage, as if in respect for the privacy of Polly's grief. Then, at the end of the line, "Skies may not always be blue –", she broke down and herself turned upstage, whereupon the company spun round to face the audience and sang fortissimo, 'But one thing is clear as can be . . .'. As they completed the refrain Diana turned front, threw down Tony's hat in a dramatic gesture of rejection and ran off-stage. The company turned to observe her flight and, as they sang the last note, all raised their upstage arms in the direction of her exit. Slow curtain.

The effect was extraordinary. It was funny, in its exploitation of outdated stage conventions, and almost absurd, and yet at one and the same time it was inexpressibly moving. Vida had accomplished what I thought was the impossible: simultaneous laughter and tears. For the first time I began to think that perhaps *The Boy Friend* might turn out to be something beyond a private joke. Among the company there was also a growing feeling that they were involved in more than a temporary divertissement to give the Players' members a change from Victoriana, and Joan Sterndale Bennett for one, who had suffered misgivings to begin with, particularly about her own rôle and how to play it, was now convinced that something remarkable was in the making:

'The thing that gave it to me was when we all sat down one afternoon and watched Larry and Annie Wakefield doing the Charleston. It was so marvellous that we all stood up and cheered, and I thought, "If the rest of us can come up to that, we've got a good show." But I don't think any of us had any idea that it would go any further.'

Besides, as it stood, the show was too short to be presented on its own. 'We all thought it was worthy of a bigger audience,' Tony Hayes told me. 'I said to Vida, "The only problem is that it will have to be lengthened," and she said, "Oh, I'm sure Sandy will be able to do that. We'll cross that bridge when we come to it. Let's get this one on." '

*   *   *

For Sandy —
with all our love

Angela &
Celia

Above: Lee and Helda, the first
Nineteen Twenties Act

Left: The Rudolph Valentino
sketch in *See You Later* at the
Watergate Theatre, 1951. *L.
to R.:* Christopher Hewett,
Diana Maddox, Dennis Wood

Wilson and Rose in cabaret, 1952

Photo credit: Ian Colquhoun

Joannie Rees and Vida Hope

As dress rehearsals drew near, the cast began to concern themselves over their clothes and make-up with the same absorption that they had shown over acquiring the performing style of the period. For the girls this meant a radical change, not only of their outward appearance, but of their basic shape. At that time, in 1953, Fashion represented the antithesis of the 1920s: waists were at the natural level and were small, often pinched in by corselettes, to emphasise the fullness of the skirt, which was worn to calf-length or below and frequently given extra bulk by two or three layers of starched petticoats; bosoms were likewise emphasised, if necessary with the aid of 'falsies', and a reinforced brassière was an essential component of every girl's wardrobe. Although shorter hair-styles, such as the so-called 'urchin' cut, were beginning to appear, hair in general was worn long and dressed in buns, chignons, fringes and 'pony-tails'. Make-up was, in fashion terms, 'naturalistic': full red or crimson mouths, eyebrows darkened and thickened, and eyes 'doe-shaped' in imitation of the current ideal, Audrey Hepburn. Shoes tended to be low-heeled or even flat, to complement what was referred to as the 'ballerina' skirt, and the over-all effect was of girlish, slightly picture-book, femininity.

All this had to be jettisoned. The first problem was how to lock flat, and this was solved by Diana in consultation with Reggie Woolley. She discovered that Marks and Spencer sold cheap elasticated 'roll-ons' which, when worn back to front, did the trick perfectly. 'Very painful for someone like me,' Violetta remembers. 'I was one of the largest ladies in the show, and I was always having to push my bosom down.' Nylon stockings, now in universal use, were unknown in the Twenties, and genuine silk stockings had to be found. Skirts were worn at knee-cap level and dance movements would reveal the girls' underwear, so that too had to be accurate: perusal of fashion magazines revealed that the correct wear was directoire knickers, a modified type of bloomer caught by elastic a little way above the knee. Hair was of course short, and all the girls, with the exception of Anne Rogers who was wearing a wig, went to the hair-dresser and uncomplainingly had a shingle. 'There was nothing strange about it,' Maria Charles felt. 'We were *all* going to have our hair done, so we did – just as we *all* flattened our busts.' Over the matter of make-up Vida consulted her mother who had been on the stage at the time: such short-cuts as pan-cake had not been invented, and everyone had to use grease-paint. Mouths were shaped into a 'cupid's bow', and eyebrows were soaped out and then drawn in a perfect arch. False eye-lashes were also unheard of; instead hot-black was used, its application involving a complicated process of melting it in a spoon over a candle flame, dipping a pin-head in the liquid and dropping it in beads onto the eyelashes. Natural-coloured hands and arms were considered unladylike and this was remedied by washing on a preparation called 'wet-white'. The dresses were belted round the hips and had the straight up-and-down 'chemise' look, while the cloche-shaped hats had to be pulled down to just above eyebrow level to conceal all the hair, an essential point which Fred Stone took it upon himself to check carefully every night of the run.

'When the first dress rehearsal started,' Malcolm Goddard remembers, 'and the girls came on in their hair-cuts and short dresses, we all fell about. We thought they looked hysterical. The next day we laughed a little. But on the third day our eyes had got used to them and we thought they looked jolly pretty.'

Things were rather easier for the boys, their only problem being the difference in make-up, but it was tackled with equal thoroughness. Jimmy Thompson had an old book on the subject, published by Samuel French: 'There was a diagram of a juvenile face of the period, with little red dots at the corners of the eyes and a touch of rouge on the chin and the ear-lobes, and arched eyebrows. Malcolm and I dedicated ourselves to creating this look without making it appear artificial in any way. Then we pomaded our hair – in 1953 it was still the right length – so that when you combed it, all the lines could be seen.'

'In those days at the Players,' Joan Sterndale Bennett remarked, 'we were *used* to doing things absolutely right. To hell with whether a hair-style suited you or not, as long as it was correct. I always said, "If you wear the correct hair-style, you can look marvellous; if you wear what you think suits you, you'll look stupid." '

The opening night was to be Tuesday, April the Fourteenth, and on the previous Sunday Vida had scheduled two dress rehearsals, one in the afternoon, to be followed by a photo-call, and the second in the evening, after the cast had had their supper. Jon and I arrived at the Players that evening to find the stage set for the last act – the Terrasse of the Café Pataplon – and the company posing for the last few photographs. It looked enchanting: Reggie had constructed the set almost entirely of white trellis work, covered with climbing roses, and across it hung a line of Chinese lanterns. The boys and girls were all in fancy dress, and Joan wore a beautiful beaded gown, surmounted by a fan-shaped head-dress of ostrich feathers. It was a perfect picture and in the middle of it were Tony and Diana, as Pierrot and Pierrette, at the moment when Polly is about to rediscover her Boy Friend.

As I looked at Diana, I couldn't help feeling that although she is supposed to appear forlorn at this point, she was rather over-doing it, and when I remarked on it to Jon, he agreed. It seems that Vida had also noticed that something was wrong and, turning to Johnnie Heawood, said, 'What's the *matter* with that child? I've never heard of anyone looking pale under their make-up, except in novels, but she does.' The photo-call ended and the company broke for supper. Jon and I went out to the pub for a drink, and when we came back we were told that Diana had collapsed on a sofa at the side of the stage and was now lying on the car-park attendant's bed in a room above the box-office. She maintained that she was ill and could not go on, and had asked for her doctor to be called. At first I was incredulous, but when I went up to see Diana, she just turned her head away and refused to talk to me. I tried cajoling her, to no effect, and then I got angry, but the result was the same. She simply said she was ill and had to see her doctor. Gervase had been trying to contact him, but there was no reply:

'I said to Diana, "I can't get hold of him. Do you really need a doctor?" and she said "Yes." So I said the only thing I could do was to get on to Charing Cross Hospital. I dialled 999 and they sent an ambulance. It came down Villiers Street, ringing its bell, and these two chaps came in and said, "Now, what's wrong with you?" There she was, lying in full 1920s make-up and costume, and they put her on a stretcher and took her down to the ambulance, and off she went to hospital.'

It seems unlikely that I shall ever know exactly what caused Diana's collapse, but, by piecing together the story from the other people concerned, I feel it must have been more psychological than physical. To me it came as a complete surprise, but to others, such as Violetta, who had often worked with her before, it was not altogether unexpected:

'We all thought it might happen – knowing Diana. Sometimes, during the Joys, she would suddenly go off and have a sort of faint – it was a proper one, but brought on by herself. It was her form of nerves, her way of getting out of the present.'

Joan Sterndale Bennett also knew her well and was very fond of her: 'I adored Diana. People did. But you could wring her bloody neck at times. When people saw it happen, they couldn't believe their eyes. Diana would suddenly sink to the floor, and you'd say, "Oh, get up, Diana!" But she wouldn't; she just lay there, gasping.'

Tony Hayes first had an inkling that something was wrong during rehearsals. Like most of the cast, Diana had been ill and was at home: 'She 'phoned me and asked me if I'd care to come round and go over one of our scenes together. She said, "I'll be in bed, but it doesn't matter." When I arrived, I could see that she wasn't happy, but I couldn't think why. But there was no quarrel; we got on very well together. Then, when it came to the dress rehearsal and she tried on the clothes, I could see that she was miserable.'

The costumes seem to have been a principal cause of Diana's débâcle. She had insisted to Reggie Woolley that she should make her own at home:

'She had ideas about what she should wear, and she also designed her second-act dress. But it was really fatal, because Diana was very curvacious, which was the wrong shape for the period. She was a neurotic lady, but she was also very intelligent, and she could have realised, when she saw herself in the costumes, that the show wasn't right for her.'

Whatever the reason, Diana had gone, and we were faced with an opening night in forty-eight hours' time, and no leading lady. To me her loss seemed a death-blow: without the one person whose original conception it was, who had helped in its creation and for whom it had been written, how could *The Boy Friend* survive? But as far as the Players were concerned, the show had somehow to go on: the first night had been announced, the Press had been invited, the tickets had been sold and it was too late to postpone it. Meanwhile the company had finished their supper and were sitting in the auditorium, waiting to be told what was going to happen. Vida went into consultation with Johnnie Heawood:

' "Well, darling," she said to me, "what do you think we ought to do? Should we put the understudy on?" And I said, "I didn't know we had one." "Well, we don't," said Vida, "but I've asked that lovely girl who's doing *Never Too Late*, you know –" "Yes, I know," I said. "Anne Rogers. And she's not doing it very well." "Well, I asked her to watch the part of Polly." '

It seems that Vida must also have had apprehensions, because one day, when Diana was away ill, she had suddenly said, 'Who else can sing? Who can hit a top C?' Anne Rogers was the only one to put her hand up, and Vida said, 'I suppose we had better have someone to cover', and that was all. Now Anne was asked to play the part for the second dress rehearsal. Vida and Johnnie settled down to watch the performance:

'She said to me, "If the child is any good, we'll play her on Tuesday." "But how can we do that?" I said, "You must be mad." "Well, we'll see." Then the dress rehearsal began. Annie Rogers made her entrance, carrying the book, and read her first line, "Hello, everyone. Where have you been?" She looked at the script and had to hold it towards the light to read the print. Then she came down to the footlights and said, in her lovely Cheshire accent, "Miss 'Ope, would you mind very mooch if I put the book down?" And Vida, who was slightly deaf, said to me, "What did she say?" I told her. "Oh, what a darling girl!" she said. "Tell her yes." And Annie went through the entire production, word, note and step perfect. At the end of it Vida turned to me and said, "There you are, darling. We have our leading lady." '

Anne herself was unaware that any decision had been taken:

'After the rehearsal Tony Hayes carried my case to Charing Cross Station, to see me off on the underground. He asked me if I would like to play the part of Polly, and I said, "Not 'arf!" I think he already knew that I would have to go on.'

Now that Anne was going to be Polly, Maria could take over Fay's number, *It's Never Too Late*, and from then on it became Dulcie's, as had always been intended. But it was necessary to find someone at once to take on the part of Fay, someone who would work hard and learn fast, as there was a dress rehearsal with an invited audience scheduled for the following evening. Johnnie remembered a girl who had been with him in the film of *Where's Charley?* He described her as 'one of those gutsy little peaches one meets from Australia', and her name was Joan Gadsdon:

'I was living in Redcliffe Gardens, and I happened to be home that night. I hadn't got a job and I didn't know what to do. Then the 'phone rang, and Heawood said, "Gadsdon! Can you get down to the Players at nine o'clock in the morning? Dress fittings from nine to ten, then you learn the show from ten until five o'clock, and you go on at seven." And I said to him, "When in doubt, say yes." Then I felt sick in my stomach and I thought, "Can I do it? Well, I'll have to." '

By coincidence she had heard about the show from Jon, and had come to see me about having an audition, but we were already cast. When I went to the Players the next day, I was amazed to find that she was now in the company. Under Johnnie's guidance and with the help of the other boys and girls, she worked through all the dance routines in the Supper Room, while Vida took Anne through her part on the stage. By five o'clock they were both ready to go on. The invited audience that night was meagre and unresponsive, but the show at least went smoothly. Watching Anne as Polly, I began to feel that the loss of Diana was perhaps not a total disaster. Joan Gadsdon, as Johnnie had predicted, was the perfect choice for Fay: she looked exquisitely pretty, and appeared to have learned every move and step. There was nothing to stop us opening, as planned, on Tuesday night.

But first, because there was a play opening at the Garrick Theatre on the same evening, we had to give a performance for the Press on

Tuesday afternoon. Critics are a cold audience under the best of circumstances, and the time of day was no help; but we had asked a few friends in as well, and the laughs we were hoping for began to come. The company felt encouraged, and although I had no idea what the critics' reaction might be, I knew that, given a responsive audience, the show could work. Only Anne was upset. After *Poor Little Pierrette* she had come off the stage in tears, because they had laughed. In her innocence she had never realised that it was meant to be funny, and even when she began to be aware of the humour in her part, she still retained the appearance of wide-eyed sincerity which helped immeasurably towards the success of the show. By a strange irony Diana's departure had not destroyed *The Boy Friend* but improved it. As Jimmy Thompson put it, many years later:

'She need never have any regrets about doing what she did, because she wasn't right for the part. However truthfully Diana played it, it didn't come out as true as everyone else did. She was brilliant, but she lacked heart.'

There was one more small, but important, mishap before the curtain finally rose on the opening night. By some extraordinary oversight the character of Tony Brockhurst, the Boy Friend of the title, and the name of Tony Hayes who was playing him had been entirely omitted from the programme, and the Players' front-of-house staff spent the last few moments before the audience arrived frantically writing it in.

When my mother, Jon and I took our seats, I was delighted to find that Hermione was sitting just in front of me: her presence nearby seemed like a talisman. As arranged, there was a half hour of Joys to start the evening, followed by an interval, after which came *The Boy Friend*. Stan Edwards, our pianist, and the drummer, Eric Giles, took their places. As the lights began to dim, Hermione turned round to me and whispered, 'Good luck, darling. It's going to be marvellous.' The overture struck up, and we were away.

Any first night is a momentous occasion to those involved in it, and the first night of a hit is an experience so astounding that descriptions of it are bound to appear overwrought and exaggerated. So I will only say that from the moment the curtain rose – or rather parted – on Reggie Woolley's set of the Villa Caprice, with Violetta perched on the edge of the sofa, telephone receiver in one hand and feather duster held aloft in the other, the audience adored *The Boy Friend*. And the more the show progressed, the more they adored it. Now that I was seeing it under ideal conditions, I could really appreciate the miracle that Vida and Johnnie had conjured out of such apparently slight material: every effect, every touch of business, every move, every posture was not only correct and true but also worked to the advantage of the script and songs. Everything was complementary and cumulative, so that when one point had been made another followed it in perfect rhythm, so that a chuckle became a laugh, became a guffaw, and ended in applause. Not content with clapping at the end of numbers, the audience would applaud in the middle, at a particularly happy piece of choreography or a felicitous grouping. But it was not only the laughter and applause that delighted me; it was the affection which greeted *The Boy Friend*, the same affection with which we had all created it.

Not surprisingly, the company responded in full measure and gave the performances of a life-time, and moment after moment remains with me, like snapshots from a particularly precious family album. The girls, Maisie, Dulcie and Fay, making their first entrance, carrying their dress boxes and chattering like starlings – not *to* each other but just into space. The heralding of Polly's appearance: the girls facing downstage, one arm raised in a vapid wave, saying 'Hello, Polly!' directly to the audience, as the leading lady enters through the French windows *behind* them (and Anne Rogers, such was the effect of this entrance, received a leading lady's round of applause). The final bars of the *Boy Friend* number, as the boys and girls linked arms to high-kick in slow tempo, then turned into line and, each clutching his neighbour's posterior, came to rest on the final note, faces horizontal, grinning firmly out front. Joan Sterndale Bennett singing off-stage, after Maisie's 'Cave, girls! Here comes Madame Dubonnet!', then sweeping on through the double doors, still singing, and holding a large bouquet, to centre stage to receive her applause, then marching swiftly to a jardinière by the proscenium and depositing the whole bunch (specially wired into a picturesque arrangement) into a base, as she admonishes the girls, 'Tiens, tiens, mes enfants! This is no way to be'ave!' Joan confounded my doubts at her casting by bestowing on the character all the sparkle and chic that I could have wished for, and in her opening scene with Polly she had some delicious business with a rose, sniffing it quizzically and finally tucking it into her waist-band, a touch that immediately informed the audience that the severe school mistress was also a beguiling woman of the world. Maisie, played to the limit of provocative daffiness by Ann Wakefield, in the lead-up to the Charleston, responding to Bobby's avowal that she is the only girl he wants to dance with at the Ball by skipping clear across the stage on a silvery laugh to land at the opposite corner in a coy attitude: 'I don't believe it!' Madame Dubonnet reappearing through the French windows – and one of Vida's cleverest touches was that a character rarely came on from the logical entrance but from the one that would give the best effect – and starting back, hand to mouth, with a strangulated gasp on recognising Polly's father as her old flame, and then, in the dance that follows their song, *Fancy Forgetting*, revolving in slow waltz tempo at a vertiginous angle, her neck supported by Percy's outstretched hand. And Tony and Polly in their entire scene together, in which the tender idiocy of their first encounter was both funny and touching: Tony, on first seeing Polly's face, letting go by one hand of the dress-box and falling down a step from the French windows into a classic attitude of thunderstruck adoration, to be topped a few moments later when he hands the box to Polly and, as love strikes them paralysed, it drops to the floor between them.

Vida was always particularly pleased with the first act of *The Boy Friend*, and felt that both in writing and production it was a model of construction. But everything else on that first night seemed to work too, only one number, Maisie's song and dance with the boys, *Safety in Numbers*, failing to get its share of applause. *A Room in Bloomsbury* was enhanced by an encore in which Polly and Tony create the home of their dreams in mime, an idea which had suddenly come to Vida out of the blue and which, she later discovered from Binnie Hale, was standard procedure in 1925. The end of Act Two, which had so impressed me in rehearsal, had exactly the effect intended: the audience didn't know whether to laugh or cry. Maria had dreaded causing a laugh on one line: when Polly confides that Tony, whom she now suspects of being a thief, has stolen something from her (i.e. her heart), Dulcie has to say, 'Not your gold bangle?' The audience did laugh, and Maria was mortified, but Vida comforted her afterwards by saying, 'It was the right *kind* of laugh. It was a laugh of love.' Maria and John Rutland triumphed with *It's Never too Late to Fall in Love*, even though, having only learned it the day before, she dried on one line. And Vida had devised for her a kind of multiple exit whereby she ran towards the wings, tittering skittishly, returned to blow a kiss to Lord Brockhurst and then repeated the whole process twice before finally disappearing with a dotty little skip and jump. Musically I think *Poor Little Pierrette* received the most ingenious treatment in the score. I had written it as a straight solo for Mme Dubonnet and left it at that, but Vida had decided to make it not only a duet with Polly but the occasion for a vocal battle between the two actresses, complete with descants, harmonies and counter-melodies, and culminating in a top note held as the two of them circled the stage in opposite directions to reach the footlights in time for the final phrase, arms and voices rising higher and higher to a ringing crescendo; while all this went on, Fred Stone posed upstage, majestically in profile against the backcloth and puffing a large cigar. Even the curtains were part of the pattern, and included a 'picture call' with all the company frozen in appropriate attitudes, and a principals' call with the leads apparently taken by surprise in the act of congratulating each other. My last impression of that night is Hermione, shooting to her feet in front of me and shouting 'Bravo! Bravo!'

Both Vida and I were called on stage, and Jimmy Thompson remembers to this day, word for word, the speech she made:

' "We're so glad you liked our little offering. It's been a labour of love which we've taken to our hearts and hugged there. It's been a surprising production, because all along the line we kept losing people. Only nine days ago Jimmy Thompson joined the cast –" and I got a smattering of applause. "Then we lost our Percy, and Fred Stone valiantly took over at four days' notice –" That got a jolly round. "And then of course came the dress rehearsal when we lost our leading lady, and Joan Gadsdon walked into this theatre yesterday morning, knowing nothing of the production, and tonight has given a faultless performance –", a tremendous roar of approval, "– and little Maria Charles took over the duet with Lord Brockhurst," and of course after the way that number had gone the house practically fell in. "Then –", beautiful actress that she was, with a little sob in her throat, "true to the tradition of the Twenties –" I always remember that alliteration – "the understudy, Anne Rogers, stepped into the lead, to become a star overnight." And that was it: they all went mad. I remember the curtains went back and forth so many times, we were all crying – except I think Anne herself kept remarkably cool! Then afterwards we went into the Supper Room and we all got plastered. I remember riding up Regent Street at about three in the morning, with the windows of the taxi-cab down, yelling to all the passers-by, "If you haven't seen *The Boy Friend*, you haven't lived!" We didn't have to read the notices. We just knew.'

The Road
to the
West End

THE critics did in fact, with one exception, wholeheartedly echo the response of the first-night audience. The *Telegraph* said that *The Boy Friend* was 'quite brilliantly evocative of the age of cloche hats and the Charleston. The lyrics, dances and tunes are a very clever imitation and – most important – the whole affair is vastly enjoyable for its own sake without reference to its antecedents.' The *Guardian* considered that Vida's production was 'something of a satirical masterpiece', and went on to say, 'Not everyone cares for burlesque, but when it is well done, as here, it can give great pleasure. That is something rather rare in the Theatre just now, and worth offering to a wider audience . . . One would like to see at least the first act of *The Boy Friend* incorporated in some Coronation revue.' The *Daily Mail*, commenting that the 1920s were now fair game for satire, said that I had not 'missed a trick or a high kick' and the *Standard* complimented me on preserving 'the butterfly lyricism of the period as well as the cloche hats and the Charleston.' All the company were praised, but Anne Rogers was singled out for special mention, partly because of her dramatic elevation into the lead at the last moment, but mostly because she was, quite simply, perfect in the part of Polly. The *Observer* judged her 'delightful as the simpering Goldilocks wooed by a page-boy who is (would you believe it?) the heir to millions', the *News of the World* called her 'a marvel of a minx' and another critic referred to her as 'everything our uncles meant by Boat Race Night', while the *News Chronicle* published a photograph of her beside an article headed 'New Star for the West End?' in which she was described as 'a major discovery'. The whole thing was neatly summed up in the *Spectator*: 'For the middle-aged this is a bitter-sweet show; for the under-forties it ought to be the funniest thing in town. The Players should do two things: extend the run beyond three weeks, and buy some pink ruched garters for the girls.' Only *The Times* found *The Boy Friend* quite lacking in charm and condemned it as 'an Aunt Sally of simple construction which a clever company has no difficulty in knocking down again and again.'

As a result the show was a sell-out for every night of its run at the Players. People even sat on the concrete steps at the side of the stage. Don Gemmell, who had begun to realise the potentialities of the show early on, was now convinced that it could reach a wider public:

'I used to go in at night and see it – watching the stage at first. Then I started watching the audience, and I noticed that the youngsters were enjoying themselves enormously and on the way out were rushing to the box-office and saying, "I must get two for next Thursday. I want my aunt to see this." And the over-forties were also having a good time, but shedding tears. Suddenly one realised, "This has got everybody!" '

Gervase Farjeon was equally convinced:

'Immediately after the Press show I felt it had a future, and then after the first night it was confirmed. All the first nights of *The Boy Friend* were fantastic, but that shook us more than any. Right from the start we began asking West End managements to come and see it, and I think most of them came. There wasn't any great difficulty in getting them there, but their reaction was that it was too short for one thing and then there were no stars.'

One management said that they might be interested if the girls' costumes were brought up to date and we put in a comedian: Norman Wisdom was suggested. I was finally convinced myself by now that *The Boy Friend* could be a success commercially, and as the run progressed and the audiences' enthusiasm remained unabated, it was disheartening to realise that, unless a West End management made us some kind of offer, the show would probably disappear for good when it closed at the Players. Night after night Jon and I would go down to the theatre and watch most of it from the back of the auditorium with Don. Then afterwards I would be asked to meet another prospective management in the Supper Room, where I would be complimented, while Don, Reggie or Gervase dispensed drinks, but always told at the end that, however good the show may be, it was not for the general public. Some managements came more than once, and it must have been plain to them that the people who crammed the Players every evening were hardly a specialised audience, but their answer remained the same: *The Boy Friend* was delightful, charming, witty and brilliant, but they didn't want it.

Only one man did want it, and he was the man who, of all people, deserved to get it. One evening towards the end of the run I was told that Jack Waller was in the audience and wanted to see me after the show. I met him at the bar at the back of the auditorium rather than in the crowded Supper Room: he looked older and a little frail, but his voice had the same incisive rasp and he was bubbling with enthusiasm.

'It's a great show, boy, a great show! All it needs is to be lengthened. Tell yer wot I'll do: I'll give yer the original script of *Nanette* as a guide. Use anything yer like and make it a full-length show, and then I'll do it.'

I had once, during the production of *Caprice*, suggested to Jack that if he revived *No, No, Nanette* in period costume, with an all-star cast, it would be a hit all over again. He pooh-poohed the idea – luckily for me, since, if he had taken it up, *The Boy Friend* would never have needed to be written. But now here he was, all ready to go, and quite certain that under his aegis we could recreate the glories of the era he knew so well. I introduced him to the Players' management in the hope that he might provide the show's salvation. Gervase felt as I did that he was at any rate the one who deserved it:

'He was marvellous and he was the only one who really was enthusiastic. He used to strut about the office, with his fingers in his waistcoat, as if he was the manager of the theatre and owned the show and everything. But we made a lot of inquiries among West End theatre owners, and he wasn't in very good favour. It was sad in a way because he was the one person who knew what it was all about.'

And so Jack's offer had to be reluctantly turned down. There was no possibility of extending the run at the Players, because by now most of the leads had accepted engagements in 'Summer Season', a four or five months' run in concert-party or variety at sea-side and holiday resorts in various parts of the country. As a final gesture the Players decided to give a special show on the Sunday after we closed, to which as many stars and Theatre people as possible would be invited. The audience was full of famous names, but for me the most important presence was that of Noël Coward, the man whom I had admired above all others and whom I had once so fervently hoped to emulate. To have him in the audience was, for me, a triumph in itself, and when I met him afterwards and heard him praise my work, I was totally tongue-tied with awe and excitement. Later I was told that, as he came up the aisle after the show, he turned to his companion and said, 'There you are, you see. We *were* right: we had *charm*!'

After the performance everyone retired, as usual, to the Supper Room and I found myself sitting next to a young woman with jet-black hair and eyes the colour of aquamarine who introduced herself to me as Vida's agent, Joan – or Joannie, as she preferred to be called – Rees. She reminded me that we had met once before, briefly, outside the Irving Theatre, where another client of hers, Lorraine Clewes, had been performing a song of mine in a revue. She then went on to tell me with great emphasis that in *The Boy Friend* I had written a master-piece which would without doubt be a success of international propor-tions and make me world-famous. Since it seemed, at that moment, unlikely that *The Boy Friend* would ever be seen again anywhere, I felt that she was being a little optimistic, but I thanked her as sincerely as I could. It was then, when she asked me to repeat what I said, that I realised she was, like Vida, rather deaf.

It had been a memorable evening but, in some ways, a sad one owing to the uncertainty of *The Boy Friend*'s future. The cast dispersed to their various destinations after being assured by the Players that they would be contacted as soon as there was any news of a West End production. They all, without exception, said that they wanted to be in it again and would keep themselves free for the autumn. We all said goodbye to each other and, although all the evidence pointed to the contrary, I think we still felt that somehow or other this would not be the last of *The Boy Friend*.

As a result of my success at the Players, I had been approached by the Watergate to write a new musical for the autumn. John and Mary had left, and it had been taken over by a completely new management headed by Emmy Tillett of the concert agency, Ibbs and Tillett, and she had asked Norman Marshall, who had made such a success of the Gate Theatre in the Thirties, to be her artistic director. The whole enterprise was obviously being conducted on a much grander scale than previously, as was apparent from the new scheme of decoration: striped wall-papers and candelabra abounded, and the atmosphere was no longer a mixture of the chic and the bohemian but one of poshness and Culture. However I was very glad of the offer, which gave me carte blanche in my choice of subject, and as a change from *The Boy Friend* I felt I should do something modern and topical. A current issue, which had even been debated in Parliament, was the import of American 'horror comics' and the effect these magazines were having on small children, which had been the subject of a book called *Seduction of the Innocent*. I decided that this could make the basis of a musical and took, as the pivot of the plot, the fate of an old-fashioned boys' magazine, like *The Ranger* or *The Magnet*, which I called *The Buccaneer*. To the distress of its owner, Mrs Barraclough, the widow of the founder, it is threatened with extinction by a take-over bid from an unscrupulous American Tycoon, called Mr Maximus, who wants to turn it into a horror-comic. She confides in the ancient Mr Donkin, who has been writing *The Buccaneer*'s leading serial, The Adventures of Captain Fairbrother, for the last fifty years, and in her secretary, Mabel. Mabel

determines to prevent *The Buccaneer*'s demise and enlists the aid of her
fiancé, Peter, who is tutor to a wealthy infant prodigy, Montgomery
Winterton. Montgomery's mother, a flighty divorcée, is persuaded,
having taken a fancy to Peter, to back *The Buccaneer*; but Montgomery
has made it a condition that he will be the new editor, and with the
assistance of Mr Maximus's daughter, Marilyn, he attempts to turn
the magazine into what he calls 'the children's *New Statesman*'. After
various complications, including Mabel's estrangement from Peter on
learning of his involvement with Mrs Winterton and Marilyn's
betrayal of Montgomery to her father, Mr Donkin is visited in a dream
by Captain Fairbrother who tells him that the children must mount a
rally in Trafalgar Square, and *The Buccaneer* is saved.

It was nothing more than a light-hearted fable, but I felt it would
give me the opportunity of commenting on various aspects of the
contemporary scene. The Watergate management was pleased with
the idea and I set to work on it as soon as *The Boy Friend* had closed.
At about the same time Vida and I were also asked by the London
Club Theatre Group to compile a late-night revue for the Edinburgh
Festival in August. My main concern was still the survival of *The Boy
Friend*, but at least I had plenty of work to keep me occupied in the
meanwhile.

1953 was of course Coronation Year, and among several West End
shows produced to celebrate the occasion was a revue called *High
Spirits* which was a re-working of the best material from the shows at
the Watergate's rival, the Irving Theatre. It was presented at the
Hippodrome, now the Talk of the Town, and the cast was led by Cyril
Ritchard, Diana Churchill and Ian Carmichael. I had known Peter
Myers, who, along with Alec Grahame and David Climie, had written
most of the numbers, since the early days of *Slings and Arrows*, and he
arranged for Jon and myself to have tickets for the first night. We
were seated rather far back in the circle, and, although some of the
material was still effective, I felt that most of it was diminished by
being transferred to such a large stage. The décor was by Osbert
Lancaster, and clearly a great deal of money had been spent, but the
result was thin and unsatisfying. I came out of the Hippodrome feeling
disappointed and disgruntled. How was it that some West End
management could take a theatre that size and spend that amount on
presenting a mediocre revue, when *The Boy Friend*, costing about a
quarter as much, could not find a home anywhere? When we got home,
my resentment exploded, and I railed on to Jon until he finally turned
on me in exasperation.

'Well, why don't you do something about it?'

'What can I do?'

'For a start, you can go and see that agent of Vida's. If she told you *The Boy Friend* was so marvellous, perhaps she can tell you how to get it on again.'

'All right,' I said, 'I will.'

I rang Joannie Rees the next day and arranged to see her that afternoon. I had decided, rather craftily I considered, that I would begin by asking her to represent Jon and myself for cabaret and then mention *The Boy Friend* as an afterthought. My experience with Cassel-Gerard had not endeared me to agents, and I had no intention of signing my life away again in a hurry.

But it was clear from the start of our meeting that Miss Rees was quite prepared for any eventuality. She lived, and still continues to live, in a mews house of Knightsbridge, and from the photographs that adorned the walls – including one that was twice life-size and in colour – I discovered that she had herself been an actress. She was for a time one of the more successful alumnae of the Charm School which I had satirised in *Thanks, Mr Rank*, but she had been suddenly struck deaf in mid-career and, rather than give up the Theatre entirely, had very bravely decided to become an agent. With the help of sponsors, among whom was Harold Huth, she had set up business in her own home, where she was attended by a plump and eager young secretary called Lucy and an elegant Siamese cat called Chi-Chi, who had a trick of dipping her paw in the milk-jug and licking it, as she demonstrated when Lucy served tea.

Over this unusual, not to say bizarre, organisation Joannie herself presided with a manner that fluctuated between little-girl innocence, when she would sit on the floor at one's knees, her blue eyes wide open in an expression of rapt attention, and career-woman mastery, when she would stride up and down, arms folded, one hand clutching a cigarette-holder charged and lit by the faithful Lucy, occasionally glancing over her shoulder at the mirror which covered one end of the room, while she rapped out her views on the situation, in the style of Barbara Stanwyck or Ida Lupino at their peak. I was both amused and astounded, and by the time I left, rather shakily, down the narrow stairway into the mews, Joannie had convinced me that she would take care not only of our cabaret act but of *The Boy Friend*, *The Buccaneer* and anything else that I chose to put in her way. Over the years our relationship has varied between the cosy and the cataclysmic, but I have never had any deep cause to reject the impulse that took me to tea with her that afternoon.

Coronation Day itself was dull and rainy, and we spent most of it at

Nancy Spain's house, watching the event on television. It was the first time that such an occasion had been fully televised, and the close-ups of the young Queen, her head weighed down by the crown, looked, in Jon's words, like a Byzantine icon.

Afterwards Nancy, who had been to see *The Boy Friend* at the Players and loved it, pressed me for news of its future. I told her there was none.

'But something must be done about it!' she protested. 'Who can we approach? I say, what about old Noël? He saw it. He can do something.'

She had already told us of her friendship with the Master and described how, when they were both staying at the Ritz in Paris, he would summon her to his suite at what he called 'trouser-time', when she would be required to help him off with those garments as he lay on his bed and into a silk dressing-gown, after which cocktails would be served.

'Why don't you just write to him,' she urged me, 'and tell him that nothing's happening? I'm sure he'd see you.'

Also to mark the occasion of the Coronation, Noël Coward was playing in a limited season of Bernard Shaw's *The Apple Cart* at the Haymarket Theatre. I had seen it and been overwhelmed by his totally authoritative performance as King Magnus, partnered in the boudoir scene by Margaret Leighton's Orinthia. After Nancy's suggestion had been reinforced by Jon, I wrote a letter to Mr Coward, reminding him that we had met at the Players and also that I was the nephew of Virginia Vernon, and asking him if he could spare the time to see me and give me his advice on the subject of *The Boy Friend*, which I understood him to have admired and which, at the moment, seemed to have no future.

His reply was prompt and asked me to present myself at the Haymarket before the evening performance. I arrived early and was told by the stage-door keeper to wait outside until Mr Coward arrived. After a few moments he did so, driving himself, and, jumping out of his car, took me by the elbow and steered me through the stage-door and into his dressing-room. I was naturally nervous, but he immediately put me at my ease, sat me down and, as his dresser began removing his jacket, asked me to tell him exactly what the trouble was. Although he was undressing, making up and putting on King Magnus's costume as I spoke to him, I never for a moment felt that his attention wandered, and he only interrupted me once when, wearing just his underpants, he surveyed himself in the mirror and remarked, 'Looking even more like an ageing Chinese madam than usual.'

At the end of my recital he turned from his dressing-table and said to me very firmly:

'Now listen to me, my dear Sandy. You are to go down to the Players' Theatre and you are to say that Noël Coward thinks it's a crying shame that *The Boy Friend* is not on in the West End. You can use my name in any way that you think fit. And if that doesn't do the trick, come back and see me again, and we'll think of the next step.'

I thanked him and rose to go, but he had not finished.

'And what are you working on now?'

I had a feeling that this was of more interest to him than the future of *The Boy Friend*. In Coward's philosophy, to keep working was the important thing. Whatever the disappointments and set-backs of the past, one must simply turn to and start something new. Fortunately I was able to tell him that I had just completed a new score, *The Buccaneer*.

'Come to dinner next Wednesday and play it to me.'

It was a command as well as an invitation, but I had the courage to ask if I could bring Jon with me to help me sing the numbers.

'Of course,' he said, and I was given the address of the house in Gerald Road and told to come there after the evening performance of *The Apple Cart*.

We arrived before he had returned home from the theatre. Wednesday was matinée day and it was reasonable to expect that Coward would be a little weary after giving two performances of one of Shaw's most demanding parts; on the contrary, we had just been served with a drink when he bustled in, accompanied by Graham Payn, full of life and enthusiasm, and over dinner he kept up a continuous flow of discussion and gossip which was as instructive as it was entertaining. He also gave me an example of the perfect manners for which he was renowned. A salad was served and I was so absorbed in the conversation that I failed to notice that a salad plate was provided and put it on my bread plate. Coward was served next and, without the flicker of an eyelid, did the same.

After dinner Jon and I took our places at one of the two grand pianos on a platform at the end of the studio and performed the whole score of *The Buccaneer*. After every number Coward made some sort of comment, usually complimentary, but invariably to the point. When Jon had sung the love song, *Unromantic Us*, of which I was particularly proud, he said, 'Very pretty. But very Rodgers and Hart.' He was of course absolutely right. At the end of it he and Graham Payn applauded enthusiastically and we were asked to have some brandy. For an hour or more Coward talked away about his favourite subject, work. He was giving me the fruits of his wisdom and experience and I tried my best to retain it all. 'Don't,' he told me at one moment, 'write all the lyric before the music. The lyric imprisons the melody. Let the music be free.' When I thought of the complexity of some of his lyrics, I realised what skill it must have taken to construct them on an existing tune. His last words, even if they no longer apply, will remain with me for ever:

'There are three good lyric-writers today,' he said, wagging an emphatic finger, 'Cole – myself – and you.'

I was overwhelmed. A moment later Graham indicated the time. It was nearly three a.m. Reluctantly the Master admitted that he had to go to bed. We rose to say goodbye. He kissed us both chastely on the cheek, and Graham ushered us out. We were both so exhilarated that we walked as far as Hyde Park Corner before hailing a cab. When we reached home, I went out into the garden. It was a brilliant night and in a melodramatic, but sincere, gesture I stood in the middle of the lawn and shook my fist at the stars:

'Now it's got to happen,' I said out loud. 'It's *got* to happen!'

Whether or not my use of Coward's name had had its effect, the Players were in touch with me soon afterwards and told me that they had had no success in finding a West End management for *The Boy Friend*; instead they would like me to make it into a full-length show which they would present at the Players for a season in the autumn, during which every London management would be given the opportunity to see it again. It was disappointing, but it did mean that at least *The Boy Friend* would reappear. After consulting with Joannie Rees, I agreed to the plan, and while the Players set about contacting the cast, I began work on lengthening the show. It was an unusual undertaking, because most musicals, as I was to learn later, normally need cutting rather than expanding, and I was also aware that several people had said that, although *The Boy Friend* was too short to fill an evening, to lengthen it would ruin it. However I had always visualised it as a three act show, and the expansion happened just as easily as the original.

One of the key points was the character of Hortense, the maid. With only the opening chorus and a few lines of dialogue to work on, Violetta had made her into such an endearing personality that the audience would obviously enjoy seeing more of her. I therefore brought her on, 'on her afternoon off', in the second act, on the Plage, where she surprises Tony kissing Polly and thus becomes privy to the whole affair, but is sworn to secrecy by Polly. Her discretion is taxed immediately by the boys and girls who are convinced she knows the identity of Polly's Boy Friend; but she evades their questions by the simple means of performing a number, *It's Nicer in Nice*, a title which Geoffrey and I had briefly toyed with for our abortive 1920s musical. In the last act Hortense became the dea ex machina who induces Tony to stay at the Ball and persuades Polly to come and meet him there, thus engineering the happy ending.

In the second act I interpolated a comedy scene between Percy and Mme Dubonnet in which she attempts to teach him to swim. They are observed by the prurient eye of Lord Brockhurst, to Percy's embarrassment, and this provided a new introduction to the Blues number. In the third act I expanded a duologue between Percy and Mme Dubonnet to include further reminiscences of their Armistice Night romance and a dancing reprise of *Fancy Forgetting* and a few moments later I added some lines on to the end of the scene where Bobby proposes to Maisie which brought on the other girls and boys and led, quite arbitrarily, into a big dance number, *The Riviera*. The third act was still not long enough, and there was nothing more that I could reasonably add in the way of dialogue, so, drawing again on my memories of Valentino, I decided to introduce a speciality act, Pépé and Lolita, who would dance the Carnival Tango for the entertainment of the guests at the Café Pataplon. The final moments of the act were re-written to include an announcement by Percy that Mme Dubonnet had just consented to become his wife and a mass acceptance by the girls of the boys' earlier proposal of marriage. It was now a happy ending on a grand scale, with no loose strings at all.

I submitted the revised version to the Players and to Vida, and they were delighted. The first night was planned to take place on October 14th, with a two week rehearsal period beforehand. In the meanwhile Vida and I were kept busy with the preparation of the revue for Edinburgh. We decided to use the best of the numbers from the two Watergate revues, and I added some topical material about the Festival and Scotland. Vida asked Eric Berry and John Rutland to be in it, and for the third man she cast a young actor called Digby Wolfe. The girls were not so easy to find, and I decided on my own to break the silence that had existed between Diana and myself since her departure from *The Boy Friend* and ask her if she would consider coming to Edinburgh. She seemed pleased to hear from me, no reference was made to the past, and when I suggested the idea of her appearing in the revue, she said she would love to. I passed the news on to Vida, who was more than agreeable. What subsequently happened I am still uncertain, but I was eventually told that the management felt Diana was too unreliable to have in the show. I could understand their attitude, but I regretted very much that she was not being given a chance to redeem herself. Besides, I was missing her and, in spite of her strange behaviour, I badly wanted to work with her again. Instead I suggested to Vida that she consider Fenella; the audition was successful, and she was cast. Lisa Lee, Barbara New and Hermene French completed the company.

As Vida was engaged on the revue, I could not suggest her for *The Buccaneer*. Norman Marshall announced that he would direct it, but also informed me that he could only do it in conjunction with another production on which he was engaged, and, perhaps unwisely, I refused to agree. Eventually the job was given to an Australian actor, Lloyd Lamble, whom Jon had suggested. He was an unknown quantity to me, but the Watergate management seemed satisfied and the production was planned for September, which meant that I would have to come down from Edinburgh as soon as the revue had opened to attend rehearsals. The cast Lloyd assembled looked on the whole very promising, and I was particularly impressed by two of the girls, both of whom had only recently finished their training as actresses: Sally Bazley, a breath-takingly pretty soprano, who was to play Mabel, and a wild-looking brunette with a strong Welsh accent, called Rachel Roberts, who had been cast, in spite of her youth, as the rich Mrs Winterton.

Rehearsals for the revue were going smoothly, with the exception of one incident which I think constituted the only row that Vida and I ever had during the ten years of our association. She had decided to include the monologue by the judge of amateur dramatics which Joan Sterndale Bennett had performed so beautifully at the Watergate, but had given it, rather to my surprise, to Digby Wolfe. As usual, I stayed away from rehearsals, and in any case I was preoccupied with *The Buccaneer*, since it was a new show and most of the revue was well-tried material. One afternoon Vida asked me to attend a run-through in the crypt of a church in Soho, where we were rehearsing. The show seemed to be taking shape nicely: Fenella was doing well, particularly with a new number I had written for her, in which the secretary of an American government official suspected of Communist affiliations pleaded for mercy from 'Dear Mister McCarthy', and all the rest of the cast were working out. But then Digby came on to deliver his monologue and I suddenly realised that, without a word to me, it had been completely re-written. I said nothing, but at the end of the run-through asked Vida if we could have a word together outside. She was obviously on the defensive, because as soon as I made my complaint about the re-writing she turned on me with extraordinary ferocity and said that if I wasn't pleased with her work she would resign on the spot.

'What's more,' she went on, 'you can find someone else to direct *The Boy Friend*, because I'll resign from that too.'

I was absolutely appalled and left at once without another word. Nothing more was said about the matter; the monologue remained as it was and, as I expected, laid an egg in Edinburgh. I discovered that it was Digby himself who had re-written it, and it was as a writer, on American television, that he later made his name. But his talent at the time lay in other directions and Vida, like every other woman on whom he cast his eye, had temporarily succumbed to it. I laughed about it later, but partly from relief, because the thought of her abandoning *The Boy Friend* had, in the words of Lady Brockhurst, 'quite unnerved me'.

We called the revue *See You Later*, but I never felt that it came up to the standards of the Watergate shows, although the notices in Edinburgh were good on the whole and the business was satisfactory. One disadvantage was the theatre, which was normally a cinema and far too large for an intimate revue, and the other was the enforced presence of a popular Scots actor, Duncan Macrae, who performed two interminable monologues which slowed up the action and conflicted totally with the show's style. We also came up against the Festival authorities, when the local papers published huge photographs of Lisa, in déshabille, playing Dulcie Gray's old rôle of the ageing French diseuse; they considered this let down the cultural tone, and I was rather inclined to agree, but of course the publicity did the revue no harm at all. I regretted having to leave Edinburgh after the opening night and miss seeing some of the other Festival offerings, but apart from that I was quite glad to get back to London and *The Buccaneer*. Revue had been great fun in its time and had been an excellent training ground as well as providing my entrée into the Theatre, but the success of *The Boy Friend* had given me the taste for something different, and now I was anxious to discover what would happen to my first effort at writing a new musical as opposed to a period pastiche.

In the event I was disappointed. For one reason and another, *The Buccaneer*, in its original form, simply did not work, and the critics had no hesitation in pronouncing it a let-down after the promise of *The Boy Friend*. Some of them said it kindly, but *The Times*, probably delighted to have its doubts about my talents confirmed, dismissed it as 'poor stuff', while conceding that 'two or three of the songs allow one to see a little of what Mr Wilson may do when he has completed his experiments.' I could discern for myself that the structure of the piece, with its rather artificial situations and conventional misunderstandings, needed a good deal more in the way of musical embellishments and production effects than was possible with the limited resources of the Watergate. Only my mother was imperturbably devoted to it, bringing the more docile residents of Brooke House Hotel to see it, whether they wanted to or not, thus supplying the bulk of the audiences; and every time she came, at the moment when Montgomery is asked how he managed to induce so many children to attend the rally in Trafalgar Square and replies, 'We told them Charles and Anne were coming', she announced her presence by clapping loyally and loudly.

I was also disappointed by the fact that Lloyd Lamble, whose production, in my opinion, lacked strength and style, seemed reluctant to come back to the show after the opening and make some attempt to improve it. When he did finally appear one evening, I cornered him in the bar after the performance and told him, perhaps too frankly, what I thought of his attitude, which led to my being barred from the theatre for the rest of the run. It was a sad ending to what had been a very happy and productive association; but the Watergate, in its high-class guise, no longer had the kick that made it such an exciting place to work in originally. As the New Watergate it continued to function until its disappearance in 1955, when the entire block was demolished. Not surprisingly, I was never asked to work there again. But I was invited to its closing night, to see the last performance of John Cranko's revue, *Cranks*, after which Emmy Tillett graciously condescended to sell me the poster of *The Buccaneer*.

The Players had managed to secure all the original leads of *The Boy Friend*, with one exception: Joan Sterndale Bennett had accepted a part in a play, *The Gentle Rain*, and was on a pre-West End tour. So we were faced with the problem of recasting the vital rôle of Madame Dubonnet. Vida's suggestion, as usual, surprised me: Totti Truman Taylor, a tall fair-haired actress with the features and bearing of a Renaissance princess, whom I knew best as a habitué of one of the local pubs in Belsize Park, where she could always be found on Saturday mornings, accompanied by her friend, a religious sculptress known as Bezer, who affected a long black cloak and a Henry the Fifth hair-cut. She seemed a far cry from Joan, but I had learned by now to trust Vida's judgement completely, and Totti was cast. Now that Hortense was to appear throughout, it was no longer possible for Violetta to double the rôle of Lady Brockhurst, and Vida gave it to a straight actress, Beryl Cooke, whom she had first seen in repertory, when Beryl was acting with Vida's father:

'She rang me one day and said, "Oh, darling, you must come down to the Players. We've got this marvellous show." So I went to see it, the tiny edition, and I said, "Oh, love, this is a winner. You mustn't ever let it go. And if you do it again, please remember me for the old lady." '

It had also been decided to add another girl, whom I christened Nancy. Juliet Hunt was given the part and was known for many months afterwards as 'The New Girl'. Another boy, Pierre, joined Alphonse and Marcel, and these parts were all recast, as Malcolm and Jimmy were no longer available. Instead we had Geoffrey Webb, Jack Thompson and Stephen Warwick, who was also engaged to appear as Pépé and dance the Carnival Tango. His partner, Lolita, was to be Joan Gadsdon.

The first rehearsal at the Players was like a family reunion, and everyone congratulated me on the new additions to the show. I was struck again by the enthusiasm and devotion with which these people approached their work. They all knew how much was at stake: if the show did not succeed this time and if no management took it in a full-length version, this had to be the end of it. On this occasion the critics were not to be asked to review it. 'I told them,' said Don Gemmell, 'that we were doing it with the hope of a transfer and if you see it three times, you'll get fed up. Come if you like, and gossip about it all you please. But don't write about it.'

A lot of the work for the new edition devolved upon Johnnie Heawood. For *It's Nicer in Nice* he created a miniature Follies routine, in which Violetta skipped and cavorted round the stage in company with the boys and girls, receiving her calls at the end in a plethora of bobs and kisses which she herself remembered from her childhood, when a touring revue visited the village in the Pyrenees where she was living. As for *Safety in Numbers*, which had been a weak spot in the first version, Johnnie turned it into a show-stopper by the simple expedient, which Ann Wakefield suggested, of putting Maisie into ballet shoes and giving her, at the climax of the dance, a tap routine on point. I had based *The Riviera*, the new dance number in Act Three, on *The Varsity Drag* in *Good News*, and here Fred Stone's advice was again invaluable because he had been in the chorus of that show. To my astonishment Vida and Johnnie managed to prolong it into four choruses, followed by an encore in which the boys and girls snaked round the stage like a train, whispering the words. There was also a new dance for Tony in Act Three, a solo with a dress box, in which, to the melody of *A Room in Bloomsbury*, his mood changed from anxiety to exultation at the thought of seeing Polly again. For the Tango Johnnie conceived the notion that Pépé and Lolita detested each other and would lose no opportunity of expressing their feelings during the number: the result was a dance that was both spectacular and hilarious. Joan Gadsdon, with her flashing good looks, was a natural for Lolita, but Vida had some trouble inducing Stephen Warwick, who was by nature rather modest about his appearance, to assume the necessary Valentino-esque bravura. Finally she said to him one day, 'Darling, just imagine that someone terribly rich has gone mad about you and given you a gold cigarette case studded with diamonds.' The result was electrifying.

The lengthened finale, with its multiple happy endings, had several delicious moments, but the one I treasured most was when Percy, preparing the way for the announcement of his betrothal to Mme Dubonnet, says to his daughter, 'Polly, I too have some news.' Anne, who was posed in profile gazing adoringly into Tony's eyes, turned her face out front and said, in a tone of utter flatness, 'Have you, Daddy? How thrilling!' and smartly returned her attention to Tony.

Everyone at the Players seemed convinced that the new version would be a success, and Vida and Johnnie were so confident that they began devising names for the foreign productions which they were sure would follow its West End première. In Paris it would be called *Les Jeunes Filles*, in Berlin *Polly und Seine Freunden*, and in Scandinavia, quite simply, *Bok*.

Now that I could see the whole piece assembled, I had no doubt at all that it not only still worked, but was an improvement on the original, and the reception on the first night at the Players confirmed my feelings. Totti's interpretation of Mme Dubonnet was different from Joan's, but just as effective in its way, and Beryl made a forbidding and yet human Lady Brockhurst. All the new songs were enthusiastically applauded, and the extra dialogue slotted smoothly and imperceptibly into the action. The only passage that failed to work was the comedy scene in the second act, where Dubonnet taught Percival to swim, and I decided that, for any future production, it must be re-written.

That *The Boy Friend* now had possibilities as a complete show there seemed no possible doubt, and it was with growing dismay and despair that we realised that, as far as West End managements were concerned, the story was going to be repeated, but this time with a different refrain. '*The Boy Friend*,' they told us, one after another, 'is charming, witty, delightful, and so on and so on. But it belongs in a club theatre, not on the West End stage.' The same performance was enacted night after night in the Supper Room: Don, Reggie and Gervase dispensing drinks to one management's representative after another, while I listened to their compliments. But the result never varied: thanks a lot, but no thanks. The weeks went by, and the show played to packed houses and rapturous curtain calls; but no-one wanted it, and Christmas was approaching, when most of our cast would have to leave for other jobs in pantomime.

One evening, towards the end of the run, a quiet-spoken young man appeared at the Players. He was the business manager of the Embassy, Swiss Cottage, which I had often visited with my mother before the War and which was still my local theatre. It was now being run by Anthony Hawtrey and his wife, Marjorie, and the young man had come to see *The Boy Friend* on their behalf. His name was Pat Freeman:

'We were looking for a Christmas show. We normally did our own pantomime, but Tony had just had his first heart attack and couldn't produce anything. Somebody had told us about this show at the Players and I said I'd go down and find out if it was the sort of thing we wanted. I saw it and absolutely adored it, but there were other managements there and I felt, "Oh, they're all going to want it. There isn't going to be much chance for us." But I queued up afterwards to see Gervase, and when the others had had their say, I talked to him and said, "No doubt they all want you to go into their lovely theatres, but if by any chance they don't, we'd love to have you at the Embassy. Can you give me a ring in the morning?" I went back and told Tony, "It's marvellous, but I'm sure we won't get it." But the next morning Gervase rang.'

Before a deal could be made, it was necessary to consult the cast, and Vida took it upon herself to sound them out. She told them quite frankly that we had been offered a Christmas season at the Embassy, which might lead to a West End transfer, but there was no guarantee whatsoever that this would happen; it was simply a way of keeping *The Boy Friend* going a little longer, and after Christmas they could well find themselves out of work. Although for most of them it meant giving up the chance of longer and more lucrative engagements in pantomime, they all said they wanted to stick by *The Boy Friend*. But Ann Wakefield and Fred Stone discovered that they had pantomime contracts from which they could not be released, and they were obliged, with great reluctance, to leave the cast. Tony Hayes had also had a contract to play in pantomime at Coventry:

'It was very good money, but I hated the idea of *The Boy Friend* transferring without me. So I talked it over with my wife and she said, "You'd be mad to leave it. We don't have any children. If nothing happens, if it doesn't transfer, it doesn't matter. But you would be so angry with yourself if it did and you weren't in it." So I cancelled my contract.'

The only person who was not consulted about the move to the Embassy was Totti Truman Taylor. Joan Sterndale Bennett's play had closed on tour, and the Players asked her to come back into *The Boy Friend*, but someone, it seems, had forgotten to explain to Totti that her engagement was dependent on Joan's availability:

'I never thought there was any question of my not going with it – to Swiss Cottage or Timbuctoo or anywhere. But just before you went to the Embassy they told me that Joan was coming back. Well, all things happen for the best. It was a lovely experience, and I learned a lot from being directed by Vida. If I were playing it now – if I were younger – I'd give it a glint. I sang *Fancy Forgetting* romantically; but now I'd do it with a hint of – you know! But the part I'd love to play now is Lady Brockhurst. I have that command, that aristocratic voice – "Disappearing from Oxford – in the *Hilary Term*!" '

To replace Fred Stone the Players engaged Hugh Paddick. Auditions were held to find a new Maisie and the choice finally fell on Denise Hirst, a deliciously pretty girl with the air of a slightly crazy débutante. For the rest of the company, and for Vida and Johnnie, these changes of cast meant yet another full rehearsal period, but they set about it without a word of complaint. Johnnie's only problem was Denise's apparently constitutional disability to master the basic step of the Charleston:

'At one point I said to Vida, "Darling, there's nothing for it. We'll simply have to break the child's pelvis and re-set it." Fortunately it suddenly came to her one day, and we were able to leave her intact.'

Instead of the 'bathing lesson' scene in the second act, I wrote in an encounter between Percy and Lord Brockhurst in which the latter attempts to start up a flirtation with Mme Dubonnet. It contained a line which, thanks to John Rutland's timing, was to become one of the biggest laughs in the show: on being informed by Percy that Mme Dubonnet is a Head Mistress, Lord Brockhurst replies: 'I say! You *are* in luck, aren't you?' The scene ended with the Brockhursts making a memorable exit in march-time after Lady Brockhurst's reprimand: 'Remember, Hubert, *we* are *British*!'

The first night at the Embassy took place on December 1st. The Press were asked, and *The Times* had agreed to send a different man from the one who had disliked it so much at the Players. Ken Tynan, after a spell as a director, was now a theatre critic and had vociferously championed the show from the very start. There was a consciousness on everyone's part that this was the last throw for *The Boy Friend*, and many people who had seen it more than once at the Players were there at the Embassy, willing and praying for it to be a success. At one moment during the first act the enthusiasm coming from the audience was so intense that several groups of aficionados began to laugh even before the lines were out of the players' mouths. Nothing irritates the critics more than displays of partisanship, and I began to fear for the effect this might have on our notices; but after the interval the fans exercised a little self-control and from then on the performance sailed through to a triumphant final curtain.

In Pat Freeman's opinion nothing in the Theatre since has compared to the excitement of that first night:

'Tony Hawtrey was still so ill that he couldn't even get down the stairs from his flat above the theatre. But he could hear the shouting and the screaming and the general pandemonium. We went up to his bedroom afterwards and Miriam Karlin said to him, "Now at last you can relax and go to South Africa and get better, because this is going to run for ever." Tony said, "Yes, I suppose so. I haven't really seen the contract." So we went down to the safe to get it, and it was only then that we found that the Players could give us a six weeks' notice to leave the Embassy.'

When we finally staggered up the road and collapsed at home over a cup of tea, Jon said to me, 'You realise that if this is handled right, you'll have a meal ticket for life.' I could not really take in what he was saying, and in any case there was still no guarantee that tonight's reception would bring us a transfer to the West End; I simply knew that, in a normal theatre and in front of a public audience, *The Boy Friend* had proved that it could succeed.

Almost before I woke up the next morning, the situation had changed completely. Within an hour or two of the appearance of the notices the Players had been rung up by eight managements making offers for *The Boy Friend*; one of them, Peter Daubeny, had even telephoned from Paris. But now it dawned on them that they no longer needed a management. 'Why should they have it?' said Reggie. 'They could have had it for nothing, but they didn't have the courage. All we want now is the right theatre.' And now suddenly, as Gervase discovered, theatres were also miraculously available:

'It was fantastic. I'd never known anything like it – although of course the whole thing was new to me. Whereas normally it's practically impossible to get an "in" to any West End theatre, now we could have had almost any one we wanted. It was at that point that I decided to concentrate on Bronny.'

Bronson Albery, who had arranged my entrance to the Old Vic School, had been to see the second production of *The Boy Friend* at the Players. He had been dragged there, rather against his will, by the actor, Brian Oulton, and his wife, Peggy Thorpe-Bates, who were both passionate admirers of the show and never stopped agitating on its behalf and bringing potential backers down to the Players to see it. Bronny had enjoyed it but he too had considered that it belonged in a club theatre and not in the West End. His son, Donald, who was now in management on his own account, had also refused it. Now Bronny was offering Gervase one of his theatres, the Criterion.

'I had family associations with the Alberys. My father was brought up with them. He worked for Lady Wyndham and he knew Bronny, and he had had shows at Wyndhams – *Diversions* was there during the War. And I'd known Bronny since I was a child. He offered me the Criterion, but he suggested the possibility of Wyndhams. But Graham Greene's play, *The Living Room*, which Donald had produced, was still on there and was doing quite well. However once I'd got an inkling that there was a chance of getting it, I said I didn't want to go to the Criterion. Of course Donald wasn't very pleased about our going to Wyndhams, but he happened to be away on holiday at the time, and his father was able to push him out.'

Within a few days the deal was made: the Players' Theatre would present *The Boy Friend* themselves, at Wyndhams, by arrangement with Bronson Albery. The two productions at the Players had both opened on the fourteenth of the month. By a curious coincidence the West End first night was arranged for January the Fourteenth, 1954.

Meanwhile the Embassy was enjoying the biggest success in its history. All day long there were queues at the box office, and the cast and everyone connected with the show suddenly discovered they had friends in all walks of life who happened to want tickets. As I was living so near, I was able to drop in when I felt like it and see who was in the audience. One night, at the final curtain, a lady charlestoned down to the front of the circle, blew kisses to the cast and shouted, 'It was *my* period!' Princess Margaret, then the leader of her own social set, came and was observed to beat time to the music with her cigarette holder. The Embassy had a club attached to it, for whose members they gave Sunday night performances, which meant that working actors and actresses could come and see the show. One Sunday evening I arrived at the theatre to see the stately, cloaked figure of John Gielgud waiting on the steps outside. But the most significant encounter happened during the interval one night, when I was having a drink in the bar. Somebody came up to me and said, 'There's a person over there whom I think you ought to meet.' I was led to where, perched on a table with her legs crossed, glass held high, and wearing a yachting blazer, was that legendary figure of the Twenties, Nancy Cunard.

One morning Vida, who lived nearby in Belsize Crescent, rang me:

'Darling, are you doing anything? If not, why don't we get dressed up and go down to Wyndhams. I want to have a look at the stage.' I agreed and she arranged to pick me up in a cab in half an hour's time. I put on my only dark suit, and when Vida arrived, she was wearing a hat and her latest and most precious acquisition, a fur stole. We drove down to Wyndhams and walked through the alley-way to the stage-door, the same alley-way that I had so often wandered down in my explorations of theatre-land when we first came to London. To the stage-door keeper's enquiry Vida replied, 'This is Mr Sandy Wilson, the author of *The Boy Friend*, and I am his producer,' and we swept in. On stage was the set of *The Living Room*, which, as its name implies, was an elaborate interior, built with complete realism. Neither of us had seen the play, and we wandered round the stage, examining the scenery and wondering how *The Boy Friend* would look in its new home. At one point Vida opened a door. 'Look!' she cried, with a gurgle of laughter. 'They've even got a real loo! That must be where Mary Jerrold sits when she goes off!' She took my arms and we wandered off into the wings, giggling happily. As we left I thought I heard a voice from the darkened auditorium calling out something, but I paid no attention. Vida suggested that we go into the pub near the stage door and have a celebratory drink. It was only much later that I discovered that the voice had belonged to Donald Albery. He was auditioning for his new production, *I Am a Camera*, and what he had called out was, 'Can we have the next one please?' Not surprisingly, his opinion of *The Boy Friend*, never very favourable, deteriorated even more after that morning.

Although the production would be virtually the same as it had been at the Players, there were several things that had to be done before we opened in the West End. The scenery had to be repainted and the costumes, some of which were beginning to fall to pieces, refurbished. The music, hitherto played just on piano and drums, was re-orchestrated by Phil Cardew for a four-piece band, the most that could be accommodated in the tiny pit at Wyndhams. Understudies were engaged to cover the leads and to appear as passers-by and guests in the second and third acts. Although he was content to take the show as it was, Bronson Albery did insist on two rather trivial alterations. Geoffrey Webb, playing Alphonse, appeared at the Carnival Ball as Charlie Chaplin; Bronny considered this ugly, and poor Geoffrey, who had spent weeks perfecting an imitation of the famous Chaplin walk, was made to change into the relatively uninteresting costume of a matador. Bronny also decided that Anne Rogers' Pierrette frock should have its waist raised to the natural level, to make her prettier; but this would have looked

Above: The Boy Friend, London 1954. *Top Row:* Denise Hirst, Maria Charles. *Bottom Row:* Juliet Hunt, Joan Gadsdon

Left: The Boy Friend, London 1954. Anthony Hayes and Anne Rogers

Left: The Boy Friend, New York 1954. Julie Andrews and John Hewer sing 'I Could be Happy with You'

Below: The Boy Friend, New York 1954. *Top Row:* Millicent Martin, Stella Claire. *Bottom Row:* Dilys Laye, Julie Andrews, Ann Wakefield

glaringly inaccurate, and Reggie Woolley would only consent to raise it an inch or so. Our one other problem at Wyndhams was the sound. At the last dress rehearsal Vida said to Tony Hayes, ' "I don't know what we're going to do, dear. The orchestra sound like mice," and I felt so depressed. I thought, "This lovely show is going to be ruined, because no-one will be able to hear the music." ' But overnight two loudspeakers were installed at the sides of the stage, so that the cast could hear the orchestra, and the instrumentalists were raised on a platform built into the pit. On the afternoon of January 14th the company were summoned for a final band-call. After that there was nothing else to do but fill in the time until the evening. Most of them went home, to try to relax and prepare themselves for the moment for which they had been praying and which had been so long in coming. But one of them, the 'over-night star', Anne Rogers, had other things on her mind:

'I didn't realise how important it was. It was drizzling with rain that day, and after the rehearsal broke, about three o'clock, I thought, "I'm not going home, all that way to Shepherd's Bush. I'll go and have a look at the shops." So I was walking round Soho, and I met one of the musicians from a broadcast I'd done and said hello, and he said, "My God, haven't you got an opening night tonight? What are you doing, walking round in the rain?" I said, "I'm going to have something to eat." He said, "You're going to *eat*?" And I said, "Yes", and I did. I went into a little cayf on the corner and had a bloody great steak. With those costumes I knew it would be all right, because it wouldn't show. I wish I could still do that, but now I wouldn't be able to keep it down. I do think it would be a help, because it's that emptiness inside your tummy that makes you nervous!'

A few days earlier I had heard from Charles Stromberg that he would be coming down to London from his parish in the North for the first night, as he had managed to get a ticket in the upper circle. He was also going to a matinée of the revue at the Lyric, Hammersmith, and we arranged to have lunch together, as we used to before the War, when we met at the beginning of the school holidays for our visits to the cinema. I was so pleased that he was going to be there: it was a link with the past, with the time when I had first had the dream that looked as if it was beginning to come true.

My mother had decided to go out to Christian, in Bulawayo, over Christmas and she had not yet come home and so would miss the first night. Jon and I took two girl friends, and before the performance we had dinner Au Jardin des Gourmets. Some people at the next table who were also going to Wyndhams recognised me and wished us luck.

H [225]

It was *The Boy Friend*'s fourth first night, and the culmination of a train of events that had started two years before with Diana's chance remark to me about a 1920s show. Or had it started earlier than that, much earlier, when I had lain awake at school and tried to remember how the Charleston went? Or even before that, as I listened to the gramophone playing *Tea for Two* and *I Want to be Happy*?

To describe once again what the performance was like and how the audience enjoyed it would, I am afraid, be tedious. I shall only repeat what Maria Charles told me recently: 'If anybody asks me what was the best night of my life, I just say, "I was in *The Boy Friend* on the first night at Wyndhams." ' At the end of it, I was called on stage and even from the upper circle Charles could see how nervous I was:

'You were deathly pale. I've never seen you look so frightened.'

I have no idea now what I said. I had been instructed by the company manager that Bronson Albery only occasionally permitted authors to take a call and that any speech I made must be as brief as possible. There was so much I wanted to say, but I imagine that I just uttered the conventional words of thanks to the audience and the company. What I would have liked to tell the audience was how much I owed to those people, to the Players, to Vida and Johnnie, to the actors and actresses, who had shown such faith in my show, who had given up so much for it, in the face of continual disappointments and frustrations, because they believed that one day, somehow, it would be a success. I wanted to say that for them tonight was not just a reward for their hard work, their loyalty and their devotion; it was their due.

As for me, when the excitement was over and when the reviews next day confirmed once and for all that *The Boy Friend* was a hit, I could only say to myself, with a sigh of relief and satisfaction, 'Well – it's about time!'

And
to
Broadway

WHILE *The Boy Friend* was still at the Embassy, there were one or two tentative offers from American producers; but they suggested alterations to the show which I was not prepared to make, and in any case it was obviously wiser to wait until we had opened in the West End. By the time we reached Wyndhams I had already made up my mind that if *The Boy Friend* were to be produced in America, it would have to be the same in every respect – production, design, choreography – as it was in London, and unless this could be guaranteed there would be no deal. From *Oklahoma!* onwards London had seen exact reproductions of Broadway's hit musicals; I wanted Broadway to see an exact reproduction of *The Boy Friend*. Joannie Rees was in total agreement with me, and she entertained no offers from anyone who was not prepared to give us this guarantee. In fact the majority of American producers were wary of the show; they felt it was all right for English audiences, but was not big and brassy enough for Broadway. Alistair Cooke, the English ex-patriot who broadcasts a weekly American newsletter on the BBC, went on record as saying that any Broadway impresario who took *The Boy Friend* to New York needed his head examined. But we were prepared to wait, and one day, a few weeks after we had opened in the West End, Joannie told me that she felt the right American producers had come our way, in the persons of Cy Feuer and Ernest Martin.

Feuer and Martin's first success on Broadway had been *Where's Charley?*, a musical version of *Charley's Aunt*, starring Ray Bolger. They followed that with *Guys and Dolls*, probably one of the best to appear in that golden era of the American Musical. *Where's Charley?* was not put on in London until several years later, although the film version had already been made here in 1952, but *Guys and Dolls* was produced at the London Coliseum in the spring of 1953, with some of the original Broadway cast and, among the dancers, Johnnie Heawood. The production was in the hands of Feuer and Martin's amiable and eager factotum, Arthur Lewis, and during rehearsals Johnnie mentioned to him in passing that he had just choreographed a 'little piece' at the Players' Theatre, and would Arthur be interested in seeing the Sunday night performance at the end of the run?

' "I would like that very much, John. Yes, why not?" Arthur replied in his warm-hearted way. So I took him to see *The Boy Friend* on that particular evening, and I think he enjoyed it very much. Well, it was a very gala evening. And that really is the end of the story, except that Arthur was sent back by Feuer and Martin at the end of the year to have a disciplinary look at *Guys and Dolls*, and I said to him "Arthur, do you remember that little musical play?" "Indeed I do!" he said, "I've never stopped talking about it." "Well, it just so happens that we're now playing at the Embassy, Swiss Cottage, in a full-length version, and I think it works better. Funnily enough we play on Sundays." So off we went the following Sunday night, and when we came out Arthur gripped my arm and said, "Promise me you won't let anyone get the American rights." '

Johnnie told him that there was nothing much he could do about that: we were moving to the West End, and after that it would be up to any American producer who wanted *The Boy Friend* to make a bid for it. Arthur accordingly decided to do something on his own initiative, and when we opened at Wyndhams, he booked a box and cabled Feuer and Martin to come over and see it. They did so and agreed that Arthur's opinion of the show was absolutely correct and they must secure the rights for Broadway.

My first meeting with Cy and Ernie took place at the Savoy Hotel where they had taken a suite during the negotiations for the American production. As soon as I entered the room I realised that I was in a new world, which was nevertheless familiar to me from the Cinema: the world of American Show Business. Cigar smoke floated in the air, the telephone rang persistently, one waiter was clearing breakfast, while another appeared with drinks and sandwiches, and in the midst of it were the two producers: Cy Feuer, short, compact, with a grey crew-cut and glasses, and Ernie Martin, tall, bulky and black-haired. They were both charming, and Cy was particularly welcoming, bubbling with enthusiasm for the show in a way that reminded me a little of Jack Waller. Drinks, coffee, cigarettes, cigars, sandwiches were pressed on me, as they both assured me, with tremendous sincerity, that *The Boy Friend* was perfection, an exquisite jewel of a show, which they intended to reproduce faithfully for us, down to the smallest facet, the last bead on Madame Dubonnet's frock, the last wave in Polly's wig: they loved every bit of it, and they wanted every bit of it to be exactly the same on Broadway. Vida was to direct, Johnnie was to choreograph, and Reggie's designs were to be used; and I was to come over to New York for the whole rehearsal period, to ensure that everything was as I wanted it.

I was overwhelmed by their enthusiasm, which seemed to me to be totally genuine. After the strictures and reservations I had heard from London managements, this open-handed and open-hearted attitude was wonderfully refreshing, and what was more these people were not eager novices but hardened professionals with three hits (the third, *Can Can*, had just opened on Broadway) to their credit. I had no hesitation in agreeing with Joannie that they were the ones to present *The Boy Friend* in America.

To begin with, they planned to do the show some time in the following year, when it might be possible, if the Players agreed, to take most of the English company to New York. At that time American Equity allowed a foreign show to import forty per cent of its cast, and by a bit of juggling and introducing a few more extras into the crowd scenes this could be adjusted to cover most of *The Boy Friend*'s principal characters. But a message came from New York that a revival of *Good News* was planned for the autumn: if this were to happen before *The Boy Friend*, most of the wind would be taken out of our sails. It was immediately decided that we must be the first musical to open on Broadway in the Fall season. This would mean finding another theatre, as the Music Box, the one considered most suitable, would not be available; instead we were to open at the Royale, a considerably larger theatre, but still, I was assured, reasonably intimate. The date was to be September the Thirtieth, the first opening of the season after Labour Day week-end, when, I was informed, New Yorkers considered the summer is over. The contracts were signed and Cy and Ernie gave a large party at the Savoy to celebrate, at which I was photographed, in an apparent state of manic glee, shaking hands with both of them at once.

Since the Players, quite understandably, would not release any of the London company so early in the run, we had to set about finding a new cast for Broadway. Under the existing agreement we could bring over nine members: Polly, Tony, Maisie, Dulcie, Nancy, Fay, Madame Dubonnet, Percy and Lord Brockhurst. Bobby van Husen, being an American anyway, could naturally be cast in New York, and we were promised an actress of French extraction to play Hortense. There were several expatriate English character actresses working in New York among whom it would be easy to find a Lady Brockhurst, and the three

French boys, Alphonse, Marcel and Pierre, would of course be played by American dancers. Vida suggested that Geoffrey Hibbert, her original choice for the part, who was now free again, should be considered for Lord Brockhurst, and this was readily agreed to. Arthur Lewis, who had seen Ann Wakefield playing Maisie at the Players, was very anxious that she should be brought back into the show for Broadway, and urged Cy and Ernie to see her. Ann was still up in Manchester, playing the lead in *Goody Two Shoes* for Emile Littler:

'I was living at an ironmonger's-cum-funeral parlour – a famous "digs" that Ian Carmichael had recommended. I walked in one day after a matinée, and the landlady told me I had had a call from the Savoy Hotel. It was Cy and he wanted me to come down to London at the week-end. "We'll put you up for the night," he said. Well, I'd always wanted to stay at the Savoy, so I arrived there and went up to their room. They were ordering trays and trays of food: Ernie looked a bit like Cary Grant, and Cy reminded me of Cagney, and they were very business-like. They said, "We've heard a lot about you from Arthur Lewis. Would you be interested in coming to New York?" I said, "I certainly would." '

Ann was signed, but only after a certain amount of wrangling with Emile Littler who also had her under contract to play pantomime the following year and had to be paid off. Extensive auditions were now going on at the Coliseum to find the other girls. Stella Claire, a dancer from the Sadlers Wells ballet with a bewitching pekingese face, was cast as Fay, and one day, when I was seeing Cy and Ernie at the Savoy, the ballet mistress from *Guys and Dolls* arrived with one of the chorus, a rather plain girl called Millicent Martin. She was highly recommended for all-round efficiency and was accordingly cast as Nancy, who is required to cover the other girls, should one of the leads be off. The rôle of Dulcie was more difficult to fill. Vida had virtually created it for Maria, and she was now, in all our minds, completely identified with the character. Among the actresses who were suggested was Dilys Lay, a very young and dynamic girl whom I had seen and admired in one or two club theatre revues. She seemed a likely choice, but both Vida and Feuer and Martin wanted to make sure:

'I did five auditions for Dulcie over a period of five months. I learned *Never Too Late*, and Geoff Hibbert and I turned up every month, on the hour, and did it. At the end of five months we were all called again. I remember Geoff, who always shook, bless his heart! – when he put his hands on my shoulders during the number we both vibrated – and I sat holding hands in the stalls at the Coliseum, not knowing whether we had got it or not. Then Arthur Lewis gave us a great chat on what to expect in America, and we knew we were going. Vida was very fond of Maria Charles, as you know, and I'll always remember her saying, "I never thought I'd find another mouse-face," and I fell in love with her from that moment. Though I must admit I said to myself afterwards, "Mouse-face? But you're beautiful!" '

The next problem was to find a Polly. We auditioned numerous girls, and, as Johnnie Heawood put it, 'most of them were charming and delightful, but none of them had what we were looking for. Of course what we really wanted was Anne Rogers: we wanted a duplicate. One day at the Players Vida was chatting with Hattie Jacques, saying, "I don't know what I'm going to do. There's no-one like Annie." And Hattie said, "Well, I've been working for years on a radio show called *Educating Archie*, and there's a little creature on it by the name of Julie Andrews. She's playing Cinderella at the London Palladium. Why don't you go and see her?" '

Vida did so, was impressed, and asked me to have a look at her too. Jon and I went to a matinée and I could see at once that, while quite different in physical type from Annie, she had the right aura of radiant innocence to play Polly. I was already familiar with her phenomenal singing voice, having first seen her on stage in a revue called *Starlight Roof* at the huge London Hippodrome, when, still a small girl in a party frock and large white shoes, she had filled the theatre with a soprano of astonishing range and purity. I told Vida that I felt she could well be the answer, and Julie was asked to come to the Coliseum for an audition. Her mother, Barbara Andrews, a rather forceful lady with red hair, came with her and sat in the pit to accompany her.

'It was pure *Gypsy*,' was Johnnie's impression. 'We asked her to dance and Barbara stood up and said, "Go on, Julie. Show them your tap." And Julie, being very modest, said, "I don't think I can." But she did, and at the end of this rather difficult audition, Vida whispered to me, "That's it. We've found her." And we came down the aisle of the Coliseum, that vast, empty establishment, and she said, "Miss Andrews, I think you have the most perfect theatre manners of any young person I have ever met." And she was right: Julie *had* perfect manners, against, let's face it, fearful odds.'

For the part of Percy it was suggested that Fred Stone might be brought back, but Hugh Paddick had only been contracted to play four months at Wyndhams and the Players made Freddie a counter-offer to return to the London production. Characteristically he played safe, since there was no knowing how *The Boy Friend* might fare in New York, and went to Wyndhams in May. Instead we asked Eric Berry, whose excellent qualities were already familiar to us from the two revues, and he was fortunately free and keen to go to America.

Finding a new Tony was almost more of a head-ache than discovering a new Polly, since Tony Hayes had brought to the part, out of his own experience, a style and a personality which had almost ceased to exist among present-day performers. There were plenty of young men who could sing, plenty more who could dance, and some of them were perfectly capable of acting. But few of them could do all three, and none of them had the period feeling that was essential to the part. Johnnie Heawood suggested casually to Cy that he should go down to the Players one evening and see a friend of his, John Hewer, who was in the bill:

'Cy told me that he thought John had charm, but he was doing something like *Any Old Iron*, one of his rorty, shouting Cockney numbers – certainly not the song for Tony, who is supposed to be upper-crust. Hewer didn't look at all like that, with a red nose, check trousers and a big bow tie. So I said to Cy, "He has many sides to his nature," and I told Hewer to come along to the Coliseum and sing *They Didn't Believe Me* which he happened to be able to sing probably better than anyone in the world. "Woo him," I said. And he did, and Cy said, "God, the guy really gets you, doesn't he? Can he dance?" And I said, "He *moves* very well." '

In fact John Hewer had hardly any dancing experience and could not tap a step. I had first met him at the Comedy, during rehearsals of *Slings and Arrows*, when I wrote a number for him at very short notice, on Diana's suggestion. It was performed for one preview and then taken out, but I could see that John had a lot of skill with a song as well as a very endearing personality. One evening at the Players he had laughingly suggested to Vida that if she couldn't find a Jack Buchanan type to play Tony, she might fancy someone who could play him like Bobby Howes. This had rung a bell with her, and after auditioning for Ernie as well, John was given the part. With the help of Tony Hayes a tap-dance instructor was found, and John spent the next three months learning, step for step, the two routines which he would be required to do in *The Boy Friend*.

Now the only rôle left to cast was Madame Dubonnet. After seeing a number of candidates, Vida's choice fell upon a singer and comedienne who was currently appearing as the comic at the Windmill Theatre, the only woman ever to have done so. Her name was Eileen Murphy and she was to play a crucial part off-stage in the events that led to *The Boy Friend*'s opening on Broadway:

'I had never seen it, but I knew it was an enormous success. I had a girl friend, Coleen Clifford, in *Guys and Dolls* and she told me they were looking for a Madame Dubonnet, and I said, "Oh, really?" because I was auditioning for something else, something I wanted very badly. But she said, "I'll speak to Johnnie Heawood." I never expected to hear any more, but to my amazement Vida rang me and asked me if I would audition for her at the Coliseum, and because I wasn't aware of America and everything I hadn't any nerves but just gave an audition and enjoyed it. Everybody was terribly kind and flattering, and eventually I was engaged and that was that. So then I went to see the show at Wyndhams and I was delighted. I thought, "Wonderful! It's right up my street, and it'll be the greatest fun in the world to go to America with it." '

It was arranged that Vida would sail to New York towards the end of July to complete the casting, and I would follow in mid-August. Johnnie Heawood had been put under contract by Feuer and Martin with a view to choreographing their next show, and he would be there ahead of us. Shortly after *The Boy Friend* opened at Wyndhams, Jon and I, on advice from Peter King, had formed a limited company, both to take care of what promised to be a huge increase in my earnings and also, we hoped, to produce my future work. Jon would therefore be coming with me to New York in his official capacity as company director, but, as far as I was concerned, I had no intention of going there alone anyway. The whole thing was an adventure, and an exciting one, but it also had its frightening side, because none of us had ever been involved in such a high-powered operation, and, much as I appreciated Cy and Ernie's enthusiasm for *The Boy Friend*, I was beginning to detect in their behaviour a certain lack of humanity.

Now that everything was fixed up, Jon and I decided to take a holiday on the Continent. Apart from my visits to Paris and my overseas service, I had never been abroad, and the means to travel was one of the best benefits that the success of *The Boy Friend* had brought me. Jon, like most Australians on their arrival in Europe, had already been to France and Italy, and he mapped out an itinerary: we would fly to Nice by night, take a train to Rome, and then on to Naples and Capri, returning via Rome to Juan-les-Pins for a week or so, and flying back to London. Before we went I decided that it would be a good idea to take our new leading lady out to dinner. Together with Vida and Derek Twist, I invited Julie and her current admirer, the actor Neil McCallum, to the Royal Court Theatre Club, then a restaurant and cabaret run by Clement Freud. Throughout the evening I was struck again by Julie's perfect behaviour: a combination of schoolgirlish innocence with a control and poise far in advance of her years. As I watched her and listened to her, I wondered if we might be about to assist at the birth of a new star, someone as remarkable in her way as Gertrude Lawrence. Then, in a moment of insight unusual for me, I realised that this girl would be a star anyway, with or without our assistance. It was nothing that she said or did, and she certainly betrayed no symptoms of egotism or ambition; she simply had about her an unmistakeable air of cool, clear-cut determination. For Julie, I could tell, it was going to be the top or nothing.

Our holiday went more or less as planned. I was thrilled by my first glimpse of the Riviera by night: it actually was, as everyone has described it, like a diamond necklace strung along the Mediterranean. While waiting for the train to Rome, we walked down to the Plage at dawn and I saw, for the first time, the actual settings I had imagined for *The Boy Friend*. When we reached Rome that evening we discovered that there was a train leaving for Naples in a few minutes; so we decided to catch it instead of staying the night in Rome. We had dinner on board and found ourselves at the same table as a middle-aged American lady who was plying a paper fan with great rapidity. She introduced herself to us as Marion Abbott Kimball and announced that she was travelling to Taormina to stay with 'two darling boys' who owned a villa there, one of whom I happened to know vaguely in London. We told her that we were going to New York in the autumn for the opening of my show, and she made us promise to get in touch with her when we arrived there. As the train approached Naples we left her in the dining-car, still fanning herself energetically.

By the time we returned to London a few weeks later, I was feeling fit and ready for whatever ordeal lay ahead. Vida was sailing on the *Ile de France*, and the whole *Boy Friend* company were at Waterloo to see her off on the boat train. She had promised to keep a diary of her trip and send one copy to Derek, one to Wyndhams, and one to Joannie. That evening on board ship she wrote:

'At last this terrifying day has come and I am due to embark on this incredible adventure, which means so much to me personally and to the dear *Boy Friend* and has now gone beyond my own intimate circle and become almost a source of national pride. The whole of Britain waits for the show to conquer New York. And can we ever do it again? I wonder . . .

'All my darling cast came to see me off. Will there ever be such a feeling in any show – this strange family thing that we have: what happens to one is important to all the rest. They are so loyal and wonderful to me that, as I looked at that galaxy of good looks, charm, talent and kindness, I realised that, however good and nice the American company are, they will never be my only original "children". I love them so dearly that when they sang *I Could Be Happy with You* for me as the train was due to leave, I was overwhelmed. They are always making me cry . . .'

A few days later I had a letter from her. Her first contact with Americans, on board the ship, had not been very encouraging. McCarthyism still flourished and she found that her fellow passengers were deeply suspicious of the British and their socialist notions: even 'your little Queen', as they referred to her, needed watching:

'I must admit at the moment I feel full of apprehension,' Vida wrote, 'and try as I may I cannot accept the Americans as anything more than children. I just wouldn't begin to know what they will make of *The Boy Friend* – not much, I shouldn't think, judging by this boat. They seem to lack all sense or appreciation of subtlety. But perhaps I'm being mean and New York will prove quite different.

'Darling boy, I miss you like stink, and I shall be the happiest girl in the world when I come to meet you off *your* boat. It doesn't seem right somehow that I should be out here working alone on what is our joint baby. Never mind; when you arrive, it will all seem normal and ordinary again . . .'

I had rather fancied sailing on the *Queen Elizabeth* or the *Queen Mary*, but earlier in the year I received a letter from a friend of mine, Michael Edwards, whom I had known at Harrow, to tell me that he was working for the American shipping line in London and that, if I cared for the idea, he would like to arrange my passage on their new boat, the *United States*, and assured me that I would have the best of treatment and any publicity I required. This sounded like a good idea: to travel on an American boat would give us a foretaste of what to expect in New York, and, as neither of us had travelled first class before, it would be comforting to do it in the guise of VIPs.

We sailed on August 12th and I also decided to keep a diary, for my own benefit, but only managed to do so until we reached New York:

'The leave-taking was very sketchy on my part because of having to pose for photographs, kissing Ann Wakefield, Eileen Murphy and Joannie and smiling at the same time until my face ached. Mother had brought me some magazines wrapped in a plastic Union Jack which appealed to the Press tremendously, and Joannie and I posed with it draped across our chests . . .

'When we came on board ship we were greeted by a reporter from the *Daily Sketch* – quite a satisfactory interview except that, as is so often the case, he hadn't seen *The Boy Friend* and didn't have a clue what it was about. All he could say was that the title sounded "queer" and "gay". So I had to emphasise that it wasn't that kind of show at all . . .'

The passenger list was almost entirely made up of Americans returning from holidays in Europe and we were put at the Purser's table with three middle-aged ladies who were lively and amusing and rather more intelligent than the people Vida had been blessed with on the *Ile de France*. We both ate and drank an enormous amount, and I was staggered by the size and extravagance of the menus. The ship, while built on rather austere lines – it was rumoured that she could be converted to a troop-carrier at a moment's notice – struck me as being elegantly and tastefully designed, and the service was cheerful and efficient. The only other Show Business people on board were Ozzie and Harriet Nelson, who at the time had a popular family series on TV in the States. When we were introduced to them, she was flattered by my remembering her as Harriet Hilliard, singing *Get Thee Behind Me, Satan* in the Astaire-Rogers film *Follow the Fleet*; but her husband expressed strong disapproval when I told him how much I had enjoyed *Call Me Madam*. He considered it 'un-American'. We made friends with a family, Harriet and Leon Mnuchin and their daughter Renée, who were returning to New York from a European holiday during which Leon, who had a collection of modern art, had purchased, among other things, a statue by Maillol. I was duly impressed. They made us promise to get in touch with them in New York and come and stay for the week-end at their house in Scarsdale.

We were due to arrive early on the morning of August 17th. At six a.m. I looked out of the port-hole and had my first glimpse of America in the rising sun. Jon was having a shower, but I hauled him out to see the famous sky-line. It looked very pretty and quite unreal, like a delicately painted back-drop. At eight o'clock we disembarked and found Vida, Johnnie and Arthur Lewis waiting on the dockside to greet us. Vida and Johnnie looked well and sunburned, but were obviously very glad that I had arrived. With Vida we drove to the hotel where we were all staying, the Park Chambers, on the corner of Sixth Avenue and 58th Street. It had been recommended to us by various theatre people in London as being unpretentious and reasonable, with a staff who were well disposed towards the English – all of which turned out to be quite true. Once we were alone with Vida in our room and coffee had been sent up, she began to enlarge on the horrors of New York, the Americans and, in particular, of Cy Feuer and Ernie Martin.

On first arriving in New York, she had been given every kind of hospitality by both of them, taken to dine at Sardi's and invited to their houses for drinks and meals. And then after three days they had both quite suddenly and without informing her in advance disappeared to California to work on their next show with Cole Porter, leaving Vida alone in New York, apart from Johnnie Heawood. It was the middle of August, when New York is suffocatingly hot, Vida knew hardly anybody, and the living allowance she had been given was barely enough for her basic needs. Some of her time was taken up with auditioning and casting the remaining parts in the show, which had not been easy owing to the dearth of the right kind of acting talent on Broadway; but she had found an excellent Bobby in Larry Howard, who, she informed us, was an absolute dish and looked like Dirk Bogarde when he was young. Lady Brockhurst was to be played by an English actress, Moyna McGill, the mother of Angela Lansbury. It had been very difficult to find a good Hortense, but Vida had finally settled on a girl who was currently appearing with Tom Ewell in *The Seven Year Itch*, called Paulette Girard. The boys were Buddy Schwab, Jerry Newby and Joe Milan, the latter, being dark and extremely good-looking, to dance the Tango. So far all was well, but when the time came to cast understudies and walk-ons, she discovered, to her astonishment, that she was being asked to audition actresses not as understudies to Madame Dubonnet but to play her, since Ernie Martin had decided that Eileen Murphy was not right for the part and would have to be replaced. Vida quite naturally refused to take this seriously and made it quite clear that Eileen was to play and that was that. But it turned out that, while all the other English members of the company had received their visas, Eileen's had not come through.

One evening, Arthur Lewis had taken Vida out to dinner at Sardi's and, in the course of the meal, had casually told her that Cy and Ernie had decided to find a new Madame Dubonnet in New York. Vida now completely lost patience and told him that she would have it out with Ernie who was due back in New York the next day. On arriving at the Feuer and Martin office she was confronted by Ernie, Arthur, Ira Bernstein, Feuer and Martin's casting director, and their business manager, Monty Schaff, a thick-set gorilla-like man who reminded us all of a Hollywood hoodlum. Before they could begin to brow-beat her, she told them firmly that *she* was going to do the talking and they would have to listen to her for a change, and for one and a half hours she made them do so, at the end of which Ernie Martin rather weakly agreed to arrange Eileen's visa and bring her over from England with the rest of the cast.

Vida was triumphant but exhausted. She had already discovered that Americans, far from being quick and business-like as we had been led to believe, took endless time to get anything done, largely because every decision, on even the smallest matter such as the shape of heel on the girls' shoes, appeared to them to present what Vida described as a 'prahblem', which necessitated hours of discussion and argument, often ending in a shouting match, at which point they would decide to do what she had suggested in the first place. On top of that she was bitterly home-sick and missing Derek very much, but now we were with her and probably everything would be all right from now on.

She left us to unpack and have a rest, and I began to have my first forebodings about the future. But Jon was determined to be cheerful and, looking out of the window, drew my attention to the sign on a hotel roof a block or two away.

'Look,' he said, 'that's a good omen!'

The sign read: The Wyndham Hotel.

That day was, I regret to say, the last one recorded in my diary:

'After lunch, as we were both feeling very tired, we went and lay in Central Park which, we have been warned, is a den of vice by night and not much safer by day. However we both slept quite peacefully, only to be woken by a coloured mother calling out to her small boy, "Conrad! Conrad! If yo' run down there again, yo'll break yo' neck!"'

'For dinner we had been asked with Vida to go to Sardi's, with Arthur and Ernie and his wife. Vida walked there with us from the hotel. A few blocks down Sixth Avenue she stopped us and, with a gesture, said, "Look – there it is!" "It" was Times Square, and it is indescribable – Vulgarity exalted to such a degree that it becomes Magnificence.

'Sardi's was crowded when we got there, and we had to wait quite a while for our table. It has no particular atmosphere, and is not very elegant to look at. The caricatures of Theatre People which cover the walls are entertaining, but otherwise I was a little disappointed. The food was lavish, but not of very high quality.

'Mrs Martin turned out to be Nancy Guild, whom I saw in several films about ten years ago. She was very charming, but a little superficial, and I had the impression that the whole evening was "laid on" to make us feel we were at home and didn't really mean a great deal, but I may be wrong.'

After dinner we looked in at the Royale, where *The Boy Friend* was to open and which was currently occupied by *Sabrina Fair*. It seemed rather austere and unwelcoming in comparison with Wyndhams, and the stage, like so many Broadway theatres, was wider and shallower than is usual in London; but the larger orchestra pit would undoubtedly be an advantage, and the auditorium did have a certain intimacy. When we came out, Ernie asked us what we would like to do to round off the evening. We said we wanted to go to a drug-store, and we were led into Howard Johnson's where malted milks and ice-cream sodas were ordered – 'Very democratic!' I said in my diary.

Vida was also busy supervising the physical side of the show, the scenery, wardrobe and the lighting, which was in the hands of one of Broadway's top experts, Abe Feder, whom Vida considered a genius. It was all very different from the original production at the Players, where Reggie Woolley had assembled the sets largely from stock: one piece of scenery, the arch at the back of Act Three, had done service in an Arts Council tour of *Macbeth* and had at one point fallen into the sea when the company visited South Africa. The costumes had been assembled from the Players' wardrobe, supplemented by loans from friends and relatives, and the girls' frocks and bathing costumes had been run up on a sewing machine by Mary Bennett, with some assistance from the girls themselves. Even with the replacements and refurbishings that were necessary when we transferred to Wyndhams, the whole production cost barely two thousand pounds. The estimated cost for Broadway was the equivalent of sixty thousand pounds. While they were in London, Cy and Ernie had arranged for a film to be made of an entire performance, given without audience at Wyndhams one afternoon, which must in itself have cost a pretty penny. They did this to ensure that they had a complete record of the London production, and they supplemented it with still photographs of every item of the wardrobe, including hats, shoes and jewellery. Meanwhile Reggie, whose system was to rout about among his stock and use whatever struck him as suitable, was obliged to make detailed drawings of every piece of scenery, including a small, solitary pillar which had been lying around at the Players for years and which he had added, on the spur of the moment, to the set for Act Two. All this had to be reproduced, at tremendous cost, by the top costumiers and scenic studios in New York, and, needless to say, the result never achieved the slightly dowdy charm and authenticity of the original.

While this was going on, Jon and I were busy exploring New York, which I found, and still find, an exciting and alarming city. What struck me at once on my first visit was how foreign it was. I had mistakenly assumed that, because we had a common language, I would feel more at home there than in, say, Paris or Rome; but the opposite was the case. The language was the same, roughly, but the habits, attitudes, standards and manners were totally alien. The next thing that astonished me, coming from a country where austerity was a very recent memory, was the profligate luxury of everything. The shops were like gigantic treasure chests, overflowing with the loot of the world, where we spent hours just gazing and marvelling. The restaurants were similarly lavish: every dish was a mountain of food, coated with sauces, relishes and garnishes, but unfortunately, when one got down to eating it, tasting of practically nothing. We learned early on that the best food in New York is also the cheapest, and we lived for most of the time on delicious hamburgers, malted milks and ice-cream sodas at the corner drug-stores. Drink was another matter: it was extraordinary to be able to drop into a bar at any time of the day or night and order a perfectly mixed manhattan, martini or, particularly in the stifling heat, a glass of ice-cold beer. Until I went to New York drink was something which I enjoyed when it was available but never missed very much when it was not. Now it began to be a regular part of my life and has remained so, for better or for worse, ever since. It was only when we had been in America for a few weeks that I realised that the strength of spirits is much higher there than in England: those dry martinis that we knocked back so casually every evening each contained the equivalent of a triple gin in an English pub. At first I was shocked by the way Americans added a mere dash of vermouth to their cocktails; in England I had been used to what was called a 'gin and French' or a 'gin and It'. But before long I was agreeing with them that it was a much better drink, and I cultivated a taste for very dry martinis which I have, perhaps regrettably, never lost.

We also went to the theatre, but, as it was still high summer, there was not a great deal to see, most of the few shows remaining open being 'hold-overs' from a previous season. The first one we went to was of course Feuer and Martin's latest hit, *Can Can*. We were given seats at the front of the stalls – or 'orchestra' as it is called there – near the percussion section, and the opening bars of the overture nearly gave me a heart attack. The show itself turned out to be an unbelievably vulgar farrago of clichés about the oh-so-naughty French in Gay Paree, barely redeemed by a few of the Cole Porter numbers and atrociously performed by a second-rate cast, with the exception of the red-headed soubrette, Gwen Verdon. My spirits sank at the thought that the people who were responsible for this abomination now had their hands on *The Boy Friend*. The next musical we saw was not much better, a period hotch-potch called *By the Beautiful Sea* starring Shirley Booth, whom I had admired so much in the film of *Come Back, Little Sheba*. But through a girl-friend of Michael Edwards, Marcia Scott, we were introduced to Hal Prince, then flushed with his first success as a producer, *The Pajama Game*, and he secured us tickets, which were almost unobtainable at the time. To me it did not compare with the great American musicals I had seen in London, but it was at least fresh and bright and enthusiastically put over by a talented cast. I was more interested to see a revival of Rodgers and Hart's *On Your Toes* for which Hal also got us tickets, but, while the score still sounded fine, the book had dated badly and Vera Zorina, in the rôle she had played in London in the Thirties, was beginning to do the same.

But, in spite of these disappointments, I was finding New York a stimulating and enjoyable place to be. I was very taken with the attitude of theatre people and journalists towards the Musical: in England it was considered a rather disreputable relative of the straight theatre, something to be done occasionally for fun but not to be taken seriously; here it was treated with as much respect as the latest play by Tennessee Williams or Arthur Miller or a new production of *Hamlet*. Another thing that attracted me to New York was its size: in comparison with London, so sprawling and undefined, Manhattan seemed very compact and accessible, so that one felt within easy reach of other people, almost in the manner of village life; and I liked to stand on an avenue in mid-town and, looking east and west to the River, remind myself that the whole extraordinary place was on a rather small island. It was also pleasing to find that the types one met every day, the cab-drivers, the cops, the soda-jerks and the shop-girls were exactly, but exactly, the same as their counterparts on the screen, whose jargon and behaviour I had been perfectly familiar with for the last twenty years. It was a comfort to know that Hollywood, in this respect at least, was so utterly true to life.

Rehearsals were due to start on August 26th and the English cast were arriving by air a day or two before. But Ann Wakefield reached New York first, having insisted, rather to the management's displeasure, on sailing first class on the *United States*, since, as she put it, 'I had always seen myself arriving to do a Broadway musical on a liner, posing on the ship's rail for photographs, saying "cheese", the lot!' All the others flew in to Idlewild two days later – all, that is, except Eileen Murphy. Her visa had still not come through, but Arthur assured Vida that it was in hand and she would be arriving at the week-end. That evening he gave a dinner party for us all in an upstairs room at Sardi's, and we were all so excited and happy to be together again that it turned into a gala affair. After dinner a party of us left Sardi's, headed by Johnnie Heawood, who insisted that we should all visit his friends, Allyn Ann

McLerie and her husband, George Gaynes. When we arrived at their apartment, we realised that Hermione, who was now domiciled in America, lived in the same block, and nothing would do but we must visit her too. If she was surprised by the incursion into her bedroom at one a.m. of a horde of inebriated acquaintances from England, she disguised it perfectly and made us welcome. Vida finally managed to shepherd John Hewer and me back to the Park Chambers and our beds at about three in the morning.

The first reading took place, with Vida giving her accustomed speech at the end about authenticity and playing straight which, to her astonishment, was applauded by the American members of the cast. The only disturbing element was the rather mystifying presence of Eileen Murphy's understudy, a well-upholstered brunette called Ruth Altman. 'She stood apart from us all, as if she had the measles,' Ann remembers, 'wearing striking blue. I thought she must be somebody's wife. Then somebody said, "Eileen Murphy isn't here, so Ruth will read Madame Dubonnet." ' The American boys hit it off immediately with the English girls and took them off at the lunch-break. 'We all tumbled into that bar round the corner, Sid and Al's, and had beer and chicken sandwiches. It looked as if we were all going to have a lot of fun.' Buddy Schwab, who was playing Alphonse, had been Vida's first choice to play Bobby van Husen, but Cy Feuer had turned him down:

'On the very first day of rehearsals, during the first five minute break, Vida walked over to me and said, "I'm so glad you're doing the show," and I was bowled over! I fell in love with *The Boy Friend* from that first moment, and I think all the Americans felt the same.'

At the lunch-break I was introduced to the theatre critic of *The Saturday Review*, a tall, lanky gentleman called Henry Hewes, who reminded me of an intellectual version of Joel McCrea. He had seen *The Boy Friend* in London, enjoyed it very much, and was interested in observing what happened to it on Broadway, so had accordingly been given permission to sit in on rehearsal from time to time. After chatting about the show for a while, he asked me if there was anyone I particularly wanted to meet in New York. I replied, without hesitation, 'Yes. Richard Rodgers,' and he said he would see if he could arrange a lunch date.

Although Vida never requested it, I felt that my presence at rehearsal might be needed more often than at home and that it might be a help to her and Johnnie to know that I was available, even if there was nothing much for me to do. Because of the rumoured revival of *Good News*, Cy Feuer had asked me to rewrite *The Riviera*, as its resemblance to *The Varsity Drag* might get us into copyright trouble. He was also a little concerned about the *Boy Friend* number, because I had quite deliberately based its harmonic progressions on those of *The Girl Friend*. As soon as they heard about this, Chappells, who had published the music in London, immediately, and without consulting me, removed the song from their piano selection. Cy asked me to have another tune in readiness, which I agreed to, but he then decided that the matter might be best dealt with if I acknowledged my debt to Rodgers in a short programme note.

Rehearsals progressed smoothly, apart from Vida's nightly ordeal of 'the conference', whereby she, Arthur Lewis, the stage manager, the musical director, and anyone else who happened to be around and felt like pitching in, would spend half an hour or more discussing what was to be done the next day. Invariably whatever Vida suggested would present 'prahblems', which had to be evaluated, argued over and shouted about, until, as usual, when everyone had had his say, it was decided to do what she had told them in the first place. We were also a little disturbed by the comings and goings in the auditorium, which always seemed to be peopled by anonymous figures creeping around in clouds of cigar smoke and discussing business matters in very audible whispers. What made it more irritating was that it was not always *The Boy Friend* which was under discussion: Feuer and Martin were in the throes of preparing their next show, a musical version of Garbo's comedy, *Ninotchka*, for which Cole Porter had written the score. I felt they would do much better to go away and discuss it elsewhere or preferably concentrate on *The Boy Friend*, and it was the last straw when, on the arrival of Teddie Holmes, Chappells' manager in London, Arthur invited us to have a drink together and then proceeded to sing, very badly, the whole of Cole Porter's latest ballad for Don Ameche, *All of You*. At one moment during rehearsals Ameche himself, followed by two or three of his many sons, walked straight across the stage and into the auditorium while Vida was in the middle of directing a scene.

My promised lunch with Richard Rodgers was arranged by Henry Hewes, but was something of a disappointment. Rodgers, I gathered later, was far from well at the time, and was obviously not in the mood to be badgered by questions from an inquisitive young Englishman. When I asked him how he had felt about Valerie Hobson's performance in *The King and I* in London, he replied rather tersely that she was infinitely better than Gertrude Lawrence, who could never sing in tune. And when I inquired whether he was happier working with Hammerstein or Hart, he said, 'Hammerstein of course,' which rather shocked me, but, on reflection, was the only answer he could give, since he was currently collaborating with Hammerstein on their new musical,

Pipedream. But the encouraging outcome of the lunch was that Rodgers sent a message to Cy Feuer telling him not to worry about the resemblance of *The Boy Friend* to *The Girl Friend*. He realised it was meant as a tribute and there was no need for me to make any acknowledgement.

In the absence of Eileen Murphy, Vida continued to rehearse Ruth Altman in her part. Eileen's visa had come through, we were told, but, at a time when all the American tourists were returning from Europe, she was having difficulty in getting a plane to New York. Finally Joannie Rees put her on a flight from Heathrow which was due to arrive on the morning of August 30th. Eileen had been baffled and harassed by the behaviour of the American management, but Vida had constantly sent her messages of reassurance, and now at last she was on her way:

'But I flew on the only plane ever known to land at Goose Bay *and* Iceland – it went on for ever and ever. I was met at the other end by someone from the firm who took me through the crossest customs I have ever been through in my life. So then we got into a taxi and, as we drove off, four cars ahead of us jammed their brakes on and I was shot off the seat right on to my nose. The driver, to my intense amusement, put his face round the partition and said, "Are you gonna sue?" I said, "What for?", and he said, "Ya gotta sue!" And I said, "But I'm not hurt," and he said, "No – but ya *might* be!" If I'd only learned my lesson from that, I might have been better prepared for what followed.

'However I was taken to Park Chambers, where you were all staying. I was stone-deaf from the aeroplane, and it was in the middle of a New York heat wave, so I collapsed and crawled into a bath and thought, "Blessed peace! I'll take a couple of sleeping pills and face the world tomorrow." At that moment the door burst open and there was dear Vida, in a fearful state, saying, "Eileen, you're wanted at the theatre immediately. They want to throw you out of the show. They've put in this girl who was engaged as your understudy and they've been rehearsing her for days. But *you*'re going to play, and if you don't, the show's not going on. But you've got to come down tonight. And look sexy!" – which killed me, because I wanted to be sick not sexy.

'Well, I dressed myself up in a gaily coloured cotton frock – very fitting round the bust – and I had a huge fuchsia scarf that I was wound in, which made me feel very glamorous. Eric Berry came to take me to the theatre, and there were all my friends, delighted to see me, and I said to darling Julie Andrews, "I can't hear a thing, so for heaven's sake, if I'm flat or sharp, make a signal." Then we plunged into *Poor*

Little Pierrette and to my great joy Julie made a sign that I was dead on the note. Apparently at this juncture Cy Feuer, who was sitting out front, turned to Vida and said, "You're right, honey. She was worth waiting for." But there was a funny feeling prevalent . . .'

Eileen went into rehearsal the next day and I thought the matter had been settled. But on the following Friday I was asked to come to the theatre at lunch-time and watch Eileen and Ruth Altman go through the same scene with Eric, after which it would be decided once and for all who was to play Madame Dubonnet. I regarded the whole perform-ance as a farce, because I had never for a moment taken the possibility of Eileen's dismissal seriously. We had cast her and she had been signed, and that was that. But I sat through the two renditions and at the end of it the choice seemed more obvious than ever: Eileen was infinitely better than Ruth in every way. She was a little unsure of herself, which, under the circumstances, was hardly surprising; but her voice, her appearance and her manner were right, and I was convinced that Ernie Martin, who had been the only one to object to her in the first place, would now have the grace to admit that he was wrong. To my astonishment exactly the opposite occurred: both Cy and Ernie came over to us and said, 'Well, that's it, I guess. We play Ruth Altman.' There was no discussion, no argument: Eileen was out, and Ruth was in.

Very much later I learned that Vida, during the few days that she rehearsed her, had in fact been disappointed by Eileen's performance, and when faced with Cy and Ernie's decision, she had elected to give in with as good a grace as possible, while still professing her preference for Eileen. She had put up a tremendous struggle on Eileen's behalf, but now she was well into rehearsal, there was so much work to be done, and it must have seemed to her better, for the sake of the show as a whole, to try and get a reasonable performance out of Ruth and concentrate on making everyone else as good as possible. But I had no idea of her feelings at the time and could only regard Cy and Ernie's behaviour as obstinate and misguided.

Jon and I had been invited to stay for Labour Day week-end with the Mnuchins, the family we had met on the boat, at their house in Scars-dale. All the respectable clothes I had brought from England were far too thick to wear in the intense heat, so I went to Lord and Taylor's and bought a suit made of synthetic fibre which I was told, to my amazement, could be washed in the bath and worn the next day. The Mnuchins' house was like a film set: richly and tastefully decorated and bearing scarcely a trace of human habitation. Leon kept the best of his art collection in his study, where it was illuminated by a complicated system of spotlights. They entertained us lavishly and generously, but my mind refused to leave *The Boy Friend*. If Eileen could be replaced so arbitrarily, were there any limits to Cy and Ernie's interference? I had no idea what my rights were in the matter. In England the author is obliged to submit to all 'reasonable decisions' of the management. As far as I knew, it was the same in America, but I wanted to make sure. The only person that I could ask was Henry Hewes.

Eileen's own situation was now humiliating and bewildering. Having been put through a torment of uncertainty in England, she had finally reached New York, only to be told, within a matter of days, that she was no longer wanted. But instead of collapsing she decided to brave it out:

'Obviously they thought I would burst into tears, crumble and melt away on a plane back to England the next day. But I just laughed at them and said, "Don't be silly. You've engaged me and I want to play." In my innocence I thought, "This is simple. Let us go to Court." But it never got to that, because they went on rehearsing Ruth but made me go down to the theatre every day and go through my part with her understudy. To begin with, I was angry and hurt, and I cried. Then, just as I was giving up the ghost and feeling that perhaps I should commit suicide out of that fifth floor window at Park Chambers, at that precise moment a carillon burst forth from the church opposite – and do you know what they were playing? *When I Marry Mister Snow*. And I thought, "How ridiculous! This country is to be laughed at, not taken seriously." '

So she dutifully turned up at every rehearsal when Mme Dubonnet was called and sat in the stalls while Ruth Altman went through her rôle on stage.

'If they had been halfway decent, they would have said to me, "Look, Eileen, we don't fancy your face or your figure. Will you accept so much as payment and go back to London?" But they never even gave me any kind of reason why they didn't want me. They just made me feel like Quasimodo, and I had to keep getting out my photographs and saying, "This is me!" Ernie never looked at me or spoke to me. So I began to think I must remind him of someone in his youth who had had a dreadful effect on him. It was a weird experience.'

Otherwise, the show was taking shape very well. All the English company were proving themselves to be worthy counterparts to the London cast. Julie was a dream to rehearse with, picking up each precise gesture and inflection the moment it was given to her, and John Hewer, having slaved away for weeks at his tap-dancing, was bringing his own particular charm to the part of Tony. The new girls were delightful, and Dilys produced a curiously hoarse squeak in her voice which was as individual as Maria's had been in London. Geoffrey Hibbert and Eric Berry were excellent, and Geoffrey was eventually to become totally identified in my mind with Lord Brockhurst. The Americans were integrating themselves perfectly into the style of the show. Moyna McGill, a woman of great sweetness, had a little difficulty at first in conveying Lady Brockhurst's ferocity, but she managed it. Larry Howard, who was studying the Method, had, to begin with, been anxious to discuss the motivations and the background to the character of Bobby van Husen. Vida had passed him over to me and I had simply said to Larry, 'He's very rich,' which seemed to satisfy him, and he was now giving a most winning performance and making a perfect partner for Ann Wakefield. Paulette Girard's Hortense was chic and sly rather than bubbling, in the style of Violetta, but was none-the-less in keeping, and the other boys were acquiring French accents and of course, being Americans, dancing up a storm. Johnnie Heawood's new version of *The Riviera* was even more energetic and exciting than the original, and promised to stop the show. All in all, by the time we reached the dress rehearsal period, I felt that, apart from the playing of Mme Dubonnet, the show had a chance of being every bit as good as the London production.

When I told Henry Hewes about the management's behaviour, he advised me to get in touch with the Dramatists' Guild, of whose existence I was quite unaware. He also introduced me to a lawyer, Lloyd Almirall, who was experienced in theatrical affairs and was also a partner of the actor and producer, Maurice Evans. I now realised that it had been sheer folly for us to arrive in New York to do a Broadway show without legal or artistic representation of any kind. Joannie Rees was coming over for the first night but was not due to arrive until the week before we opened, by which time we would have started our previews. Since things seemed to be going smoothly at the moment, I decided for the time being I would take no action, but leave Vida and Johnnie to get on with the job undisturbed. On the advice of Lloyd Almirall, I simply reiterated to Cy and Ernie my disapproval of Eileen's dismissal and the casting of Ruth Altman.

The first complete dress rehearsal took place at the Royale Theatre on the afternoon of Saturday, September 18th. Rather as I expected, the technical rehearsals had been protracted and chaotic. 'Prahblems' abounded, and the auditorium was full of cigar smoke and gesticulating figures shouting at each other. Abe Feder was certainly a lighting genius, but his effects took an eternity to create, partly because his elaborate communications system kept breaking down and he was reduced to rushing down to the front of the stalls and bellowing for the stage manager. At one moment, during the lighting of Act Three, I asked timidly why the string of Chinese lanterns remained unlit. I was told that *The Boy Friend* was already burning more light than the London production of *The King and I* and that to illuminate the lanterns would mean engaging two more electricians at a cost of five hundred dollars a week. The lanterns, ghostly and joyless, remained unlit for the entire run. Photo-calls also took an age, in particular one that was held for the benefit of *Life Magazine*. A brutally aggressive female photographer appeared and sat on top of a step ladder in the auditorium, cursing everyone within sight; but I must confess that the results were striking. Eventually order was restored and we settled down to watch a complete performance of the show.

For a first dress rehearsal, it went remarkably well, and we all felt encouraged. There were faults in production and performance, and technical mistakes; but we had two more dress rehearsals and a week of previews in which to correct them. Vida and Johnnie had every reason to feel satisfied so far, I felt, and I was confirmed in my feelings when Albert Lewis, Arthur's father, who had been sitting just in front of me during the performance, turned round at the end and said to me, 'Well, all this show needs now is an audience.'

But Vida and I were not particularly surprised when Cy and Ernie asked us to come and have a talk with them. Another 'conference', we thought to ourselves, at which a couple of 'prahblems' will be aired, fussed over, and eventually settled: let's hope it doesn't take too long. We had been instructed to meet them in the Smoking Lounge, a dark and cheerless basement room at the front of the theatre. Cy and Ernie were already there, smoking their inevitable cigars. Vida and I seated ourselves, lit cigarettes and prepared to listen. Within a few moments it became clear that this was not to be a routine conference. With a certain amount of circumlocution, as was his habit, Cy Feuer was telling us that he was not happy with the entire show. Because of his complicated manner of explaining himself, it was a little difficult to understand why he was unhappy, but at the end of it it seemed to come down to one thing: the show lacked 'magic'. We were both nonplussed. Very few shows have any 'magic' at all at the dress rehearsal stage; one is thankful if a performance can just go through without too many hitches. Vida gave a little helpless laugh and began to explain this, which one would have thought to be unnecessary for two people who had so much experience in the Theatre. But Cy brushed her protests aside. They had seen the 'magic' in London, and they expected to see it here. Where was it? Where was The Magic? So far Ernie had said nothing, but I could see by his expression that he was preparing to weigh in, if necessary. Vida and I suddenly realised we were in some kind of a serious situation, but just what it was still seemed uncertain and unspecified. Vida, now no longer amused or nonplussed, was beginning to get annoyed, I could see. Throughout the entire rehearsal period she had been bedevilled by time-wasting discussions, arguments and squabbles. She was tired and fed up, but she had done a first-rate job, and now she began to tell them so:

'I don't know exactly what you mean, Cy,' she concluded, 'by the "Magic". I can only tell you this. In my opinion the production is in excellent shape and the whole cast are superb, with the one unfortunate exception of Miss Ruth Altman.'

Cy said nothing, just puffed hard on his cigar. But suddenly Ernie rose up from his chair, black in the face with rage, and, towering over Vida, shouted at her in the most obscene terms that she and I could take ourselves and our production out of this theatre, out of the country and back to England. It was a frightening display, and Vida, taken completely by surprise, cowered, shaking, before it. After that there seemed no point in continuing the discussion. I went over to Vida, helped her out of her chair and said, 'Come along. There's no need for us to stay here any longer.'

Jon was waiting in the foyer, and I handed Vida over to him, while I went into the auditorium. I felt weak with fear and disgust, and had no idea what I should do or say. Johnnie was on stage, taking the boys and girls through a routine. I called out to them, but I forget exactly what I said. I tried to tell them what had happened, and it was a mistake, because I was too overwrought and in any case it only concerned Johnnie. Then I rejoined Jon and Vida. She had recovered a little, and we took her arms and guided her over to Downey's where we ordered martinis. Jon had heard Ernie's outburst, but I filled in what had led up to it. After a while we decided that the best thing was to get Vida back to the hotel. We found a cab, and when we reached Park Chambers, she only got as far as the lobby where she collapsed on a chair, her head bowed to her knees and her hands dragging on the floor. I had never in my life seen a figure of such utter desolation.

A band call was scheduled for Sunday afternoon. Vida was unfit to go: the doctor who was called to treat her said that he had rarely seen such a bad case of nervous exhaustion. I went down to the Royale and had a word with the English cast: I told them Vida was unwell, but she would be returning to rehearsal very soon, and in the meanwhile I begged them not to submit to direction from anybody else. They were puzzled and a little frightened, but they agreed to do as I said. At the band call, when the whole orchestra played through the score for the first time, Cy Feuer came into his own. He was, like Jack Waller, an experienced and knowledgeable musician, but while Jack was an enthusiast, Cy was a fanatic. He stamped up and down at the front of the stalls beating time on the orchestra rail with his fist, shouting at the musical director and the artists. I was impressed by the arrangements which were far more elaborate than at Wyndhams, since we now had an orchestra of thirteen: some of the period effects were masterly and were enhanced by the marvellously authentic sound of a banjo. But it all seemed too frenetic to me, and Cy was constantly whipping the orchestra up to play faster and louder. I finally protested, as discreetly as I could – but I was, after all, the composer. Cy simply looked at me and made no reply. As far as he was concerned, the music now belonged to him.

Joannie Rees had left London and was sailing towards New York on the *Queen Mary*, quite oblivious of what had been going on. We felt sorry to spoil her trip, but decided that she had better be warned of what was awaiting her, and Jon rang her in mid-Atlantic. Vida was ordered to remain in bed by the doctor for the next day, Monday, but technical rehearsals continued at the theatre and Johnnie worked on the dance numbers. On Tuesday morning Jon and I went to meet Joannie off the boat and brought her back to the hotel. Vida was much better and the three of us told Joannie in detail what had happened. She then went off to Feuer and Martin's office, confident that she would be able to sort matters out and get everything back to normal by the next dress rehearsal which was due to take place that evening. She returned to the Park Chambers after lunch, looking crestfallen and uneasy. The news she had to tell us was that Feuer and Martin had dismissed Vida, and Cy was taking over the direction himself.

The cast had been called on stage by Cy after rehearsal and told that Vida was still unwell. He then went on to say that because this was an American production the management felt that various alterations were necessary and he would be rehearsing with them for the time being. It was all kept rather vague, and the artists were given the feeling that it was perhaps some temporary arrangement and Vida would be back. With the exception of Eric, none of the English cast had been to America before, and they were mostly young and without experience of working for a big management.

'We didn't really know what was happening,' said Dilys, 'and we were all so nervous any way, as the understudies were rehearsing upstairs while we were rehearsing on stage, and we didn't know who might be sacked next. At the end of his speech Cy said, "We've never had a flop before and we're not having one now. You're gonna work like horses and you're gonna be exhausted at the post, but you're gonna be great." '

Most of the American cast were more used to the rigours of a Broadway musical, but to Buddy Schwab it all came as a surprise: 'I was very unhappy because it was my first experience of seeing someone take over and I felt they were absolutely wrong to do so. I knew the show had been done in England very successfully, and I felt they should have left it that way.'

I decided to go to rehearsal with Joannie and see for myself what was going on. When we arrived, Cy was working with Eric Berry on stage, but we had hardly taken our seats in the auditorium before we were asked to leave. The next step was to consult the Dramatists' Guild, and they advised me that I should send a telegram to the Feuer and Martin office inquiring rehearsal times for the next day; if I received a reply, I should again go to the theatre. A telegram arrived at lunch-time, saying that rehearsals were continuing as scheduled, and that afternoon I went to the stage door of the Imperial, where we were rehearsing, as the stage of the Royale was occupied by the technicians. I had barely got inside and just had a glimpse of the girls and boys on stage when Monty Schaff, looking more thug-like than ever, confronted me and told me that I must leave. I said that, as author, it was my right to attend rehearsals and attempted to move past him. The next thing I knew was that he and Charlie Pratt, the stage manager, both fairly hefty gentlemen, had grabbed me by the arms and were propelling me to the stage door. I struggled and called out, and one or two of the girls gave frightened glances in my direction. That was the last I saw of the rehearsal. I was pushed into an office by the stage door, where Monty told me that if I tried to get inside the theatre again, he would call the police. I wanted to say, 'Go ahead and call them.' It seemed incredible that he could even make the threat, and I felt confident that he would never carry it out. Then I suddenly had doubts: these people were so tough and ruthless that perhaps they *would* put me under arrest, if I made trouble. Instead I made a last attempt to get on to the stage, but it was fruitless. Monty and Charlie simply picked me up and deposited me on the sidewalk. I got to my feet and crossed rather shakily to the bar opposite, where Jon was waiting for me, and, after a drink, told him what had happened.

Now Vida, Jon and I felt quite isolated and helpless. Lloyd Almirall had told me that we must on no account talk to the Press or make any move or statement which might be construed as being detrimental to the production, since Feuer and Martin would use it as a pretext for counter-suing, if I decided to take any legal action. It would have been possible for me to put an injunction on the show and prevent its opening, but, with all the money involved and the weight behind them of three Broadway successes, Feuer and Martin were formidable enemies and in any case, I was told, a foreign author has rarely won a law-suit in America. Now all we could do was to wait until the first night, when we would be allowed to see the show. If it failed, I would be in a much stronger position to sue the management for interfering and spoiling it. It was a miserable prospect and a beastly situation, but there seemed to be nothing we could do about it.

We did have some contact with the members of the cast who were staying at the Park Chambers. On the first evening after our banishment they came up to Vida's room, and poor Dilys cried a little. But Vida just comforted her and told her she had better go on and do as she was told. There seemed to be no question of the English company refusing to work with Cy. The only person who might have led a protest was Eric Berry, as the senior member of the cast, but he too felt that it was best to comply with the management's wishes. Johnnie Heawood, since he was under contract to Feuer and Martin for their next show, was hardly in a position to go against them; all he could do was to continue rehearsing the company and hope that something good would come out of it at the end. But it soon became apparent to him that Cy and Ernie were not going to be content with improving what was already a complete production or even with attempting to inject into it what they believed in as 'the magic'. They were going to make changes:

'It was a truly horrible experience. I was standing at the back of the stalls watching a technical rehearsal of the Charleston that Abe Feder was lighting. We had Larry Howard as Bobby – absolutely ideal casting, as he *looked* like a millionaire's son. Ernie Martin came puffing up to me and said, "Don't worry about it, John. That bum will be out of here by tonight. We've got a new boy coming in tomorrow." And I suddenly thought to myself, "I'm in the presence of monsters. Anything can happen now."

'Then they tried to fire Julie Andrews. They wanted the understudy to replace her. She was a woman of about thirty-five, if I remember rightly, who sang very nicely and moved like a Churchill tank.'

But Julie, not unexpectedly, survived. One evening I met her in the lobby of the Park Chambers as she came in from rehearsal. Because of

Ruth's limitations both as a singer and an actress Julie's duet with her, *Poor Little Pierrette*, had been one of the weak spots in the show. I asked her how it was going now. 'Oh, marvellously,' she said. 'It's just as I want it.' I said I was glad to hear that, but I wondered uneasily what she meant.

The next person to be removed was Paulette Girard, who was sharing a dressing-room with Ann Wakefield:

'I arrived there one evening to do the second preview and there was a girl making up whom I'd never met, never seen rehearse. She knew the whole part of Hortense – she'd learned it in twenty-four hours. Her name was Barbara Ashley.'

Miss Ashley went on that night, and the next day was removed and Paulette found herself back in the show, but without her number, *It's Nicer in Nice*. Now Ann herself came under fire:

'One morning Arthur came up to the dressing-room and said I would not be playing Maisie that night. Millie was going to go on "as an experiment". But I read between the lines. He said, "Do you mind helping out and doing Nancy?" I had a feeling they were playing checkers, moving one piece and then another, seeing how things looked. I went over to the bar of the Lincoln Hotel and Eric was there, and he said, "Why don't you have a brandy?" I did and felt better. And that night I played Nancy like no-one's ever played her – goddammit! After the show I was waiting in the wings and watching the cigar smoke in the stalls. Finally I couldn't stand it and I went out and I said, "All right, gentlemen. What's it going to be?" I thought, "I might as well know now and get back to England and start afresh." But Arthur came up to me and said, "It's all right, Annie. You're playing Maisie tomorrow."'

Although we had followed Lloyd Almirall's instructions and kept our mouths shut, rumours were beginning to spread in the Theatre world that all was not well with *The Boy Friend*, and there were one or two hints in the Press about a dispute between myself and the management. One morning I was rung up by Oliver Messel, the English designer, who was in New York to work on a musical version of Truman Capote's story, *House of Flowers*, which Peter Brook was to direct. I had never met him, but he told me he had heard that Vida and I were in trouble and would it help to come round and talk about it? He was living in a house belonging to Ruth and Garson Kanin, over on the East Side, and Vida, Jon and I went to lunch there the next day. Peter Brook was also there and we poured out all our misfortunes to them. They were very sympathetic, and at the end of our recital Peter said:

'What a pity you couldn't have had a producer like Saint Subber (who was presenting *House of Flowers*). He's given us a completely free hand and he couldn't be more sensitive and helpful.'

We felt very envious and said so. What none of us could know at the time was that as soon as *House of Flowers* opened in Philadelphia Saint Subber would throw out Peter, Oliver Messel, George Balanchine, the choreographer, and Truman Capote himself.

We were sitting in the garden after lunch, when a window of an upstairs room next door was thrown open and someone leaned out and called down to us in a piping Southern accent, 'Whadda yo'all doin' dahn theyah?' It turned out to be Mr Capote and he was soon with us, joining in the commiserations. Oliver then very kindly suggested that, to fortify ourselves for the ordeal, we should come and have drinks with him before the opening night of *The Boy Friend*, to which he was also going. Joannie would of course be with us, and I had been in touch with Marion Abbott Kimball, the lady with the fan on the train to Naples, and asked her to come too.

The Boy Friend was now in the midst of previews, but we none of us had any idea how they were going, since we were barred from the theatre. One night Lloyd gave Jon and me seats for *Tea-house of the August Moon*, an enormous hit produced by his partner, Maurice Evans. On our way to the theatre we deliberately walked past the Royale. The audience were streaming in and there, patrolling the pavement, was Monty Schaff, on the look-out in case we might sneak in heavily disguised. He saw us and stiffened, prepared, I suppose, for another bouncing act. But we just made funny faces at him and passed on.

At home in England there was intense interest in the fate of *The Boy Friend* on Broadway, and one paper, the *Daily Mail*, had even sent over its critic, Cecil Wilson, to cover the first night. John Barber, the critic on the *Express*, who had encouraged me from the time of the first revue at the Watergate, wrote and asked me to send an impression of my experiences in New York for him to use in the paper. He was of course unaware of what had been going on, and I wrote back to put him in the picture, but told him that, until we opened, he must keep it to himself; after that he could publish what he liked. In my last paragraph I said:

'I am heart-broken, and so is Vida, that *The Boy Friend*, which we both love so much and whose success in London has made us so happy, should make its bow on Broadway without our final blessing. If it succeeds, I shall of course be glad and I shall earn precious dollars, but that is a small compensation for the fact that we shall now never know whether our *Boy Friend*, as we originally created it, would have succeeded on Broadway as it did in London.'

By the time the first night arrived, my feelings had been so assaulted, by anger, distress, fear and frustration, that I was almost numb. I put on my new dinner-jacket, the first I had ever had made for me, as an automatic ritual, without any of the excited anticipation I had felt at all the other first nights of *The Boy Friend*. The four of us, Vida, Joannie, Jon and myself, took a cab to Oliver's, and we hardly talked all the way there, although Joannie tried hard to brighten up the atmosphere. Oliver was again a kind and charming host, and after a couple of cocktails I began to feel a little excitement. Lloyd had undertaken to meet Marion Abbott Kimball at the old Astor Hotel in Times Square, and we joined them there and all proceeded to the Royale.

We had been seated fourteen rows back in the stalls, in order, I imagine, to keep us as much out of the lime-light as possible. I believe the audience that night was fairly star-studded, but I never saw any of them. At the time when we were still on good terms, Cy had told me that Cole Porter was coming to the opening night and I was to be introduced to him. Mr Porter may have been there, but, needless to say, I never met him. We just sat in our seats, watching the theatre fill up and wondering what the show was going to be like. Eric had several times assured Vida that nothing had been altered and the spirit of *The Boy Friend* was being preserved, but I found it hard to believe him.

The lights went down and the orchestra struck up the overture. As I expected, it was too loud and brassy, but it pleased the audience and they applauded when a couple of the brass section stood up and played the 'Boop-a-doops' during *Never Too Late*. Vida glanced at me and took my hand. A few moments later the curtain rose and Paulette began Hortense's opening speech on the telephone. Then there came the chatter and laughter from the wings and the girls trooped on with their dress boxes. But these were not the girls we had known – Maisie, Dulcie, Nancy and Fay, the Perfect Young Ladies of Madame Dubonnet's Finishing School. Vida's grasp on my hand became an agonised clench. Ann, Dilys, Stella and Millie had been turned into grimacing automatons, their faces plastered with garish make-up, their voices shrill and grating, their movements jerky and ludicrous. The audience rocked with laughter, and they continued to laugh when Julie appeared, her voice 'too terribly English for words' and her expressions and gestures mannered beyond all belief. But there was no love in the laughter. They were laughing *at* the Twenties, and what we had intended as an affectionate lampoon had been transformed into a mocking burlesque.

As the show progressed, I understood what Cy Feuer had done since Vida had been dispensed with: he had kept her physical production down to the last gesture and inflection, but he had removed the heart from it. What was left was a strident, graceless parody, without a trace of the truth and sincerity which Vida had gone to such pains to create from the moment of the very first reading at the Players.

The first act ended and we pushed our way out as quickly as we could and crossed the street to a bar where Lloyd ordered us drinks. Vida, Jon and I could not restrain ourselves; we sat and cried. We were seeing a child whom we had cherished distorted into a leering monstrosity, and it was agonising. Poor Marion, who had no notion of what had been happening, was overcome with concern and sat there saying, 'This is terrible – just terrible' over and over again. None of us wanted to return to the theatre, but Lloyd and Joannie pointed out that the Press would pounce on our absence, and the result would be damaging all round. We wiped away our tears and went back across the street. But an English journalist, Evelyn Irons, must have noticed our distressed appearance, because in her story the next day she expressed surprise that we, alone in the audience, did not seem to be enjoying the show.

For without a doubt *The Boy Friend* was being a success. Only at one moment in the second act, where the removal of *It's Nicer in Nice* had upset the careful construction, did the audience's enthusiasm flag. But then Ann came on and swept them off their feet with *Safety in Numbers*, which Cy had also attempted to cut at one point. Her new partner, Bob Scheerer, was a tough, seasoned Broadway hoofer, who danced the Charleston with colossal energy but totally lacked charm; however Ann managed to preserve a little of the essential Maisie and gave what was probably the best performance of the evening. 'But the joy had gone from it,' she told me later. 'That opening night – well, we had to do it, and we did. The response was marvellous. But it was a mechanical thing. It was all slightly soiled, because the original creators could take no pride in it.'

When the moment came for Julie to do *Poor Little Pierrette* with Ruth, I realised why she had been so pleased with the way it was going. With great skill and without actually changing anything, she had turned it into a comedy solo for herself. Ruth, an amiable and accommodating woman who had been pitch-forked into an awkward situation through no fault of her own, became insignificant and little more than a stooge for Julie's virtuosity. As I had foreseen from that evening in London, *The Boy Friend* was simply another stepping-stone in the path that would lead her to stardom.

I believe the reception at the end was tumultuous. Johnnie Heawood told me later that, after the final curtain call, the audience refused to leave the theatre:

'Anton Coppola, the musical director, played the going-out music, then just said, "Letter A" to the musicians and they played the overture, then the entr'actes and then back to the beginning again, and they literally played for thirty minutes while the people gradually charlestoned their way out into the street.'

But we left as soon as we could, and we had also been informed that we would not be welcome backstage. The cast were going, as is the custom in New York, to Sardi's; but we had been asked to a party at the apartment of George Kaufman and his wife, the English actress, Leueen McGrath. This was a courageous gesture on their part, since they were deeply involved with Feuer and Martin's next show, *Silk Stockings*: they had collaborated on the book, and George was to be the director. I sat on their terrace with Leueen and she said to me, 'What has happened to you and Vida makes me worried for George. I'm afraid they'll do the same thing to him, and I don't know whether he'll be able to stand it.'

George Kaufman was sacked by Cy and Ernie early on in the tour of *Silk Stockings*, but happily managed to survive for several years longer.

In spite of the Kaufmans' generous hospitality, I must have still looked rather down in the mouth, because a little while later Oliver Messel came up to me and said,

'Cheer up, Sandy. You ought to be looking pleased. Your show is going to be a hit.'

This came as a shock. I found it hard to understand why this cultured, civilised man could not realise that I no longer cared whether *The Boy Friend* was a 'hit'. As far as I was concerned, it was a disaster, and no amount of dollars could ever compensate for the damage that had been done to it.

When we returned to Park Chambers, there was a 'phone call for me, from Sardi's: the reviews had come out, they were excellent, and Cy and Ernie were giving a party for the company. As a final irony, the only person who thought of informing me was the one who, of all of them, had suffered the most, Eileen Murphy:

'I was so savage that you weren't there. It was so awful that here was this party being given in the upstairs room at Sardi's, and the man who was responsible for the whole thing coming to life had been flung out of the theatre and wasn't even with us.'

I told her as gently as I could that we were all very tired and wanted to go to bed. At that moment nothing and no-one in the world could have got me to Sardi's. All I wanted to do was to forget the whole thing and go home.

The next morning we had a meeting with Lloyd Almirall to decide on our course of action, but the previous night had already decided it for us.

'I'm sorry, Sandy,' said Lloyd. 'You're stuck with a hit.'

It was true, and the only thing I could do was, in someone's well-known phrase about Broadway, 'take the money and go'. The only dissenting voice among the critics was that of Henry Hewes. In the *Saturday Review* he ended his notice with these words:

'What Feuer and Martin have done to this show is to make a fast, raucous burlesque out of a carefree valentine. Perhaps the ensuing box office receipts will justify the change, and make these comments seem captious. After all there is still enough left of the original to make a brilliantly funny evening, and, as Larry Hart so beautifully stated it, "Caring too much is such a juvenile fancy." Very possibly only those looking for an old sweetheart will find *The Boy Friend* a loud-mouthed date who, unlike his British cousin, *knows* he is being the life of the party.'

The Press were anxious to hint at a reconciliation between Vida and myself and the management, now that the show was a success, and she and I were photographed for *Life* walking arm in arm past the queues at the box-office, grinning broadly. On the afternoon of her departure for London, Cy and Ernie suddenly appeared at the Park Chambers with a photographer who took a picture of us apparently seeing Vida off in a blaze of good will. In fact Vida and I are clearly looking firmly at each other. As soon as the photograph was taken, Cy and Ernie walked off down the street without addressing a word to either of us.

A week later Jon and I sailed for England on the *America*. Some people were surprised that I did not stay on for a while in New York, to enjoy my success. But I did not feel there was anything about it to enjoy. Everything had happened exactly as I had imagined it when I lay awake in the dormitory at Elstree: I had written a musical which had been a hit in London and was now a hit on Broadway. The dream had come true, but, even as it did so, it had been transformed into a nightmare.

SOON after *The Boy Friend* opened at Wyndhams, Joannie Rees
was approached by the Rank Organisation about the film rights.
The approach was made through the producer, Joseph Janni, who
was later to have a very successful partnership with John Schlesinger,
and Joannie suggested that I come to meet him at her house and hear
what he had in mind. It was very encouraging: he wanted me to work
closely with the scenarist on the script, and he wanted Vida to be
co-director, with the intention of ensuring that the film would retain
as much as possible of the style and feeling of the show. Having heard
many alarming stories of how film producers ignored the author and
flouted his wishes, I was very flattered and promised to consider the
proposition seriously. British studios had for years been trying to
produce successful musicals and up to that time, apart from the Jessie
Matthews vehicles of the Thirties, had failed dismally. It would be yet
another feather in *The Boy Friend*'s cap if it could break this jinx, and
I passed on the news enthusiastically to Vida.

Not long after that Feuer and Martin came on the scene, and in the
course of their negotiations with Joannie announced that they would
like to buy the film rights along with the rights for Broadway, as they
intended going into movie production to make screen versions of their
stage hits. They were offering a substantial sum of money, and were
also implying that unless the rights were granted to them the whole
deal would be cancelled.

One morning Vida and I were summoned to another of our many
meetings with Cy and Ernie at the Savoy. As we went up in the lift, I
told her of the new situation over the film and asked her how she felt
about it.

'Darling,' she replied after a moment's thought, 'if I were you, I
would take Cy and Ernie's offer. It's very sweet of Rank to want us
both to be in on the film, but after I've done the Broadway production
I really think I shall want to have a rest from *The Boy Friend*. It would

mean another year's work on it for both of us, and at the end of that I don't think we would want to see another cloche hat for the rest of our lives. I've got other things I want to do, and I'm sure you have. Besides,' she added, 'I honestly don't see how anyone *can* make a film of *The Boy Friend*. It's so completely theatrical. You take Cy and Ernie's money, and I bet your life –' she giggled mischievously, 'they'll *never* be able to do the film!'

And she turned out to be absolutely right. When *The Boy Friend* opened in New York and was a smash hit, Cy and Ernie sat back and waited confidently for offers from all the major Hollywood studios. None came. The days of buying up Broadway successes for astronomical sums were already drawing to a close, and even the stupidest Hollywood executive must have been aware of the drawbacks of *The Boy Friend* as a screen-play. Cy and Ernie were stuck with a property they could not sell, and eventually they made a deal with Metro-Goldwyn-Mayer whereby they would themselves co-produce a series of movies, among them *The Boy Friend*, under the aegis of Metro. Not altogether to my surprise, the alliance was short-lived. My two erstwhile producers departed from Hollywood in a huff, leaving various properties behind them. Now it was Metro who were stuck with *The Boy Friend*, and for a time their only move was to announce that the part of Polly would be played by Debbie Reynolds. Miss Reynolds had already been identified with the period in Gene Kelly's *Singin' in the Rain*, and the choice seemed logical, if nothing else.

As the months went by, various other snippets appeared in the Press: Gary Cooper had turned down the part of Polly's father, and it was now being offered to Errol Flynn; Mr Flynn was not free, so David Niven was under consideration; meanwhile the whole story had been re-written to take place in Chicago during Prohibition, and Miss Reynolds' leading man was to be Donald O'Connor. I believe that in all there were seven treatments of *The Boy Friend*, none of which ever reached the screen.

Round about 1956 MGM acquired a new star from England, the enchanting Kay Kendall. Miss Kendall had recently married Rex Harrison, who had just achieved one of the biggest successes of his career, playing Higgins opposite Julie's Eliza in *My Fair Lady*. It was now announced that she would have the rôle of Madame Dubonnet in the film of *The Boy Friend*, but since Mr Harrison was due to come to London for the Drury Lane production of *My Fair Lady* and Miss Kendall insisted on accompanying him to Europe, it was decided to set the film not, after all, in Chicago but in its original location, the South of France. This sounded more promising, and I could certainly imagine Kay Kendall making a delightful Madame Dubonnet. But complications ensued, and before the production could be finally assembled, Miss Kendall died tragically, at the height of her career.

From then on *The Boy Friend* featured less and less in MGM's production schedule, and indeed the schedule itself became increasingly indefinite, as the whole Hollywood studio system began to disintegrate into independent and overseas productions. Occasionally Joannie or I would receive visits from other film producers who were convinced that, if they could obtain the rights, they could make the film of *The Boy Friend*. But MGM, having already invested so much money in the property, were now asking a prohibitive amount for the rights, and after a half-hearted attempt at bargaining even the most enthusiastic producer was obliged to give up the idea.

Somewhere in the mid-sixties, Ross Hunter, who had managed to keep Universal Studios on a more or less even keel with a series of glossy comedies and melodramas, announced his intention of making the film of *The Boy Friend* and starring in it the girl who had created Polly on Broadway, Julie Andrews, now the super-star she had always planned to be, as a result of her phenomenal success in *Mary Poppins* and *The Sound of Music*. But again the demands of MGM defeated him, and he was obliged to concoct his own tribute to the Twenties instead, *Thoroughly Modern Millie*, a top-heavy but intermittently amusing film, in which I was touched to see Julie employing many of the nuances of expression and posture which she had learned from Vida during rehearsals in that troubled summer of 1954.

Vida herself did not live to see it. A day or two before Christmas 1963 she was driving down to the cottage in Essex which she and Derek had bought soon after they were married. Her car crashed into a lorry under circumstances which were never fully explained, and she was killed instantly.

Hollywood's failure to film *The Boy Friend*, besides proving Vida right, was a boon to the stage show and, of course, to me. At that time, when the screen version of a show was playing, the studio would ensure that no stage productions were permitted. On top of this loss of revenue, there was always the risk that the film would be so awful that it would damage the value of the original. With no film version to worry us, we could happily continue to license productions of *The Boy Friend* all over the world, and I think it must have been performed almost everywhere at one time or another, with the exception of countries behind the Iron Curtain, where, after all, the Nineteen Twenties had rather different connotations. I'm sorry to say that none of Vida's and Johnnie's predictions about foreign titles came true. 'Boy Friend' turned out to be an international term, and only the definite articles were changed: *Der Boy Friend* in Germany and *Le Boy Friend* in Paris (where it was, apart from the superlative Dubonnet of Suzy Delair, a howling disaster). Only in Spain, where girls are not permitted to have boy friends, was the title changed, to *Los Novios – The Fiancés*.

Within a few years of the end of the Broadway run, Gus Schirmer directed a revival off-Broadway which was, at least in feeling and style, a good deal closer to our original than the Feuer and Martin version. From then on revivals, repertory and amateur productions and stock and student versions proliferated. In 1967 the Leatherhead Theatre, under the management of Hazel Vincent Wallace, presented a highly successful production to which Joannie Rees and I were invited. Joannie had received many offers from managements to stage a West End revival, but she was adamant that we should wait until the time was ripe. After seeing the Leatherhead production that evening, we both felt that the moment had come. We also had a management in mind: Michael Codron, a friend and a fan of *The Boy Friend* from the days at Wyndhams.

Since Vida was no longer with us, I agreed to direct it, having already done so successfully in South Africa and in repertory. At first I planned to reproduce the original as closely as possible, but, on reflecting how times had changed since then, I decided to give it a New Look without, I hoped, destroying the show's authenticity. New designs were done by the brilliant husband-and-wife team, Andrew and Margaret Brownfoot, new choreography was arranged by Noël Tovey, and I had the whole score re-orchestrated by Arthur Greenslade. Instead of trying to find replicas of the original cast we looked for new and original young people and discovered, among others, a deliciously pretty young actress called Cheryl Kennedy to play Polly, who possessed the Cockney equivalent of Anne Rogers' North Country innocence. The whole company were talented, enthusiastic and fun to work with, and we opened at the Yvonne Arnaud Theatre, Guildford, whose artistic director is Laurier Lister, the man who had taken a chance on my words and music when I first came down from Oxford.

The revival of *The Boy Friend* opened at the Comedy Theatre in London, where I had first met Hermione backstage, on November 29th 1967 and ran there for a year. I was heartened to discover that the show had lost none of its appeal and that the music was being appreciated in its own right and not just as a parody. And it was exciting to go up to the circle and the gallery and find a new generation of youngsters applauding as enthusiastically as their mothers and fathers had before them.

One evening, in the early stages of the run, I took the cartoonist and illustrator, Haro Hodson, who had designed our poster and record sleeve, to see the show. He fell in love with Cheryl from the moment she appeared and demanded to be taken round to see her afterwards. When she opened her dressing-room door, I was astonished to find her wearing her first act costume.

'What *are* you doing, Cheryl? You haven't got another show, have you?'

'Aow, naow!' she replied – and I shall not continue to reproduce her wonderful Eliza Dolittle accent. 'It's for some publicity photographs.' She was obviously in a high state of excitement. '*Twiggy*'s been in, and she's coming round!'

The next moment, with an explosion of flash-bulbs, Twiggy did indeed come round. Haro and I were swept aside, as she burst into the room accompanied by her entourage, amongst whom I was intrigued to find the veteran designer, Erté, who proceeded to compliment me on the appearance of the show. To be honest, I was much more interested in his reaction than in Twiggy's, but there was no doubt at all that she too had enjoyed it. Falling on Cheryl's neck, as if she were her long-lost sister, she announced that the whole thing was absolutely 'super' and she couldn't wait to come again.

As the two Cockney voices rose to a crescendo of mutual admiration, Haro and I discreetly withdrew.

A few months later Joannie received a communication from Justin de Villeneuve, Twiggy's discoverer, mentor and romantic partner. He wished to buy the film rights of *The Boy Friend* in which he intended to star Twiggy as Polly. Joannie replied that unfortunately they belonged to MGM and there was little likelihood of their parting with them. She had at first intended to leave the matter there, but the idea of Twiggy and me in combination appealed to her and she added a paragraph to say that perhaps Mr de Villeneuve and his protégée would like to meet me when I returned from Australia, where I was directing the revival of *The Boy Friend* in Sydney.

The meeting was duly arranged. I was invited to Justin's amazing hide-out, in a converted mews off Tottenham Court Road, for 'tea' – a term which had disturbing ambiguities; but I need not have worried, since the normal beverage was indeed served, along with a plate of biscuits, by a minion who appeared from the upper reaches of the vast studio. The famous pair sat on the floor and Justin did most of the talking, while Twiggy, arrayed in the then fashionable combination of 'gipsy' accessories – boots, patchwork skirt, blouse, bangles and kerchief – interjected the odd, always pertinent, remark. She struck me as a nice, straight-forward girl, and as soon as there was a pause in the flow of Justin's hyperboles I told her that I was sorry, but there was nothing that I personally could do about the film rights of *The Boy Friend*.

'In any case,' I went on, 'I really don't think you are right for the part of Polly. If they ever did make a film of it, you ought to play Dulcie – it's a much more amusing part. But why don't we try and think of something original for you instead?'

This seemed to intrigue them both and Justin produced a collection of remarkable photographs in which Twiggy appeared in the guise of most of the famous Hollywood stars of the Thirties. She had even got away with impersonating Greta Garbo, and the vestige of an idea began to form in my mind. A little while before, John Morley, a script-writer who was an old friend of mine from University days and with whom I was collaborating on a musical about Amy Johnson, had suggested, as a subject for another show, the Corner House Nippies, the waitresses in black frocks and white aprons and caps who had featured so much in Lyons' advertising between the wars. I suddenly saw Twiggy as a Nippy who has day-dreams of being a film star, and whenever she goes to the cinema sees herself on the screen impersonating her favourite leading ladies. John and I roughed out a scenario and submitted it to Justin and Twiggy. From the fastness of an island they had rented in the Caribbean, they cabled to say that they loved it. After that there was silence.

One morning I happened to read in the newspaper that before an audience of several hundred, including the Press, at a party at the Savoy, Twiggy, Justin and the director, Ken Russell, had announced that they would be making the film of *The Boy Friend* with Metro-Goldwyn-Mayer. Mr Russell had recently won a world-wide reputation with his version of D. H. Lawrence's *Women in Love*, and it appeared that when Twiggy and Justin had mentioned to him casually that they wanted to make a film of *The Boy Friend* he had told them that it was his ambition too, and between them, owing to their joint prestige, they had been able to make a deal with MGM.

While deploring Twiggy's and Justin's lack of manners in not communicating with me, I could not help admiring their nerve, and I sat back to await with interest and curiosity the result of this rather bizarre alliance. I had admired *Women in Love* very much on the whole, despite the tricks it played with the novel, and I had been struck by its attention to period detail, which boded well for Russell's attitude to *The Boy Friend*. But then *The Music Lovers*, his film about Tchaikovsky, opened in the West End, to be followed in due course by *The Devils*, his distortion of a magnificent play by the late John Whiting. Both were received with alarm and disgust by the more sensitive critics and I began to wonder whether this was, after all, the man best equipped to convey the delicate charm of *The Boy Friend* to the screen. At about the same time the film went into production and I was invited by MGM to attend a cocktail party at the Ritz, to celebrate the commencement of the shooting. I was warned beforehand that Mr Russell had thrown a temperament on hearing that I was to be present, but in the event, when we met in front of a battery of television cameras, he was politeness itself and told me how much he admired my music. I felt a little reassured and even managed to retain my composure when an executive of Metro, to whom I had just been introduced, bellowed at me threateningly,

'We've sunk a helluva lot of money into this picture. It's sure gotta be good!'

'It sure has,' I thought, 'otherwise you'll be out on your backside,' and passed on.

Much of the film was to be shot on location in an old theatre in Portsmouth, and within a few weeks a massive publicity campaign was launched, with photographs of the movie in production, in most of which Mr Russell appeared to figure far more prominently than the cast. I had no idea what approach he was intending to take to the subject, and I had never expected to be consulted, nor was I in fact entitled to be, since I had relinquished the rights so many years before to Cy and Ernie. But as more and more publicity stills appeared I became increasingly puzzled as to what relationship they could possibly bear to my original. Even the period in many of them seemed to be different, resembling the Thirties far more than the Twenties, and one night on television, in the course of a programme about Ken Russell conducted by Philip Jenkinson, a sequence from *The Boy Friend* was shown in which Twiggy was apparently the unwilling victim of an open-air Roman orgy, the instigators of which were my old friends from Laurier's revues, Max Adrian and Moyra Fraser (an episode that was eventually excised from the film). At the end of the programme I rang Joannie Rees, who was in a state of prostration.

'I wish I could *do* something!' she wailed. 'But I can't! I can't do *anything*!'

The only thing *I* could do was to take myself forthwith to see Mr Russell's latest offerings, which I had hitherto resisted and which were both playing in the West End. I saw *The Music Lovers* in the afternoon and *The Devils* in the early evening and then staggered home, weak with shock and nausea, to find, to my relief, that *Lil' Abner* was showing on television. But my forebodings about the film of *The Boy Friend* were now increased a thousand-fold.

Luckily I was fully occupied with the writing and production of a new musical at the Hampstead Theatre Club, which was due to open just before Christmas, at the same time as *The Boy Friend* had its première in New York. The reaction of the American critics was amost unanimously bad, and two friends sent me copies of Pauline Kael's exhaustive and scathing condemnation of the film in the *New Yorker*. I waited in trepidation for the London opening at the Empire Cinema, where I had spent so many happy hours in my youth, enjoying the masterpieces of the old MGM. An invitation to the première arrived from the Metro office, but I had already arranged to be out of London in Bristol, seeing a new musical by my friend, Julian Slade. I had decided that I could not face seeing the film on such a public occasion when I was bound to have to answer awkward questions by the Press, something which I had so far managed to avoid.

Through Chappells, who published the music, I heard that a midnight preview was to be given for ticket agencies and other business concerns. They secured me a couple of seats and I slipped into the Empire in what I hoped was total incognito. But one person recognised me immediately and came straight over to me, her pretty face distraught with anxiety. It was Anne Rogers.

'Oh, Sandy,' she whispered, 'I don't think we're going to enjoy this very mooch, are we?'

The film itself was a baffling experience. Knowing Russell's work and having seen so much advance publicity, I was prepared for it to be a travesty, but I did expect it to be an accomplished travesty, since, whatever one may think of his films, there is no denying Russell's technical expertise. But it turned out to be nothing but a mess: a wilful and at times incomprehensible confusion of Twenties and Thirties camp, through which poor Twiggy bravely twittered and pranced, almost suffocated by the welter of grotesquerie and surrounded by a cast whose unattractiveness was only rivalled by their incompetence. I could not help feeling sorry for the poor little thing. She had wanted so desperately to be Polly Browne; instead, through Justin's folly and Russell's egotism, she was only a tiny beam of pathos in a walpurgis-nacht of self-indulgence.

The night air in Leicester Square seemed so refreshing by contrast that I walked all the way home to Kensington.

Joannie, who could never bring herself to see the film, was at first extremely worried about the effect it might have on the show. But it was the opposite to what she expected. In America bookings tripled in the months following the première of the film, and MGM, concerned that the same thing might happen in England and steal the film's thunder, tried to have all stage productions stopped for the period of its release in this country. But Samuel French, who handle the rights, calmly pointed out that not only were they under no obligation to do so but *The Boy Friend* was booked from year to year by the repertory and amateur companies and there was no question of interfering with these arrangements. Joannie, encouraged by their attitude, devised a new sales slogan: 'The Real Thing. Accept no Substitutes . . .', which she admitted was vulgar, but, under the circumstances, justified.

To give Ken Russell his due, he had taken on what I already knew to be an impossible task. As Vida emphasised when the subject of a film first came up, *The Boy Friend* is essentially Theatre, relying for its effect on a style of production and performance that relates totally to a live audience. On reflection, I felt that he must have panicked in the final stages and thrown in every cinematic trick he could think of in an effort to produce something that was at least sensational.

As it had survived other crises, *The Boy Friend* survived this one, which became just another episode in its life-story – a life whose length and persistence still astonish me. On April the Fourteenth, Nineteen Seventy Four, I gave a small party to celebrate its Twenty-First Birthday, and Joannie Rees, Ann Wakefield and I drank a glass of wine to the memory of that first first night at the Players, so highly charged, as it was, with the hopes and dreams of us all.

A few weeks later I drove down to Teddington to see the local amateur group's production, in which Heather and Michael, who had first heard the score of *The Boy Friend* in that basement in Crossfield Road and had been singularly unimpressed by it, were now at last to appear in it, she as a somewhat too fetching Lady Brockhurst and he as a heroically-profiled Percival Browne.

During the celebrations afterwards I found myself musing on my relationship with *The Boy Friend*: it seemed to me to be much the same as I had described, rather crassly, in its best-known song: *I Could be Happy with You, If You Could be Happy with Me*. And, by and large, happiness had won.

Index

WITHDRAWN

No longer the property of the
Boston Public Library.
Sale of this material benefits the Library.